Second Workshop on Hybrid Approaches to Translation 2013

Sofia, Bulgaria
8 August 2013

ISBN: 978-1-62993-002-2

Printed from e-media with permission by:

Curran Associates, Inc.
57 Morehouse Lane
Red Hook, NY 12571

Some format issues inherent in the e-media version may also appear in this print version.

Printed by Curran Associates, Inc. (2013)

For permission requests, please contact the Association for Computational Linguistics at the address below.

Association for Computational Linguistics
209 N. Eighth Street
Stroudsburg, Pennsylvania 18360

Phone: 1-570-476-8006
Fax: 1-570-476-0860

acl@aclweb.org

Additional copies of this publication are available from:

Curran Associates, Inc.
57 Morehouse Lane
Red Hook, NY 12571 USA
Phone: 845-758-0400
Fax: 845-758-2634
Email: curran@proceedings.com
Web: www.proceedings.com

Preface

This second edition of the Workshop on Hybrid Approaches to Translation (HyTra) is co-located with the 51st Annual Meeting of the Association for Computational Linguistics (ACL 2013) in Sofia. It further progresses on the findings of the first edition which was held as a joint 2-day event together with the Workshop on Exploiting Synergies between Information Retrieval and Machine Translation (ESIRMT) at the 13th Conference of the European Chapter of the Association for Computational Linguistics (EACL 2012) in Avignon.

The aim of the HyTra workshop series is to bring together and share ideas among MT researchers who combine data-driven statistical approaches with linguistic knowledge models. We open the floor for researchers and groups who develop and improve machine translation systems across different paradigms: rule-based, example-based, statistical or hybrid. The workshop provides a platform for publishing their work, and contributes towards building a research community in the field of hybrid MT, around sharing a common vision, methods, evaluation benchmarks and tools. The uniting focus for this community is a new cross-paradigm view of the area of machine translation, seeing the potential to move the technology beyond the state-of-the-art by combining ideas and models developed in different fields of computational linguistics and artificial intelligence. This workshop gives an opportunity to motivate the cooperation and interaction between them, and to foster innovative combinations between the two main MT paradigms: statistical and rule-based.

The advantages of rule-based MT are that its rules and representations are geared towards human understanding and can be more easily checked, corrected and exploited for applications outside of machine translation such as dictionaries, text understanding and dialog systems. But (pure) rule-based MT has also severe disadvantages, among them slow development cycles, high cost, a lack of robustness in the case of incorrect input, and difficulties in making correct choices with respect to ambiguous words, structures, and transfer equivalents.

The advantages of statistical MT are fast development cycles, low cost, robustness, superior lexical selection and relative fluency due to the use of language models. But (pure) statistical MT has also disadvantages: it needs large amounts of data, which for many language pairs are not available, and are unlikely to become available in the foreseeable future. This problem is especially relevant for under-resourced languages. Recent advances in factored morphological models and syntax-based models in SMT indicate that non-statistical symbolic representations and processing models need to have their proper place in MT research and development, and more research is needed to understand how to develop and integrate these non-statistical models most efficiently.

The translations of statistical systems are often surprisingly good with respect to phrases and short distance collocations, but they often fail when preferences need to be based on more distant words. In contrast, the output of rule-based systems is often surprisingly good if the parser assigns the correct analysis to a sentence. However, it usually leaves something to be desired if the correct analysis cannot be computed, or if there is not enough information for selecting the correct target words when translating ambiguous words and structures.

Given the complementarity of rule-based and statistical MT, it is natural that the boundaries between them have narrowed. The question is what the combined architecture should look like. In the past few years, in the MT scientific community, the interest in hybridization and system combination has significantly increased. This is why a large number of approaches for constructing hybrid MT have already been proposed offering a considerable potential of improving MT quality and efficiency. Mainly, the following hybrid MT systems can be identified: (1) SMT models augmented with morphological, syntactic or semantic information; (2) Rule-based MT systems using parallel and comparable corpora to improve results by enriching their lexicons and grammars and by applying new methods for disambiguation; (3) MT system combination based on different paradigms (including voting systems); (4) automatic and semi-automatic pre-editing and post-editing approaches, including re-ordering systems.

There is also great potential in expanding hybrid MT systems with techniques, tools and processing resources from other areas of NLP, such as Information Extraction, Information Retrieval, Question Answering, Semantic Web, Automatic Semantic Inferencing.

Given this context, relevant topics for the workshop series include the following:

- ways and techniques of hybridization
- architectures for the rapid development of hybrid MT systems
- applications of hybrid systems
- hybrid systems dealing with under-resourced languages
- hybrid systems dealing with morphologically rich languages
- using linguistic information (morphology, syntax, semantics) to enhance statistical MT (e.g. with hierarchical or factored models)
- using contextual information to enhance statistical MT
- bootstrapping rule-based systems from corpora
- hybrid methods in spoken language translation
- extraction of dictionaries and other large-scale resources for MT from parallel and comparable corpora
- induction of morphological, grammatical, and translation rules from corpora
- machine learning techniques for hybrid MT
- describing structural mappings between languages (e.g. tree-structures using synchronous/ transduction grammars)
- heuristics for limiting the search space in hybrid MT
- alternative methods for the fair evaluation of the output of different types of MT systems (e.g. relying on linguistic criteria)
- system combination approaches such as multi-engine MT (parallel) or automatic post-editing (sequential)
- open source tools and free language resources for hybrid MT

From this range most contributors of the current workshop have chosen to present work about how SMT may be improved by adding linguistic knowledge and representation respectively. For some of the papers this means to add morphological or morpho-syntactic representation levels - and to define the lexicon- and language-models for these representations instead of considering inflected words or chunks of inflected words; for others this (also) means to incorporate pre-processing components for reordering the input (that, possibly, has been morphologically analyzed before). This set of papers where SMT is taken as a basis is complemented by a few papers dedicated to integrating statistical information – mainly about lexical selection and disambiguation - in RBMT systems; and by another few papers concentrating on extracting information for MT from monolingual resources (including analysis learning for RBMT). A small number of contributions include general considerations about hybrid architectures as such. However, a clear trend in the sense of a convention about hybridity coming into being cannot be entailed from the contributions, not yet. This encourages continuation of the series.

This second HyTra workshop has been supported by the Seventh Framework Programme of the European Commission through the Marie Curie actions HyghTra ("A Hybrid Hygh-Quality Translation System"; grant agreement no.: 251534 - PIAP-GA-2009-251534-HyghTra), IMTraP (Integration of Machine Translation Paradigms, grant agreement no.: 2011-29951), AutoWordNet ("The Automatic Generation of Lexical Databases Analogous to WordNet"; grant agreement no. 254504) and CrossLingMind ("Automated analysis of opinions in a multilingual context"; grant agreement no. 300828). It has also been supported in part by Spanish "Ministerio de Economía y Competitividad", contract TEC2012-38939-C03-02 as well as from the European Regional Development Fund (ERDF/FEDER).

We would like to thank all people who contributed towards making the workshop a success. Our special thanks go to our invited keynote speakers: Hermann Ney (RWTH Aachen), Will Lewis and Chris Quirk (both Microsoft Research); as well as to our above mentioned sponsors, to the members of the program committee who did an excellent job in reviewing the submitted papers despite a very tight schedule, and to the ACL 2013 organizers, in particular the workshop general chairs Aoife Cahill and Qun Liu and the publication team including Roberto Navigli, Jing-Shin Chang, and Stefano Faralli. Last but not least, we would like to thank all authors and participants of the workshop, who have made this second edition of HyTra very successful.

Sofia, Bulgaria, August 2013

Marta R. Costa-jussà, Reinhard Rapp, Patrik Lambert, Kurt Eberle, Rafael E. Banchs, Bogdan Babych

Organizers:

Marta R. Costa-jussà, Institute for Infocomm Research, Singapore
Reinhard Rapp, Universities of Aix-Marseille, France and Mainz, Germany
Patrik Lambert, Barcelona Media Innovation Center, Spain
Kurt Eberle, Lingenio GmbH, Germany
Rafael E. Banchs, Institute for Infocomm Research, Singapore
Bogdan Babych, University of Leeds, UK

Invited Speakers:

Hermann Ney, RWTH Aachen, Germany
Will Lewis and Chris Quirk, Microsoft Research, USA

Program Committee:

Alexey Baytin, Yandex, Moscow, Russia
Núria Bel, Universitat Pompeu Fabra, Barcelona, Spain
Pierrette Bouillon, ISSCO/TIM/ETI, University of Geneva, Switzerland
Michael Carl, Copenhagen Business School, Denmark
Marine Carpuat, National Research Council, Canada
Josep Maria Crego, Systran, Paris, France
Oliver Čulo, University of Mainz, Germany
Andreas Eisele, DGT (European Commission), Luxembourg
Marcello Federico, Fondazione Bruno Kessler, Trento, Italy
Christian Federmann, Language Technology Lab, DFKI, Saarbrücken, Germany
Alexander Fraser, University of Stuttgart, Germany
José A. R. Fonollosa, Universitat Politècnica de Catalunya, Barcelona, Spain
Tony Hartley, Toyohashi University of Technology, Japan, and University of Leeds, UK
Maxim Khalilov, TAUS, Amsterdam, The Netherlands
Kevin Knight, University of Southern California, USA
Philipp Koehn, University of Edimburgh, UK
Udo Kruschwitz, University of Essex, UK
Yanjun Ma, Baidu Inc., Beijing, China
José B. Mariño, Universitat Politècnica de Catalunya, Barcelona, Spain
Maite Melero, Barcelona Media Innovation Center, Barcelona, Spain
Bart Mellebeek, University of Amsterdam, The Netherlands
Haizhou Li, Institute for Infocomm Research, Singapore
Chris Quirk, Microsoft, USA
Paul Schmidt, Institute for Applied Information Science, Saarbrücken, Germany
Anders Søgaard, University of Copenhagen, Denmark
Uta Seewald-Heeg, Anhalt University of Applied Sciences, Köthen, Germany
Nasredine Semmar, CEA LIST, Fontenay-aux-Roses, France
Wade Shen, Massachusetts Institute of Technology, Cambridge, USA
Serge Sharoff, University of Leeds, UK
George Tambouratzis, Institute for Language and Speech Processing, Athens, Greece
Jörg Tiedemann, University of Uppsala, Sweden
Dekai Wu, The Hong Kong University of Science and Technology, Hong Kong, China

Table of Contents

Workshop Program

Thursday, August 8, 2013

8:50–9:00 Workshop Opening

Workshop on Hybrid Approaches to Translation: Overview and Developments
Marta Ruiz Costa-jussà, Rafael Banchs, Reinhard Rapp, Patrik Lambert, Kurt Eberle and Bogdan Babych

9:00–9:50 Keynote Speech 1

Statistical MT Systems Revisited: How much Hybridity do they have?
Hermann Ney

Session 1: Morphology

09:50–10:15 *Hybrid Selection of Language Model Training Data Using Linguistic Information and Perplexity*
Antonio Toral

10:15–10:40 *Machine Learning Disambiguation of Quechua Verb Morphology*
Annette Rios Gonzales and Anne Göhring

10:40–11:00 Coffee Break

Session 2: Syntax I

11:00–11:25 *Improvements to Syntax-based Machine Translation using Ensemble Dependency Parsers*
Nathan Green and Zdeněk Žabokrtský

11:25–11:50 *Using unlabeled dependency parsing for pre-reordering for Chinese-to-Japanese statistical machine translation*
Dan Han, Pascual Martinez-Gomez, Yusuke Miyao, Katsuhito Sudoh and Masaaki NAGATA

Session 3: Syntax II

11:50–12:15 *Reordering rules for English-Hindi SMT*
Raj Nath Patel, Rohit Gupta, Prakash B. Pimpale and Sasikumar M

12:15–12:40 *English to Hungarian Morpheme-based Statistical Machine Translation System with Reordering Rules*
László Laki, Attila Novak and Borbála Siklósi

12:40–14:00 Lunch Break

Thursday, August 8, 2013 (continued)

14:00–14:50 Keynote Speech 2

Controlled Ascent: Imbuing Statistical MT with Linguistic Knowledge
William Lewis and Chris Quirk

14:50–16:00 **Session 4: Poster Session**

14:50–15:15 Poster Booster Presentations (5 minutes per poster)

Unsupervised Transduction Grammar Induction via Minimum Description Length
Markus Saers, Karteek Addanki and Dekai Wu

Integrating morpho-syntactic features in English-Arabic statistical machine translation
Ines Turki Khemakhem, Salma Jamoussi and Abdelmajid Ben Hamadou

Experiments with POS-based restructuring and alignment-based reordering for statistical machine translation
Shuo Li, Derek F. Wong and Lidia S. Chao

Building bilingual lexicon to create Dialect Tunisian corpora and adapt language model
Rahma Boujelbane, Mariem Ellouze khemekhem, Siwar BenAyed and Lamia Hadrich-Belguith

A Hybrid Word Alignment Model for Phrase-Based Statistical Machine Translation
Santanu Pal, Sudip Naskar and Sivaji Bandyopadhyay

15:30–16:00 Coffee Break (to occur concurrently with poster session)

Thursday, August 8, 2013 (continued)

Session 5: Semantics

16:00–16:25 *Lexical Selection for Hybrid MT with Sequence Labeling*
Alex Rudnick and Michael Gasser

16:25–16:50 *Two Approaches to Correcting Homophone Confusions in a Hybrid Machine Translation System*
Pierrette Bouillon, Johanna Gerlach, Ulrich Germann, Barry Haddow and Manny Rayner

Session 6: Multi-level Approaches

16:50–17:15 *Uses of Monolingual In-Domain Corpora for Cross-Domain Adaptation with Hybrid MT Approaches*
An-Chang Hsieh, Hen-Hsen Huang and Hsin-Hsi Chen

17:15–17:40 *Language-independent hybrid MT with PRESEMT*
George Tambouratzis, Sokratis Sofianopoulos and Marina Vassiliou

17:40–17:50 Conclusions and Wrap-up Session

Workshop on Hybrid Approaches to Translation: Overview and Developments

Marta R. Costa-jussà, Rafael E. Banchs
Institute for Infocomm Research[1]
Reinhard Rapp
Aix-Marseille Université, LIF[2]
Patrik Lambert
Barcelona Media[3]
Kurt Eberle
Lingenio GmbH[4]
Bogdan Babych
University of Leeds[5]

[1]{vismrc,rembanchs}@i2r.a-star.edu.sg, [2]reinhardrapp@gmx.de,
[3]patrik.lambert@barcelonamedia.org, [4]k.eberle@lingenio.de,
[5]b.babych@leeds.ac.uk

Abstract

A current increasing trend in machine translation is to combine data-driven and rule-based techniques. Such combinations typically involve the hybridization of different paradigms such as, for instance, the introduction of linguistic knowledge into statistical paradigms, the incorporation of data-driven components into rule-based paradigms, or the pre- and post-processing of either sort of translation system outputs. Aiming at bringing together researchers and practitioners from the different multidisciplinary areas working in these directions, as well as at creating a brainstorming and discussion venue for Hybrid Translation approaches, the HyTra initiative was born. This paper gives an overview of the Second Workshop on Hybrid Approaches to Translation (HyTra 2013) concerning its motivation, contents and outcomes.

1 Introduction

Machine translation (MT) has continuously been evolving from different perspectives. Early systems were basically dictionary-based. These approaches were further developed to more complex systems based on analysis, transfer and generation. The objective was to climb up (and down) in the well-known Vauquois pyramid (see Figure 1) to facilitate the transfer phase or to even minimize the transfer by using an interlingua system. But then, corpus-based approaches irrupted, generating a turning point in the field by putting aside the analysis, generation and transfer phases.

Although there had been such a tendency right from the beginning (Wilks, 1994), in the last years, the corpus-based approaches have reached a point where many researchers assume that relying exclusively on data might have serious limitations. Therefore, research has focused either on syntactical/hierarchical-based methods or on trying to augment the popular phrase-based systems by incorporating linguistic knowledge. In addition, and given the fact that research on rule-based has never stopped, there have been several proposals of hybrid architectures combining both rule-based and data-driven approaches.

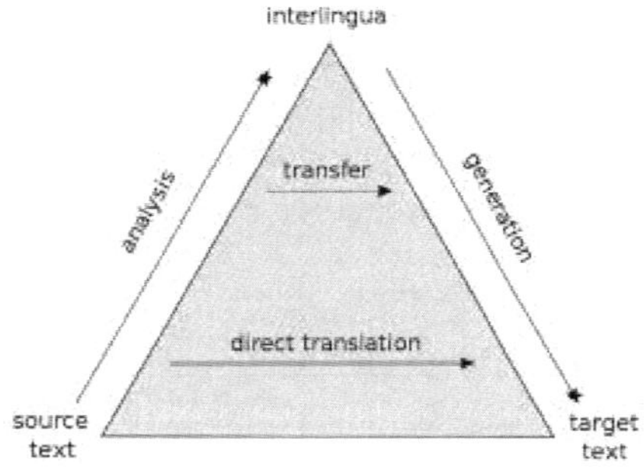

Figure 1: Vauquois pyramid (image from Wikipedia).

In summary, there is currently a clear trend towards hybridization, with researchers adding morphological, syntactic and semantic knowledge to statistical systems, as well as combining data-driven methods with existing rule-based systems.

In this paper we provide a general overview of current approaches to hybrid MT within the context of the Second Workshop on Hybrid Approaches to Translation (HyTra 2013). In our overview, we classify hybrid MT approaches according to the linguistic levels that they address. We then briefly summarize the contributions presented and collected in this volume.

The paper is organized as follows. First, we motivate and summarize the main aspects of the HyTra initiative. Then, we present a general overview of the accepted papers and discuss them within the context of other state-of-the-art research in the area. Finally, we present our conclusions and discuss our proposed view of future directions for Hybrid MT research.

2 Overview of the HyTra Initiative

The HyTra initiative started in response to the increasing interest in hybrid approaches to machine translation, which is reflected on the substantial amount of work conducted on this topic. Another important motivation was the observation that, up to now, no single paradigm has been able to successfully solve to a satisfactory extent all of the many challenges that the problem of machine translation poses.

The first HyTra workshop took part in conjunction with the EACL 2012 conference (Costa-jussà et al., 2012). The Second HyTra Workshop, which was co-organized by the authors of this paper, has been co-located with the ACL 2013 conference (Costa-jussà et al., 2013). The workshop has been supported by an extensive programme committee comprising members from over 30 organizations and representing more than 20 countries. As the outcome of a comprehensive peer reviewing process, and based on the recommendations of the programme committee, 15 papers were finally selected for either oral or poster presentation at the workshop.

The workshop also had the privilege to be honored by two exceptional keynote speeches:

- *Controlled Ascent: Imbuing Statistical MT with Linguistic Knowledge* by Will Lewis and Chris Quirk (2013), Microsoft research. The intersection of rule-based and statistical approaches in MT is explored, with a particular focus on past and current work done at Microsoft Research. One of their motivations for a hybrid approach is the observation that the times are over when huge improvements in translation quality were possible by simply adding more data to statistical systems. The reason is that most of the readily available parallel data has already been found.

- *How much hybridity do we have?* by Hermann Ney, RWTH Aachen. It is pointed out that after about 25 years the statistical approach to MT has been widely accepted as an alternative to the classical approach with manually designed rules. But in practice most statistical MT systems make use of manually designed rules at least for preprocessing in order to improve MT quality. This is exemplified by looking at the RWTH MT systems.

3 Hybrid Approaches Organized by Linguistic Levels

'Hybridization' of MT can be understood as combination of several MT systems (possibly of very different architecture) where the single systems translate in parallel and compete for the best result (which is chosen by the integrating meta system). The workshop and the papers do not focus on this 'coarse-grained' hybridization (Eisele et al., 2008), but on a more 'fine grained' one where the systems mix information from different levels of linguistic representations (see Figure 2). In the past and mostly in the framework of rule-based machine translation (RBMT) it has been experimented with information from nearly every level including phonetics and phonology for speech recognition and synthesis in speech-to-speech systems (Wahlster, 2000) and including pragmatics for dialog translation (Batliner et al., 2000a; Batliner et al., 2000b) and text coherence phenomena (Le Nagard and Koehn, 2010). With respect to work with emphasis on statistical machine translation (SMT) and derivations of it mainly those information levels have been used that address text in the sense of sets of sentences.

As most of the workshop papers relate to this perspective - i.e. on hybridization which is defined using SMT as backbone, in this introduction we can do with distinguishing between approaches focused on morphology, syntax, and semantics. There are of course approaches which deal with more than one of these levels in an integrated manner, which are commonly refered to as multilevel approaches. As the case of treating syntax and morphology concurrently is especially common, we also consider morpho-syntax as a separate multilevel approach.

3.1 Morphological approaches

The main approaches of statistical MT that exploit morphology can be classified into segmentation, generation, and enriching approaches. The

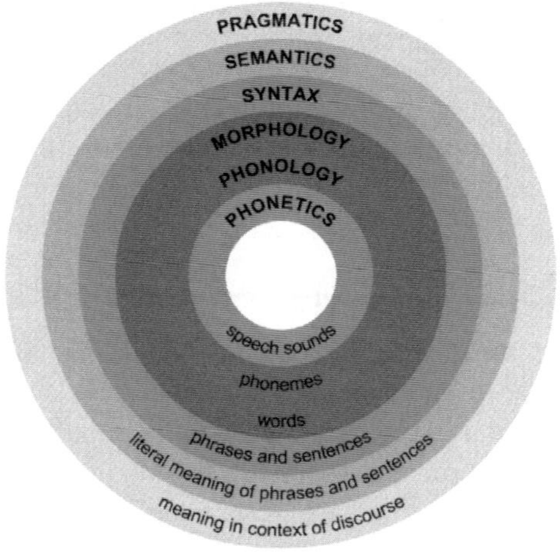

Figure 2: Major linguistic levels (image from Wikipedia).

first one attempts to minimize the vocabulary of highly inflected languages in order to symmetrize the (lexical granularity of the) source and the target language. The second one assumes that, due to data sparseness, not all morphological forms can be learned from parallel corpora and, therefore, proposes techniques to learn new morphological forms. The last one tries to enrich poorly inflected languages to compensate for their lack of morphology. In HyTra 2013, approaches treating morphology were addressed by the following contributions:

- Toral (2013) explores the selection of data to train domain-specific language models (LM) from non-domain specific corpora by means of simplified morphology forms (such as lemmas). The benefit of this technique is tested using automatic metrics in the English-to-Spanish task. Results show an improvement of up to 8.17% of perplexity reduction over the baseline system.

- Rios Gonzalez and Goehring (2013) propose machine learning techniques to decide on the correct form of a verb depending on the context. Basically they use tree-banks to train the classifiers. Results show that they are able to disambiguate up to 89% of the Quechua verbs.

3.2 Syntactic approaches

Syntax had been addressed originally in SMT in the form of so called phrase-based SMT without any reference to linguistic structures; during the last decade (or more) the approach evolved to or, respectively, was complemented by - work on syntax-based models in the linguistic sense of the word. Most such approaches can be classified into three different types of architecture that are defined by the type of syntactic analysis used for the source language and the type of generation aimed at for the target language: tree-to-tree, tree-to-string and string-to-tree. Additionally, there are also the so called hierarchical systems, which combine the phrase-based and syntax-based approaches by using phrases as translation-units and automatically generated context free grammars as rules. Approaches dealing with the syntactic approach in HyTra 2013 include the following papers:

- Green and Zabokrtský (2013) study three different ways to ensemble parsing techniques and provide results in MT. They compute correlations between parsing quality and translation quality, showing that NIST is more correlated than BLEU.

- Han et al. (2013) provide a framework for pre-reordering to make Chinese word order more similar to Japanese. To this purpose, they use unlabelled dependency structures of sentences and POS tags to identify verbal blocks and move them from after-the-object positions (SVO) to before-the-object positions (SOV).

- Nath Patel et al. (2013) also propose a pre-reordering technique, which uses a limited set of rules based on parse-tree modification rules and manual revision. The set of rules is specifically listed in detail.

- Saers et al. (2013) report an unsupervised learning model that induces phrasal ITGs by breaking rules into smaller ones using minimum description length. The resulting translation model provides a basis for generalization to more abstract transduction grammars with informative non-terminals.

3.3 Morphosyntactical approaches

In linguistic theories, morphology and syntax are often considered and represented simultaneously (not only in unification-based approaches) and the same is true for MT systems.

- Laki et al. (2013) combine pre-reordering rules with morphological and factored models for English-to-Turkish.

- Li et al. (2013) propose pre-reordering rules to be used for alignment-based reordering, and corresponding POS-based restructuring of the input. Basically, they focus on taking advantage of the fact that Korean has compound words, which - for the purpose of alignment - are split and reordered similarly to Chinese.

- Turki Khemakhem et al. (2013) present work about an English-Arabic SMT system that uses morphological decomposition and morpho-syntactic annotation of the target language and incorporates the corresponding information in a statistical feature model. Essentially, the statistical feature language model replaces words by feature arrays.

3.4 Semantic approaches

The introduction of semantics in statistical MT has been approached to solve word sense disambiguation challenges covering the area of lexical semantics and, more recently, there have been different techniques using semantic roles covering shallow semantics, as well as the use of distributional semantics for improving translation unit selection. Approaches treating the incorporation of semantics into MT in HyTra 2013 include the following research work:

- Rudnick et al. (2013) present a combination of Maximum Entropy Markov Models and HMM to perform lexical selection in the sense of cross-lingual word sense disambiguation (i.e. by choice from the set of translation alternatives). The system is meant to be integrated into a RBMT system.

- Boujelbane (2013) proposes to build a bilingual lexicon for the Tunisian dialect using modern standard Arabic (MSA). The methodology is based on leveraging the large available annotated MSA resources by exploiting MSA-dialect similarities and addressing the known differences. The author studies morphological, syntactic and lexical differences by exploiting Penn Arabic Treebank, and uses the differences to develop rules and to build dialectal concepts.

- Bouillon et al. (2013) presents two methodologies to correct homophone confusions. The first one is based on hand-coded rules and the second one is based on weighted graphs derived from a pronunciation resource.

3.5 Other multilevel approaches

In a number of linguistic theories information from the morphological, syntactic and semantic level is considered conjointly and merged in corresponding representations (a RBMT example is LFG (Lexical Functional Grammars) analysis and the corresponding XLE translation architecture). In HyTra 2013 there are three approaches dealing with multilevel information:

- Pal et al. (2013) propose a combination of aligners: GIZA++, Berkeley and rule-based for English-Bengali.

- Hsieh et al. (2013) use comparable corpora extracted from Wikipedia to extract parallel fragments for the purpose of extending an English-Bengali training corpus.

- Tambouratzis et al. (2013) describe a hybrid MT architecture that uses very few bilingual corpus and a large monolingual one. The linguistic information is extracted using pattern recognition techniques.

Table 1 summarizes the papers that have been presented in the Second HyTra Workshop. The papers are arranged into the table according to the linguistic level they address.

4 Conclusions and further work

The success of the Second HyTra Workshop confirms that research in hybrid approaches to MT systems is a very active and promising area. The MT community seems to agree that pure data-driven or rule-based paradigms have strong limitations and that hybrid systems are a promising direction to overcome most of these limitations. Considerable progress has been made in this area recently, as demonstrated by consistent improvements for different language pairs and translation tasks.

The research community is working hard, with strong collaborations and with more resources at hand than ever before. However, it is not clear

Morphological	(Toral, 2013) (Gonzales and Goehring, 2013)	Hybrid Selection of LM Training Data Using Linguistic Information and Perplexity Machine Learning disambiguation of Quechua verb morphology
Syntax	(Green and Zabokrtský, 2013) (Han et al., 2013) (Patel et al., 2013) (Saers et al., 2013)	Improvements to SBMT using Ensemble Dependency Parser Using unlabeled dependency parsing for pre-reordering for Chinese-to-Japanese SMT Reordering rules for English-Hindi SMT Unsupervised transduction grammar induction via MDL
Morpho-syntactic	(Laki et al., 2013) (Li et al., 2013) (Khemakhem et al., 2013)	English to Hungarian morpheme-based SMT system with reordering rules Experiments with POS-based restructuring and alignment based reordering for SMT Integrating morpho-syntactic feature for English Arabic SMT
Semantic	(Rudnick and Gasser, 2013) (Boujelbane et al., 2013) (Bouillon et al., 2013)	Lexical Selection for Hybrid MT with Sequence Labeling Building bilingual lexicon to create dialect Tunisian corpora and adapt LM Two approaches to correcting homophone confusions in a hybrid SMT based system
Multilevels	(Pal et al., 2013) (Hsieh et al., 2013) (Tambouratzis et al., 2013)	A hybrid Word alignment model for PBSMT Uses of monolingual in-domain corpora for cross-domain adaptation with hybrid MT approaches Overview of a language-independent hybrid MT methodology

Table 1: HyTra 2013 paper overview.

whether technological breakthroughs as in the past are still possible are still possible, or if MT will be turning into a research field with only incremental advances. The question is: have we reached the point at which only refinements to existing approaches are needed? Or, on the contrary, do we need a new turning point?

Our guess is that, similar to the inflection point giving rise to the statistical MT approach during the last decade of the twentieth century, once again there might occur a new discovery which will revolutionize further the research on MT. We cannot know whether hybrid approaches will be involved; but, in any case, this seems to be a good and smart direction as it is open to the full spectrum of ideas and, thus, it should help to push the field forward.

Acknowledgments

This workshop has been supported by the Seventh Framework Program of the European Commission through the Marie Curie actions HyghTra, IMTraP, AutoWordNet and CrossLingMind and the Spanish "Ministerio de Economía y Competitividad" and the European Regional Development Fund through SpeechTech4all. We would like to thank the funding institution and all people who contributed towards making the workshop a success. For a more comprehensive list of acknowledgments refer to the preface of this volume.

References

Anton Batliner, J. Buckow, Heinrich Niemann, Elmar Nöth, and Volker Warnke, 2000a. *The Prosody Module*, pages 106–121. New York, Berlin.

Anton Batliner, Richard Huber, Heinrich Niemann, Elmar Nöth, Jörg Spilker, and K. Fischer, 2000b. *The Recognition of Emotion*, pages 122–130. New York, Berlin.

Pierrette Bouillon, Johanna Gerlach, Ulrich Germann, Barry Haddow, and Manny Rayner. 2013. Two approaches to correcting homophone confusions in a hybrid machine translation system. In *ACL Workshop on Hybrid Machine Approaches to Translation*, Sofia.

Rahma Boujelbane, Mariem Ellouze khemekhem, Siwar BenAyed, and Lamia HadrichBelguith. 2013. Building bilingual lexicon to create dialect tunisian corpora and adapt language model. In *ACL Workshop on Hybrid Machine Approaches to Translation*, Sofia.

Marta R. Costa-jussà, Patrik Lambert, Rafael E. Banchs, Reinhard Rapp, and Bogdan Babych, editors. 2012. *Proceedings of the Joint Workshop on Exploiting Synergies between Information Retrieval and Machine Translation (ESIRMT) and Hybrid Approaches to Machine Translation (HyTra)*. Association for Computational Linguistics, Avignon, France, April.

Marta R. Costa-jussà, Patrik Lambert, Rafael E. Banchs, Reinhard Rapp, Bogdan Babych, and Kurl Eberle, editors. 2013. *Proceedings of the Second Workshop on Hybrid Approaches to Translation (HyTra)*. Association for Computational Linguistics, Sofia, Bulgaria, August.

Andreas Eisele, Christian Federmann, Hans Uszkoreit, Hervé Saint-Amand, Martin Kay, Michael Jellinghaus, Sabine Hunsicker, Teresa Herrmann, and Yu Chen. 2008. Hybrid machine translation architectures within and beyond the euromatrix project. In John Hutchins and Walther v.Hahn, editors, *12th annual conference of the European Association for Machine Translation (EAMT)*, pages 27–34, Hamburg, Germany.

Annette Rios Gonzales and Anne Goehring. 2013. Machine learning disambiguation of quechua verb morphology. In *ACL Workshop on Hybrid Machine Approaches to Translation*, Sofia.

Nathan Green and Zdenek Zabokrtský. 2013. Improvements to syntax-based machine translation using ensemble dependency parsers. In *ACL Workshop on Hybrid Machine Approaches to Translation*, Sofia.

Dan Han, Pascual Martinez-Gomez, Yusuke Miyao, Katsuhito Sudoh, and Masaaki NAGATA. 2013. Using unlabeled dependency parsing for pre-reordering for chinese-to-japanese statistical machine translation. In *ACL Workshop on Hybrid Machine Approaches to Translation*, Sofia.

An-Chang Hsieh, Hen-Hsen Huang, and Hsin-Hsi Chen. 2013. Uses of monolingual in-domain corpora for cross-domain adaptation with hybrid mt approaches. In *ACL Workshop on Hybrid Machine Approaches to Translation*, Sofia.

Ines Turki Khemakhem, Salma Jamoussi, and Abdelmajid Ben Hamadou. 2013. Integrating morpho-syntactic feature in english-arabic statistical machine translation. In *ACL Workshop on Hybrid Machine Approaches to Translation*, Sofia.

László Laki, Attila Novak, and Borbála Siklósi. 2013. English to hungarian morpheme-based statistical machine translation system with reordering rules. In *ACL Workshop on Hybrid Machine Approaches to Translation*, Sofia.

Ronan Le Nagard and Philipp Koehn. 2010. Aiding pronoun translation with co-reference resolution. In *Proceedings of the Joint Fifth Workshop on Statistical Machine Translation and MetricsMATR*, pages 252–261, Uppsala, Sweden, July. Association for Computational Linguistics.

Will Lewis and Chris Quirk. 2013. Controlled ascent: Imbuing statistical mt with linguistic knowledge. In *ACL Workshop on Hybrid Machine Approaches to Translation*, Sofia.

Shuo Li, Derek F. Wong, and Lidia S. Chao. 2013. Experiments with pos-based restructuring and alignment-based reordering for statistical machine translation. In *ACL Workshop on Hybrid Machine Approaches to Translation*, Sofia.

Santanu Pal, Sudip Naskar, and Sivaji Bandyopadhyay. 2013. A hybrid word alignment model for phrase-based statistical machine translation. In *ACL Workshop on Hybrid Machine Approaches to Translation*, Sofia.

Raj Nath Patel, Rohit Gupta, Prakash B. Pimpale, and Sasikumar M. 2013. Reordering rules for english-hindi smt. In *ACL Workshop on Hybrid Machine Approaches to Translation*, Sofia.

Alex Rudnick and Michael Gasser. 2013. Lexical selection for hybrid mt with sequence labeling. In *ACL Workshop on Hybrid Machine Approaches to Translation*, Sofia.

Markus Saers, Karteek Addanki, and Dekai Wu. 2013. Unsupervised transduction grammar induction via minimum description length. In *ACL Workshop on Hybrid Machine Approaches to Translation*, Sofia.

George Tambouratzis, Sokratis Sofianopoulos, and Marina Vassiliou. 2013. Language-independent hybrid mt with presemt. In *ACL Workshop on Hybrid Machine Approaches to Translation*, Sofia.

Antonio Toral. 2013. Hybrid selection of language model training data using linguistic information and perplexity. In *ACL Workshop on Hybrid Machine Approaches to Translation*, Sofia.

Wolfgang Wahlster, editor. 2000. *Verbmobil: Foundations of Speech-to-Speech Translation*. Springer, Berlin, Heidelberg, New York.

Yorick Wilks. 1994. Stone soup and the french room: The empiricist-rationalist debate about machine translation. *Current Issues in Computational Linguistics: in honor of Don Walker*, pages 585–594. Pisa, Italy: Giardini / Dordrecht, The Netherlands: Kluwer Academic.

Statistical MT Systems Revisited: How much Hybridity do they have?

Hermann Ney
RWTH Aachen University, Aachen and DIGITEO Chair, LIMSI-CNRS, Paris
Lehrstuhl für Informatik 6
RWTH Aachen
Ahornstr. 55
52056 Aachen
ney@informatik.rwth-aachen.de

Abstract

The statistical approach to MT started about twenty-five years ago and has now been widely accepted as an alternative to the classical approach with manually designed rules. Among the attractive properties of the statistical approach is its capability to learn the translation models automatically from a (sufficiently) large amount of source-target sentence pairs. Thus the need for the manual design of suitable rules and for human interaction can be reduced dramatically when developing an MT system for a new application or language pair.

The idea of hybrid MT is to combine the advantages of both the rule-based and statistical approaches. In practice, most statistical MT systems make use of manually designed rules in order to improve the MT accuracy. We revisit the RWTH systems in order to study the effect of typical preprocessing steps based on manually designed rules. The RWTH systems cover various tasks (e.g. news, patents, lectures) and various languages (e.g. Arabic, Chinese, English, Japanese). The preprocessing steps may include a categorization of numbers, date and time expressions, a word decomposition based on morphological analysis and explicit word re-ordering based on a syntactic analysis. In general, the preprocessing steps may depend heavily on the language pair under consideration.

We will also address concepts that aim at a tighter integration of the conventional rule-based and the statistical approaches. We will consider the implications of such a tight integration for the architecture of an MT system.

Hybrid Selection of Language Model Training Data Using Linguistic Information and Perplexity

Antonio Toral
School of Computing
Dublin City University
Dublin, Ireland
atoral@computing.dcu.ie

Abstract

We explore the selection of training data for language models using perplexity. We introduce three novel models that make use of linguistic information and evaluate them on three different corpora and two languages. In four out of the six scenarios a linguistically motivated method outperforms the purely statistical state-of-the-art approach. Finally, a method which combines surface forms and the linguistically motivated methods outperforms the baseline in all the scenarios, selecting data whose perplexity is between 3.49% and 8.17% (depending on the corpus and language) lower than that of the baseline.

1 Introduction

Language models (LMs) are a fundamental piece in statistical applications that produce natural language text, such as machine translation and speech recognition. In order to perform optimally, a LM should be trained on data from the same domain as the data that it will be applied to. This poses a problem, because in the majority of applications, the amount of domain-specific data is limited.

A popular strand of research in recent years to tackle this problem is that of training data selection. Given a limited domain-specific corpus and a larger non-domain-specific corpus, the task consists on finding suitable data for the specific domain in the non-domain-specific corpus. The underlying assumption is that a non-domain-specific corpus, if broad enough, contains sentences similar to a domain-specific corpus, which therefore, would be useful for training models for that domain.

This paper focuses on the approach that uses perplexity for the selection of training data. The first works in this regard (Gao et al., 2002; Lin et al., 1997) use the perplexity according to a domain-specific LM to rank the text segments (e.g. sentences) of non-domain-specific corpora. The text segments with perplexity less than a given threshold are selected.

A more recent method, which can be considered the state-of-the-art, is Moore-Lewis (Moore and Lewis, 2010). It considers not only the cross-entropy[1] according to the domain-specific LM but also the cross-entropy according to a LM built on a random subset (equal in size to the domain-specific corpus) of the non-domain-specific corpus. The additional use of a LM from the non-domain-specific corpus allows to select a subset of the non-domain-specific corpus which is better (the perplexity of a test set of the specific domain has lower perplexity on a LM trained on this subset) and smaller compared to the previous approaches. The experiment was carried out for English, using Europarl (Koehn, 2005) as the domain-specific corpus and LDC Gigaword[2] as the non-domain-specific one.

In this paper we study whether the use of two types of linguistic knowledge (lemmas and named entities) can contribute to obtain better results within the perplexity-based approach.

2 Methodology

We explore the use of linguistic information for the selection of data to train domain-specific LMs from non-domain-specific corpora. Our hypothesis is that ranking by perplexity on n-grams that represent linguistic patterns (rather than n-grams that represent surface forms) captures additional information, and thus may select valuable data that is not selected according solely to surface forms.

We use two types of linguistic information at

[1] note that using cross-entropy is equivalent to using perplexity since they are monotonically related.

[2] http://www.ldc.upenn.edu/Catalog/catalogEntry.jsp?catalogId=LDC2007T07

word level: lemmas and named entity categories. We experiment with the following models:

- Forms (hereafter f), uses surface forms. This model replicates the Moore-Lewis approach and is to be considered the baseline.
- Forms and named entities (hereafter fn), uses surface forms, with the exception of any word detected as a named entity, which is substituted by its type (e.g. person, organisation).
- Lemmas (hereafter l), uses lemmas.
- Lemmas and named entities (hereafter ln), uses lemmas, with the exception of any word detected as a named entity, which is substituted by its type.

A sample sentence, according to each of these models, follows:

```
f: I declare resumed the session of the
 European Parliament
fn: I declare resumed the session of the
 NP00000
l: i declare resume the session of the
 european_parliament
ln: i declare resume the session of the
 NP00000
```

Table 1 shows the number of n-grams on LMs built on the English side of News Commentary v8 (hereafter NC) for each of the models. Regarding 1-grams, compared to f, the substitution of named entities by their categories (fn) results in smaller vocabulary size (-24.79%). Similarly, the vocabulary is reduced for the models l (-8.39%) and ln (-44.18%). Although not a result in itself, this might be an indication that using linguistically motivated models could be useful to deal with data sparsity.

n	f	fn	l	ln
1	65076	48945	59619	36326
2	981077	847720	835825	702118
3	2624800	2382629	2447759	2212709
4	3633724	3412719	3523888	3325311
5	3929751	3780064	3856917	3749813

Table 1: Number of n-grams in LMs built using the different models

Our procedure follows that of the Moore-Lewis method. We build LMs for the domain-specific corpus and for a random subset of the non-domain-specific corpus of the same size (number of sentences) of the domain-specific corpus. Each sentence s in the non-domain-specific corpus is then scored according to equation 1 where $PP_I(s)$ is the perplexity of s according to the domain-specific LM and $PP_O(s)$ is the perplexity of s according to the non-domain-specific LM.

$$score(s) = PP_I(s) - PP_O(s) \quad (1)$$

We build LMs for the domain-specific and non-domain-specific corpora using the four models previously introduced. Then we rank the sentences of the non-domain-specific corpus for each of these models and keep the highest ranked sentences according to a threshold. Finally, we build a LM on the set of sentences selected[3] and compute the perplexity of the test set on this LM.

We also investigate the combination of the four models. The procedure is fairly straightforward: given the sentences selected by all the models for a given threshold, we iterate through these sentences following the ranking order and keeping all the distinct sentences selected until we obtain a set of sentences whose size is the one indicated by the threshold. I.e. we add to our distinct set of sentences first the top ranked sentence by each of the methods, then the sentence ranked second by each method, and so on.

3 Experiments

3.1 Setting

We use corpora from the translation task at WMT13.[4] Our domain-specific corpus is NC, and we carry out experiments with three non-domain-specific corpora: a subset of Common Crawl[5] (hereafter CC), Europarl version 7 (hereafter EU), and United Nations (Eisele and Chen, 2010) (hereafter UN). We use the test data from WMT12 (newstest2012) as our test set. We carry out experiments on two languages for which these corpora are available: English (referred to as "en" in tables) and Spanish ("es" in tables).

We test the methods on three very different non-domain-specific corpora, both in terms of the topics that they cover (text crawled from web in CC, parliamentary speeches in EU and official documents from United Nations in UN) and their size

[3]For the linguistic methods we replace the sentences selected (which contain lemmas and/or named entities) with the corresponding sentences in the original corpus (containing only word forms).

[4]http://www.statmt.org/wmt13/translation-task.html

[5]http://commoncrawl.org/

(around 2 million sentences both for CC and EU, and around 11 million for UN). This can be considered as a contribution of this paper since previous works such as Moore and Lewis (2010) and, more recently, Axelrod et al. (2011) test the Moore-Lewis method on only one non-domain-specific corpus: LDC Gigaword and an unpublished general-domain corpus, respectively.

All the LMs are built with IRSTLM 5.80.01 (Federico et al., 2008), use up to 5-grams and are smoothed using a simplified version of the improved Kneser-Ney method (Chen and Goodman, 1996). For lemmatisation and named entity recognition we use Freeling 3.0 (Padró and Stanilovsky, 2012). The corpora are tokenised and truecased using scripts from the Moses toolkit (Koehn et al., 2007).

3.2 Experiments with Different Models

Figures 1, 2 and 3 show the perplexities obtained by each method on different subsets selected from the English corpora CC, EU and UN, respectively. We obtain these subsets according to different thresholds, i.e. percentages of sentences selected from the non-domain-specific corpus. These are the first $\frac{1}{64}$ ranked sentences, $\frac{1}{32}$, $\frac{1}{16}$, $\frac{1}{8}$, $\frac{1}{4}$, $\frac{1}{2}$ and 1.[6] Corresponding figures for Spanish are omitted due to the limited space available and also because the trends in those figures are very similar.

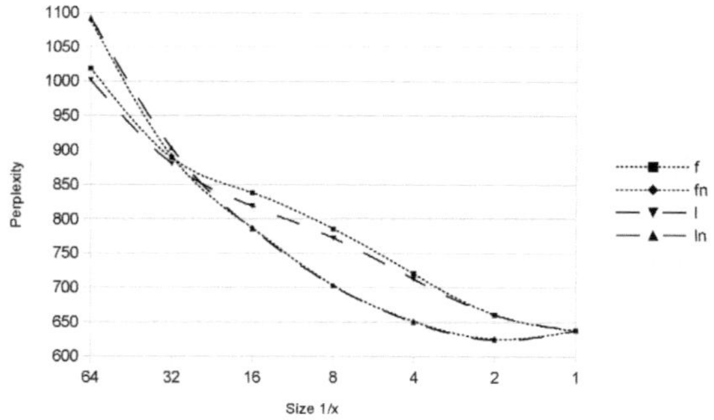

Figure 1: Results of the different methods on CC

In all the figures, the results are very similar regardless of the use of lemmas. The use of named entities, however, produces substantially different results. The models that do not use named entity categories obtain the best results for lower thresholds (up to $1/32$ for CC, and up to $1/16$ both for

[6]An additional threshold, $\frac{1}{128}$, is used for the United Nations corpus

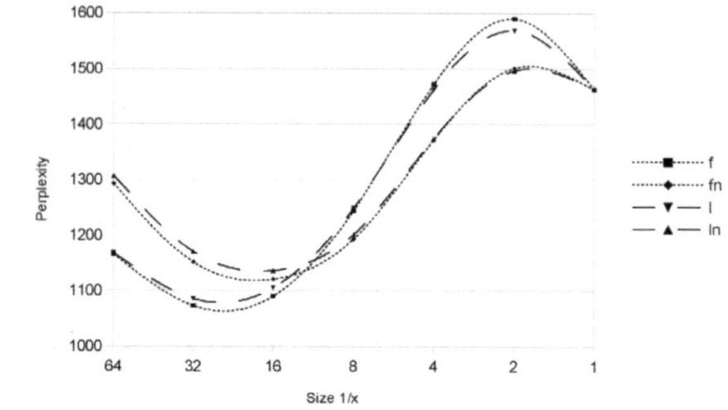

Figure 2: Results of the different methods on EU

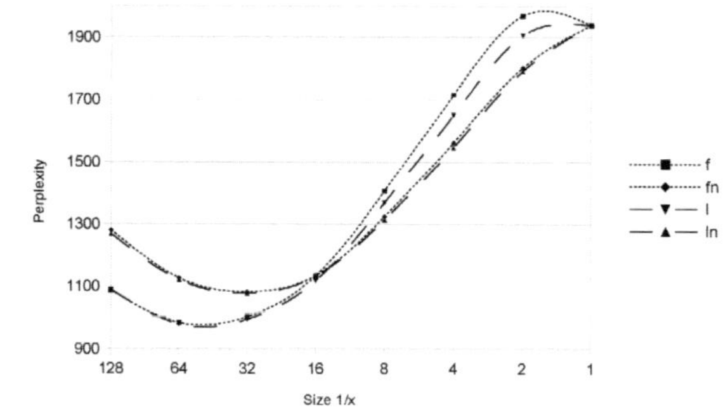

Figure 3: Results of the different methods on UN

EU and UN). If the best perplexity is obtained with a lower threshold than this (the case of EU, $1/32$, and UN, $1/64$), then methods that do not use named entities obtain the best result. However, if the optimal perplexity is obtained with a higher threshold (the case of CC, $1/2$), then using named entities yields the best result.

Table 2 presents the results for each model. For each scenario (corpus and language combination), we show the threshold for which the best result is obtained (column best). The perplexity obtained on data selected by each model is shown in the subsequent columns. For the linguistic methods, we also show the comparison of their performance to the baseline (as percentages, columns diff). The perplexity when using the full corpus is shown (column full) together with the comparison of this result to the best method (last column diff).

The results, as previously seen in Figures 1, 2 and 3, differ with respect to the corpus but follow similar trends across languages. For CC we obtain the best results using named entities. The model ln obtains the best result for English (5.54% lower

corpus	best	f	fn	diff	l	diff	ln	diff	full	diff
cc_en	1/2	660.77	625.62	-5.32	660.58	-0.03	**624.19**	-5.54	638.24	-2.20
eu_en	1/32	**1072.98**	1151.13	7.28	1085.66	1.18	1170.00	9.04	1462.61	-26.64
un_en	1/64	984.08	1127.55	14.58	**979.06**	-0.51	1121.45	13.96	1939.44	-49.52
cc_es	1/2	499.22	**480.17**	-3.82	498.93	-0.06	480.45	-3.76	481.96	-0.37
eu_es	1/16	**788.62**	813.32	3.13	801.50	1.63	825.13	4.63	960.06	-17.86
un_es	1/32	725.93	773.89	6.61	**723.37**	-0.35	771.25	6.24	1339.78	-46.01

Table 2: Results for the different models

perplexity than the baseline), while the model fn obtains the best result for Spanish (3.82%), although in both cases the difference between these two models is rather small.

For the other corpora, the best results are obtained without named entities. In the case of EU, the baseline obtains the best result, although the model l is not very far (1.18% higher perplexity for English and 1.63% for Spanish). This trend is reversed for UN, the model l obtaining the best scores but close to the baseline (-0.51%, -0.35%).

3.3 Experiments with the Combination of Models

Table 3 shows the perplexities obtained by the method that combines the four models (column comb) for the threshold that yielded the best result in each scenario (see Table 2), compares these results (column diff) to those obtained by the baseline (column f) and shows the percentage of sentences that this method inspected from the sentences selected by the individual methods (column perc).

corpus	f	comb	diff	perc
cc_en	660.77	**613.83**	-7.10	76.90
eu_en	1072.98	**1035.51**	-3.49	70.51
un_en	984.08	**908.47**	-7.68	74.58
cc_es	499.22	**478.87**	-4.08	74.61
eu_es	788.62	**748.22**	-5.12	68.05
un_es	725.93	**666.62**	-8.17	74.32

Table 3: Results of the combination method

The combination method outperforms the baseline and any of the individual linguistic models in all the scenarios. The perplexity obtained by combining the models is substantially lower than that obtained by the baseline (ranging from 3.49% to 8.17%). In all the scenarios, the combination method takes its sentences from roughly the top 70% sentences ranked by the individual methods.

4 Conclusions and Future Work

This paper has explored the use of linguistic information (lemmas and named entities) for the task of training data selection for LMs. We have introduced three linguistically motivated models, and compared them to the state-of-the-art method for perplexity-based data selection across three different corpora and two languages. In four out of these six scenarios a linguistically motivated method outperforms the state-of-the-art approach.

We have also presented a method which combines surface forms and the three linguistically motivated methods. This combination outperforms the baseline in all the scenarios, selecting data whose perplexity is between 3.49% and 8.17% (depending on the corpus and language) lower than that of the baseline.

Regarding future work, we have several plans. One interesting experiment would be to apply these models to a morphologically-rich language, to check if, as hypothesised, these models deal better with sparse data.

Another strand regards the application of these models to filter parallel corpora, e.g. following the extension of the Moore-Lewis method (Axelrod et al., 2011) or in combination with other methods which are deemed to be more suitable for parallel data, e.g. (Mansour et al., 2011).

We have used one type of linguistic information in each LM, but another possibility is to combine different pieces of linguistic information in a single LM, e.g. following a hybrid LM that uses words and tags, depending of the frequency of each type (Ruiz et al., 2012).

Given the fact that the best result is obtained with different models depending on the corpus, it would be worth to investigate whether given a new corpus, one could predict the best method to be applied and the threshold for which one could expect to obtain the minimum perplexity.

Acknowledgments

We would like to thank Raphaël Rubino for insightful conversations. The research leading to these results has received funding from the European Union Seventh Framework Programme FP7/2007-2013 under grant agreements PIAP-GA-2012-324414 and FP7-ICT-2011-296347.

References

Amittai Axelrod, Xiaodong He, and Jianfeng Gao. 2011. Domain adaptation via pseudo in-domain data selection. In *Proceedings of the Conference on Empirical Methods in Natural Language Processing*, EMNLP '11, pages 355–362, Stroudsburg, PA, USA. Association for Computational Linguistics.

Stanley F. Chen and Joshua Goodman. 1996. An empirical study of smoothing techniques for language modeling. In *Proceedings of the 34th annual meeting on Association for Computational Linguistics*, ACL '96, pages 310–318, Stroudsburg, PA, USA. Association for Computational Linguistics.

Andreas Eisele and Yu Chen. 2010. Multiun: A multilingual corpus from united nation documents. In Nicoletta Calzolari, Khalid Choukri, Bente Maegaard, Joseph Mariani, Jan Odijk, Stelios Piperidis, Mike Rosner, and Daniel Tapias, editors, *LREC*. European Language Resources Association.

Marcello Federico, Nicola Bertoldi, and Mauro Cettolo. 2008. IRSTLM: an open source toolkit for handling large scale language models. In *INTERSPEECH*, pages 1618–1621. ISCA.

Jianfeng Gao, Joshua Goodman, Mingjing Li, and Kai-Fu Lee. 2002. Toward a unified approach to statistical language modeling for chinese. 1(1):3–33, March.

Philipp Koehn, Hieu Hoang, Alexandra Birch, Chris Callison-Burch, Marcello Federico, Nicola Bertoldi, Brooke Cowan, Wade Shen, Christine Moran, Richard Zens, Chris Dyer, Ondřej Bojar, Alexandra Constantin, and Evan Herbst. 2007. Moses: open source toolkit for statistical machine translation. In *Proceedings of the 45th Annual Meeting of the ACL on Interactive Poster and Demonstration Sessions*, ACL '07, pages 177–180, Stroudsburg, PA, USA. Association for Computational Linguistics.

Philipp Koehn. 2005. Europarl: A Parallel Corpus for Statistical Machine Translation. In *Conference Proceedings: the tenth Machine Translation Summit*, pages 79–86, Phuket, Thailand. AAMT, AAMT.

Sung-Chien Lin, Chi-Lung Tsai, Lee-Feng Chien, Keh-Jiann Chen, and Lin-Shan Lee. 1997. Chinese language model adaptation based on document classification and multiple domain-specific language models. In George Kokkinakis, Nikos Fakotakis, and Evangelos Dermatas, editors, *EUROSPEECH*. ISCA.

Saab Mansour, Joern Wuebker, and Hermann Ney. 2011. Combining translation and language model scoring for domain-specific data filtering. In *International Workshop on Spoken Language Translation*, pages 222–229, San Francisco, California, USA, December.

Robert C. Moore and William Lewis. 2010. Intelligent selection of language model training data. In *Proceedings of the ACL 2010 Conference Short Papers*, ACLShort '10, pages 220–224, Stroudsburg, PA, USA. Association for Computational Linguistics.

Lluís Padró and Evgeny Stanilovsky. 2012. Freeling 3.0: Towards wider multilinguality. In *Proceedings of the Language Resources and Evaluation Conference (LREC 2012)*, Istanbul, Turkey, May. ELRA.

Nick Ruiz, Arianna Bisazza, Roldano Cattoni, and Marcello Federico. 2012. FBK's Machine Translation Systems for IWSLT 2012's TED Lectures. In *Proceedings of the 9th International Workshop on Spoken Language Translation (IWSLT)*.

Machine Learning Disambiguation of Quechua Verb Morphology

Annette Rios
Institute of Computational Linguistics
University of Zurich
arios@ifi.uzh.ch

Anne Göhring
Institute of Computational Linguistics
University of Zurich
goehring@cl.uzh.ch

Abstract

We have implemented a rule-based prototype of a Spanish-to-Cuzco Quechua MT system enhanced through the addition of statistical components. The greatest difficulty during the translation process is to generate the correct Quechua verb form in subordinated clauses. The prototype has several rules that decide which verb form should be used in a given context. However, matching the context in order to apply the correct rule depends crucially on the parsing quality of the Spanish input. As the form of the subordinated verb depends heavily on the conjunction in the subordinated Spanish clause and the semantics of the main verb, we extracted this information from two treebanks and trained different classifiers on this data. We tested the best classifier on a set of 4 texts, increasing the correct subordinated verb forms from 80% to 89%.

1 Introduction

As part of our research project SQUOIA,[1] we have developed several tools and resources for Cuzco Quechua. These include a treebank, currently consisting of around 500 sentences[2], and a rule-based MT system Spanish-Cuzco Quechua. The treebank is currently being enhanced with more annotated text and should reach about 4000 sentences upon project completion.

As for the translation system, we want to enhance the rule-based approach with statistical methods to overcome certain limitations of the prototype. The main reason to build the core system with a rule-based architecture is the lack of parallel texts in Spanish and Quechua; there is not enough parallel material to train a statistical MT system of acceptable quality, as Mohler and Mihalcea (2008) showed in their experiments. They trained an SMT system Spanish-Quechua on translations of the Bible, resulting in 2.89 BLEU points. By increasing the size of their training corpus with web-crawled parallel texts and additional Bible translations, they achieved 4.55 BLEU points.[3] Although better, the overall quality of the SMT system is still very low.

There are at least two other projects that started the implementation of MT systems for the same language pair, but in the opposite direction; the AVENUE project[4] used elicited corpora to build an MT system Quechua-Spanish. Furthermore, the language pair Quechua-Spanish has recently been added to the open-source MT platform Apertium.[5] The translation system is still at a very early stage in its development; at present, the grammar contains 30 transfer rules and a morphological analyzer.

2 Hybrid MT Spanish-Cuzco Quechua

The core of our own Spanish-Quechua MT system is a classical rule-based transfer engine, based on a reimplementation of the Matxin[6] framework that was originally developed for the translation of Spanish to Basque (Mayor et al., 2012). As not all of the necessary disambiguation can be done satisfactorily with rules alone, we plan to add statistical modules at different stages of the transfer to resolve the remaining ambiguities. The module for the disambiguation of subordinated verb

[1] http://tiny.uzh.ch/2Q

[2] available through the PML query interface (Štěpánek and Petr, 2010) at: http://kitt.ifi.uzh.ch:8075/app/form

[3] both baseline and improved SMT systems evaluated on parts of the Bible

[4] http://www.cs.cmu.edu/~avenue/

[5] http://wiki.apertium.org/wiki/Quechua_cuzqueno_y_castellano

[6] http://matxin.sourceforge.net/

forms described in this paper is the first statistical enhancement to the rule-based prototype.

3 Quechua verb forms

Subordinated clauses in Quechua are often non-finite, nominal forms. There are several nominalizing suffixes that are used for different clause types that will be illustrated in more detail in this section.

3.1 Switch-Reference

A common type of subordination in Quechua is the so-called switch-reference: the subordinated, non-finite verb bears a suffix that indicates whether its subject is the same as in the main clause or not. If the subject in the subordinated clause is different, the non-finite verb bears a possessive suffix that indicates the subject person. Consider the following examples[7]

Same subject: *Mikhuspa hamuni.*

(1)

Mikhu	***-spa***	*hamu*	*-ni.*
eat	**-SS**	come	-1.Sg

"When I finished eating, I'll come."
(lit. "My eating, I come.")

Different subject: *Mikhuchkaptiy pasakura.*

(2)

Mikhu	*-chka*	***-pti***	*-y*	*pasa*	*-ku*	*-ra*
eat	-Prog	**-DS**	-1.Sg.Poss	leave	-Rflx	-Pst
-ø.						
-3.Sg						

"While I was eating, he left."
(lit. "[During] my eating, he left.")
(Dedenbach-Salazar Sáenz et al., 2002, 168)

In the Spanish source language, subordinated verbs are usually finite. An overt subject is not necessary, as personal pronouns are used only for emphasis ("pro-drop"). In order to generate the correct verb form, we need to find the subject of the subordinated verb and compare it to the main verb. For this reason, we included a module that performs co-reference resolution on subjects. So far, the procedure is based on the simple assumption that an elided subject is coreferent with the previous explicit subject, if this subject agrees in number and person with the current verb. Of course, there are some exceptions that have to be considered, e.g. the subject of a verb in direct speech is not a good antecedent.

3.2 Other Types of Subordination

Generally, the relation of the subordinated clause to the main clause is expressed through different conjunctions in Spanish. In Quechua, on the other hand, a specific verb form in combination with a case suffix indicates the type of subordination. For example, Spanish *para que* - "in order to" has to be translated with a nominal verb form with the suffix *-na* and the case suffix *-paq* (usually called benefactive, "for"):

(3) *Ventanata kichay wayraq haykurimunanpaq.*

Ventana	*-ta*	*kicha*	*-y*	*wayra*	*-q*	
window	-Acc	open	-2.Sg.Imp	wind	-Gen	
hayku	*-ri*	*-mu*	***-na***	*-n*	*-paq.*	
enter	-Inch	-Dir	**-Obl**	-3.Sg.Poss	-Ben	

"Open the window, so the air comes in."
(lit. "Open the window for his entering of the wind")
(Cusihuamán, 1976, 210)

Finite verb forms are also possible in subordinated clauses; in this case, the relation of the subordinated and the main clause is indicated through a "linker". A linker often consists of a demonstrative pronoun combined with case suffixes or so-called independent suffixes; these are special suffixes that can be attached to any word class and their position is usually at the end of the suffix sequence. The functions of the independent suffixes include data source, polar question marking and topic or contrast, amongst others (Adelaar and Muysken, 2004, 209). In combination with demonstrative pronouns, the independent suffixes are used for linking clauses, similar to Spanish or English conjunctions. For example, the combination of demonstrative *chay* - "this" with the topic marker *-qa*, *chayqa*, is used in the sense of "if, in case that":

(4) *Munanki* ***chayqa****, Arekipatapis rinki makinapi.*

Muna	*-nki*	***chay***	***-qa,***	*Arekipa*	*-ta*	*-pis*
want	-2.Sg	**this**	**-Top**	Arequipa	-Acc	-Add
ri	*-nki*	*makina*	*-pi.*			
go	-2.Sg	machine	-Loc			

"If you like, you can also go to Arequipa by train (machine)."
(Cusihuamán, 1976, 264)

A special case is indirect speech in the Spanish source text; the Quechua equivalence of indirect

[7] Abbreviations used:

Acc: accusative	Add: additive ('too,also')
Ben: benefactive ('for')	Dir: directional
DirE: direct evidentiality	DS: different subject
Gen: genitive	Imp: imperative
Inch: inchoative	Loc: locative
Neg: negation	Obl: obligative
Perf: perfect	Poss: possessive
Prog: progressive	Pst: past
Rflx: reflexive	Sg: singular
SS: same subject	Top: topic

speech is direct speech. The conversion from indirect to direct speech is not trivial, because coreference resolution for the subject is required: if the subject of the main verb is the same as in the indirect speech clause, the verb has to be generated as first person form in direct speech.[8]

Furthermore, the form of the subordinated verb may also depend on the semantics of the main verb, e.g. complement clauses of control verbs usually require *-na*, whereas with other verbs, the nominalizer *-sqa* is used:

(5)

Ri	***-na***	*-yki*	*-ta*	*muna*	*-ni.*
go	**-Obl**	-2.Sg.Poss	-Acc	want	-1.Sg

"I want you to leave."
(lit. "I want your going.")

(6)

Ama	*-n*	*chay*	*yacha*	***-sqa***	*-yki*	*-ta*
don't	-DirE	this	know	**-Perf**	-2.Sg.Poss	-Acc
qunqa	*-nki*	*-chu.*				
forget	-2.Sg	-Neg				

"Don't forget what you learned."
(lit. "Don't forget those your learnings.")
(Cusihuamán, 1976, 125)

For all of these cases, the rule-based prototype has a set of rules to match the given context, so that the correct form can be assigned to each verb.

3.3 Relative Clauses

A special case of subordination are relative clauses; the verb in the relative clause is a nominal form that is either agentive or non-agentive. The form depends on the semantics of the nominal head and its semantic role within the relative clause. The MT system includes a specific rule-based module that uses semantic resources for the disambiguation of relative clauses. As their form does not depend on the main verb, relative clauses will not be discussed further in this paper.

4 Rule-based Disambiguation of Verb Forms

The disambiguation of subordinated verb forms depends on the previously described steps: the disambiguation of Spanish relative clauses, coreference resolution of subjects, the recognition of the given type of subordination through the Spanish conjunction and the semantics of the main verb. Such a rule-based approach is prone to error, since

		correct	incorrect
verb chunks to disambiguate:	219		
disambiguated chunks:	186	175	11
	85%	**94%**	**6%**
left ambiguous for ML:	33		

Table 1: Evaluation of rule-based verb disambiguation

it depends crucially on correct parse trees and correctly tagged verbs and conjunctions. As a precaution, we only use rule-based disambiguation in cases that can be safely disambiguated, i.e. if we find the main verb and the Spanish conjunction in the parse tree where they are to be expected. An evaluation on four texts from different genres[9] shows that the rule-based module can disambiguate 85% of the verb forms; of these, 94% are correct (see Table 1 for details).

For subordinated clauses that cannot be disambiguated with rules (15% in the 4 texts used for evaluation), we use the machine learning approach described in the following section.

5 Disambiguation with Machine Learning

5.1 Training Corpus

As the form of the subordinated verb depends mainly on the semantics of the main verb and the Spanish conjunction in the source text, we trained and evaluated different classifiers based on these features.

We extracted all verb pairs from our Quechua treebank with their corresponding forms and, if present, the linker. The Quechua roots in the treebank contain one or more Spanish translations. We used the Spanish lemmas to create the instances for training, as we might not have access to the Quechua translation of the Spanish verb during the transfer. Furthermore, we use the standardized Southern Quechua orthography (Cerrón-Palomino, 1994) in our translation system; however, the text in the treebank is written in a slightly

[8] consider this English example:
"John said he wanted to go fishing."
if John = he : "I want to go fishing", John said.
if John $\neq$ he: "He wants to go fishing", John said.

[9] Texts:
- *La catarata de la sirena* - 'the waterfall of the siren' (Andean story)
- first two chapters of 'The Little Prince'
- article from the Peruvian newspaper 'El Diario'
- Spanish Wikipedia article about Peru

different spelling. By using the Spanish version of the verbs, we avoid mapping the Quechua verbs obtained from the transfer to the orthography used in the treebank. Since most Quechua roots in the treebank contain more than one Spanish translation, we can create an instance for every combination of the Spanish translations. With this approach we extracted 444 instances from our treebank.

Since this initial training set was too small to yield satisfactory results,[10] we added synthetic training data created from the translation of the Spanish AnCora treebank (Taulé et al., 2008) with the prototype. As the dependencies in AnCora are correctly annotated, the rules of the MT system will assign the correct Quechua verb forms with high precision. We used these verb forms as additional instances for training the classifiers. The total number of instances obtained from AnCora amounts to 7366.

5.2 Setup

We used WEKA (Hall et al., 2009) and SVM^{multiclass} (Joachims, 1999) to compute the machine learning models for our disambiguation task. We trained different classifiers on 7810 instances extracted from a Quechua and a translated Spanish treebank. The class variable `form` represents the form of the subordinated verb; there are 5 different classes:[11]

- perfect: nominal form with *-sqa*
- obligative: nominal form with *-na*
- agentive: nominal form with *-q*
- switch: nominal forms with *-pti/spa*
- finite

5.3 Evaluation

We tested the classifiers on the ambiguous forms from the 4 texts that we used for the evaluation of the rule-based approach (see Table 1). Additionally, we extracted verb pairs from Quechua texts (with their Spanish translations) and assigned them the corresponding class number. With this procedure, we collected 100 instances for testing. We trained and tested different classifiers: Naïve Bayes, Nearest Neighbour (Martin, 1995) and a multiclass support vector machine (Joachims, 1999). Table 2 contains the best results for each classifier. The three WEKA classifiers were trained with default settings, whereas for SVM^{multiclass} we obtained the best results with ϵ=0.1 and c=0.02 (linear kernel).

In an ideal case of disambiguation during translation, we would have information about the lemma of the main verb ("head") and the Spanish conjunction ("linker").[12] In these ideal cases, we use the rule-based module to assign the subordinated verb form. In real translation scenarios, however, either the head or linker might be missing; a common source for errors are polysemous conjunctions, such as *que* - 'that' or *como* - 'as' , that the tagger erroneously labeled as relative pronoun or preposition, respectively. In this case, the linker cannot be retrieved from the parse tree and we have to guess the verb form based only on the lemmas of the main and the subordinated verb ("subV"). Furthermore, we might have a clearly subordinated verb form with a linker that the parser attached to the wrong head. Finding the correct head automatically is not always possible, especially within coordinations. In this case, we need to guess the verb form based only on the lemma of the subordinated verb and the linker.

Naïve Bayes achieves the highest scores, both on cross validation and on the test set (see Table 2 for details). From the 33 ambiguous verb forms in Table 1, only 22 were disambiguated with the classifiers, as the rest were either nouns erroneously tagged as verbs or had the wrong lemma, and therefore can be counted as false without further processing. From the 22 correctly tagged ambiguous verbs, Naïve Bayes classified 20 instances correctly. The rules of the MT system disambiguated 80% of the verb forms in the 4 evaluation texts correctly. Feeding the remaining ambiguous verbs to the classifier; we achieve an overall accuracy of 89% (see the results in Table 3).
The complete translation pipeline including the Naive Bayes classifier is illustrated in Fig. 1.

6 Concluding remarks

We enhanced a purely rule-based machine translation system for the language pair Spanish-Quechua with a classifier that predicts the form of subordinated verbs in the target language Quechua, based on information collected from the

[10] 36% accuracy achieved with Naive Bayes, on the same test set used in the final evaluation (see Table 2).

[11] Every instance contains the lemma of the main verb, the lemma of the subordinated verb, the linker and a number representing one of the 5 classes.

[12] The Spanish lemma of the subordinated verb is always known, since this is the verb we want to disambiguate.

	SVM ϵ=0.1,c=0.02	LibSVM default: radial	NBayes	NNge
cross-validation, 10x				
head,subV	-	43%	**58%**	48%
subV,linker	-	59%	**67%**	60%
head,subV,linker	-	47%	**81%**	75%
test set, 100 instances				
head,subV	31%	38%	**57%**	47%
subV,linker	41%	61%	**75%**	68%
head,subV,linker	46%	45%	**84%**	72%

Table 2: Evaluation of Classifiers

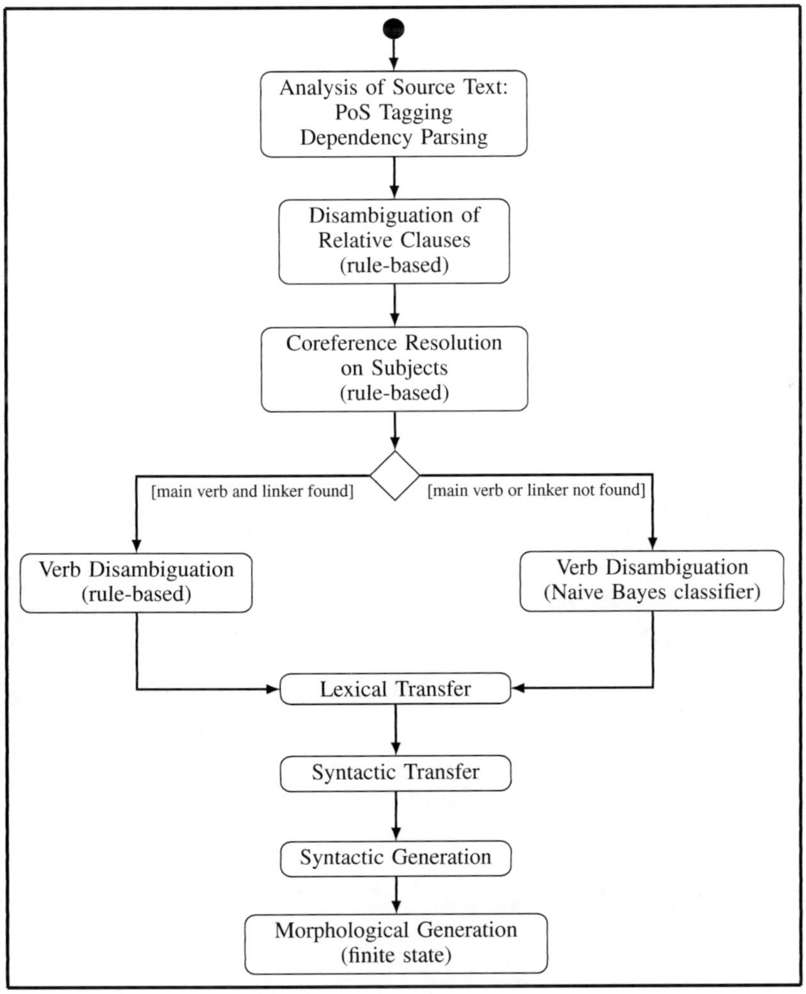

Figure 1: Translation Pipeline

		correct	incorrect
rule based:	186	175	11
		80%	5%
not disambiguated*:	11		11
ML :	22	20	2
total "verb" chunks:	219	195	24
		89%	11%

Table 3: Evaluation of Hybrid Verb Disambiguation
*11 of the ambiguous "verbs" are nouns that were erroneously tagged as verbs, had the wrong lemma or were relative clauses. We did not run those through disambiguation with ML.

Spanish input text. The MT system has rules to match the context of the subordinated verb and assign a verb form for generation. Due to parsing and tagging errors, the information needed for rule-based disambiguation cannot always be retrieved. In order to disambiguate these forms, we use a classifier that predicts the verb form even if all of the context information is not accessible. We tested three different machine learning algorithms, out of which Naïve Bayes achieved the best results. In an evaluation on 4 texts from different genres, verb disambiguation was improved from 80% (purely rule-based) to 89%, with a combination of the rule-based module and the Naïve Bayes classifier.

Acknowledgments

The authors would like to thank Rico Sennrich for his helpful advise and David Harfield for proofreading the first version of this paper. This research is funded by the Swiss National Science Foundation under grant 100015_132219/1.

References

Willem F. H. Adelaar and Pieter Muysken. 2004. *The Languages of the Andes*. Cambridge Language Surveys. Cambridge University Press.

Rodolfo Cerrón-Palomino. 1994. *Quechua sureño, diccionario unificado quechua-castellano, castellano-quechua*. Biblioteca Nacional del Perú, Lima.

Antonio G. Cusihuamán. 1976. *Gramática Quechua: Cuzco-Collao*. Gramáticas referenciales de la lengua quechua. Ministerio de Educación, Lima.

Sabine Dedenbach-Salazar Sáenz, Utta von Gleich, Roswith Hartmann, Peter Masson, and Clodoaldo Soto Ruiz. 2002. *Rimaykullayki - Unterrichtsmaterialien zum Quechua Ayacuchano*. Dietrich Reimer Verlag GmbH, Berlin, 4. edition.

Mark Hall, Eibe Frank, Geoffrey Holmes, Bernhard Pfahringer, Peter Reutemann, and Ian H. Witten. 2009. The WEKA data mining software: an update. *SIGKDD Explorations*, 11(1):10–18.

Thorsten Joachims. 1999. Making Large-Scale SVM Learning Practical. In Bernhard Schölkopf, Christopher John C. Burges, and Alexander J. Smola, editors, *Advances in Kernel Methods - Support Vector Learning*, pages 169–184, Cambridge, MA, USA. MIT Press.

Brent Martin. 1995. Instance-Based learning: Nearest Neighbor With Generalization. Master's thesis, University of Waikato, Hamilton, New Zealand.

Aingeru Mayor, Iñaki Alegria, Arantza Díaz de Ilarraza, Gorka Labaka, Mikel Lersundi, and Kepa Sarasola. 2012. Matxin, an open-source rule-based machine translation system for Basque. *Machine Translation*, (25):53–82.

Michael Mohler and Rada Mihalcea. 2008. Babylon Parallel Text Builder: Gathering Parallel Texts for Low-Density Languages. In Nicoletta Calzolari, Khalid Choukri, Bente Maegaard, Joseph Mariani, Jan Odijk, Stelios Piperidis, and Daniel Tapias, editors, *Proceedings of the Sixth International Conference on Language Resources and Evaluation (LREC'08)*, Marrakech, Marroco.

Mariona Taulé, M. Antònia Martí, and Marta Recasens. 2008. AnCora: Multilevel Annotated Corpora for Catalan and Spanish. In Nicoletta Calzolari, Khalid Choukri, Bente Maegaard, Joseph Mariani, Jan Odijk, Stelios Piperidis, and Daniel Tapias, editors, *Proceedings of the Sixth International Language Resources and Evaluation (LREC'08)*, Marrakech, Marroco.

Jan Štěpánek and Pajas Petr. 2010. Querying Diverse Treebanks in a Uniform Way. In Nicoletta Calzolari, Khalid Choukri, Bente Maegaard, Joseph Mariani, Jan Odijk, Stelios Piperidis, Mike Rosner, and Daniel Tapias, editors, *Proceedings of the 7th International Conference on Language Resources and Evaluation (LREC 2010)*, Valletta, Malta.

Improvements to Syntax-based Machine Translation using Ensemble Dependency Parsers

Nathan David Green and Zdeněk Žabokrtský
Charles University in Prague
Institute of Formal and Applied Linguistics
Faculty of Mathematics and Physics
Prague, Czech Republic
{green,zabokrtsky}@ufal.mff.cuni.cz

Abstract

Dependency parsers are almost ubiquitously evaluated on their accuracy scores, these scores say nothing of the complexity and usefulness of the resulting structures. The structures may have more complexity due to their coordination structure or attachment rules. As dependency parses are basic structures in which other systems are built upon, it would seem more reasonable to judge these parsers down the NLP pipeline.

We show results from 7 individual parsers, including dependency and constituent parsers, and 3 ensemble parsing techniques with their overall effect on a Machine Translation system, Treex, for English to Czech translation. We show that parsers' UAS scores are more correlated to the NIST evaluation metric than to the BLEU Metric, however we see increases in both metrics.

1 Introduction

Ensemble learning (Dietterich, 2000) has been used for a variety of machine learning tasks and recently has been applied to dependency parsing in various ways and with different levels of success. (Surdeanu and Manning, 2010; Haffari et al., 2011) showed a successful combination of parse trees through a linear combination of trees with various weighting formulations. To keep their tree constraint, they applied Eisner's algorithm for reparsing (Eisner, 1996).

Parser combination with dependency trees has been examined in terms of accuracy (Sagae and Lavie, 2006; Sagae and Tsujii, 2007; Zeman and Žabokrtský, 2005; Holan and Žabokrtský, 2006). Other methods of parser combinations have shown to be successful such as using one parser to generate features for another parser. This was shown in (Nivre and McDonald, 2008), in which Malt Parser was used as a feature to MST Parser. The result was a successful combination of a transition-based and graph-based parser, but did not address adding other types of parsers into the framework.

We will use three ensemble approaches. First a fixed weight ensemble approach in which edges are added together in a weighted graph. Second, we added the edges using weights learned through fuzzy clustering based on POS errors. Third, we will use a meta-classifier that uses an SVM to predict the correct model for edge using only model agreements without any linguistic information added. Parsing accuracy and machine translation has been examined in terms of BLEU score (Quirk and Corston-Oliver, 2006). However, we believe our work is the first to examine the NLP pipeline for ensemble parsing for both dependency and constituent parsers as well as examining both BLEU and NIST scores' relationship to their *U*nlabeled *A*ccuracy *S*core(UAS).

2 Methodology

2.1 Annotation

To find the maximum effect that dependency parsing can have on the NLP pipeline, we annotated English dependency trees to form a gold standard. Annotation was done with two annotators using a tree editor, Tred (Pajas and Fabian, 2011), on data that was preprocessed using MST parser. For the annotation of our gold data, we used the standard developed by the Prague Dependency Treebank (PDT) (Hajič, 1998). PDT is annotated on three levels, morphological, analytical, and tectogrammatical. For our gold data we do not touch the morphological layer, we only correct the analytical layer (i.e. labeled dependency trees). For machine translation experiments later in the paper we allow the system to automatically generate a new tectogrammatical layer based on our new analytical layer annotation. Because the Treex machine translation system uses a tectogrammatical layer, when in doubt, ambiguity was left to the tectogrammatical (t-layer in Figure 1) to handle.

2.1.1 Data Sets

For the annotation experiments we use data provided by the 2012 Workshop for Machine Translation (WMT2012). The data which consists of 3,003 sentences was automatically tokenized, tagged, and parsed. This data set was also chosen since it is disjoint from the usual dependency training data, allowing researchers to use it as a out-of-domain testing set. The parser used was an implementation of MST parser. We then hand corrected the analytical trees to have a "Gold" standard dependency structure. Analytical trees were annotated on the PDT standard. Most changes involved coordination construction along with prepositional phrase attachment. We plan to publicly release this data and corresponding annotations in the near future[1].

Having only two annotators has limited us to evaluating our annotation only through spot checking and through comparison with other baselines. Annotation happened sequentially one after another. Possible errors were additionally detected through automatic means. As a comparison we will evaluate our gold data set versus other parsers in respect to their performance on previous data sets, namely the Wall Street Journal (WSJ) section 23.

2.2 Translation

2.2.1 Data Sets

All the parsers were trained on sections 02-21 of the WSJ, except the Stanford parser which also uses section 01. We retrained MST and Malt parsers and used pre-trained models for the other parsers. Machine translation data was used from WMT 2010, 2011, and 2012. Using our gold standard we are able to evaluate the effectiveness of different parser types from graph-base, transition-based, constituent conversion to ensemble approaches on the 2012 data while finding data trends using previous years data.

[1]When available the data and description will be at www.nathangreen.com/wmtdata

2.2.2 Translation Components

To examine the effects of dependency parsing down the NLP pipeline, we now turn to syntax based machine translation. Our dependency models will be evaluated using the Treex translation system (Popel and Žabokrtský, 2010). This system, as opposed to other popular machine translation systems, makes direct use of the dependency structure during the conversion from source to target languages via a tectogrammatical tree translation approach.

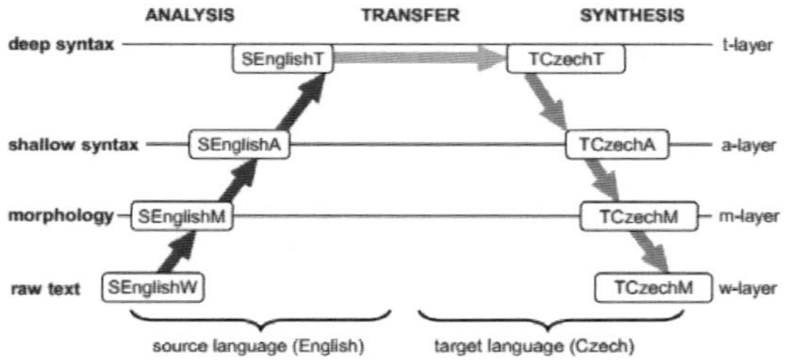

Figure 1: Treex syntax-based translation scenario (Popel and Žabokrtský, 2010)

We use the different parsers in separate translation runs each time in the same Treex parsing block. So each translation scenario only differs in the parser used and nothing else. As can be seen in Figure 1, we are directly manipulating the Analytical portion of Treex. The parsers used are as follows:

- **MST**: Implementation of Ryan McDonald's Minimum spanning tree parser (McDonald et al., 2005)
- **MST with chunking**: Same implementation as above but we parse the sentences based on chunks and not full sentences. For instance this could mean separating parentheticals or separating appositions (Popel et al., 2011)
- **Malt**: Implementation of Nivre's Malt Parser trained on the Penn Treebank (Nivre, 2003)
- **Malt with chunking**: Same implementation as above but with chunked parsing
- **ZPar**: Yue Zhang's statistical parser. We used the pretrained English model (english.tar.gz) available on the ZPar website for all tests (Zhang and Clark, 2011)
- **Charniak**: A constituent based parser (ec50spfinal model) in which we transform

the results using the Pennconverter (Johansson and Nugues, 2007)

- **Stanford**: Another constituent based parser (Klein and Manning, 2003) whose output is converted using Pennconverter as well (wsjPCFG.ser.gz model)
- **Fixed Weight Ensemble**: A stacked ensemble system combining five of the parsers above (MST, Malt, ZPar, Charniak, Stanford). The weights for each tree are assigned based on UAS score found in tuning data, section 22 of the WSJ (Green and Žabokrtský, 2012)
- **Fuzzy Cluster**: A stacked ensemble system as well but weights are determined by a cluster analysis of POS errors found in the same tuning data as above (Green and Žabokrtský, 2012)
- **SVM**: An ensemble system in which each individual edge is picked by a meta classifier from the same 5 parsers as the other ensemble systems. The SVM meta classifier is trained on results from the above tuning data (Green et al., 2012a; Green et al., 2012b).

2.2.3 Evaluation

For Machine Translation we report two automatic evaluation scores, BLEU and NIST. We examine parser accuracy using UAS. This paper compares a machine translation system integrating 10 different parsing systems against each other, using the below metrics.

The BLEU (*Bi*Lingual *E*valuation *U*nderstudy) and NIST(from the *N*ational *I*nstitute of *S*tandards and *T*echnology), are automatic scoring mechanisms for machine translation that are quick and can be reused as benchmarks across machine translation tasks. BLEU and NIST are calculated as the geometric mean of n-grams multiplied by a brevity penalty, comparing a machine translation and a reference text (Papineni et al., 2002). NIST is based upon the BLEU n-gram approach however it is also weighted towards discovering more "informative" n-grams. The more rare an n-gram is, the higher the weight for a correct translation of it will be.

Made a standard in the CoNLL shared tasks competition, UAS studies the structure of a dependency tree and assesses how often the output has the correct head and dependency arcs (Buchholz and Marsi, 2006). We report UAS scores for each parser on section 23 of the WSJ.

3 Results and Discussion

3.1 Type of Changes in WMT Annotation

Since our gold annotated data was preprocessed with MST parser, our baseline system at the time, we started with a decent baseline and only had to change 9% of the dependency arcs in the data. These 9% of changes roughly increase the BLEU score by 7%.

3.2 Parser Accuracy

As seen in previous Ensemble papers (Farkas and Bohnet, 2012; Green et al., 2012a; Green et al., 2012b; Green and Žabokrtský, 2012; Zeman and Žabokrtský, 2005), parsing accuracy can be improved by combining parsers' outputs for a variety of languages. We apply a few of these systems, as described in Section 2.2.2, to English using models trained for both dependencies and constituents.

3.2.1 Parsers vs our Gold Standard

On average our gold data differed in head agreement from our base parser 14.77% of the time. When our base parsers were tested on the WSJ section 23 data they had an average error rate of 12.17% which is roughly comparable to the difference with our gold data set which indicates overall our annotations are close to the accepted standard from the community. The slight difference in percentage fits into what is expect in annotator error and in the errors in the conversion process of the WSJ by Pennconverter.

3.3 Parsing Errors Effect on MT

3.3.1 MT Results in WMT with Ensemble Parsers

WMT 2010

As seen in Table 1, the highest resulting BLEU score for the 2010 data set is from the fixed weight ensemble system. The other two ensemble systems are beaten by one component system, Charniak. However, this changes when comparing NIST scores. Two of the ensemble method have higher NIST scores than Charniak, similar to their UAS scores.

WMT 2011

The 2011 data corresponded the best with UAS scores. While the BLEU score increases for all

Parser	UAS	NIST(10/11/12)	BLEU(10/11/12)
MST	86.49	5.40/5.58/5.19	12.99/13.58/11.54
MST w chunking	86.57	5.43/5.63/5.23	13.43/14.00/11.96
Malt	84.51	5.37/5.57/5.14	12.90/13.48/11.27
Malt w chunking	87.01	5.41/5.60/5.19	13.39/13.80/11.73
ZPar	76.06	5.26/5.46/5.08	11.91/12.48/10.53
Charniak	92.08	5.47/5.65/5.28	13.49/13.95/**12.26**
Stanford	87.88	5.40/5.59/5.18	13.23/13.63/11.74
Fixed Weight	92.58	**5.49**/5.68/**5.29**	**13.53**/14.04/12.23
Fuzzy Cluster	92.54	5.47/5.68/5.26	13.47/14.06/12.06
SVM	92.60	5.48/**5.68**/5.28	13.45/**14.11**/12.22

Table 1: Scores for each machine translation run for each dataset (WMT 2010, 2011 and 2012)

the ensemble systems, the order of systems by UAS scores corresponds exactly to the systems ordered by NIST score and corelates strongly (Table 2). Unlike the 2010 data, the MST parser was the highest base parser in terms of the BLEU metric.

WMT 2012

The ensemble increases are statistically significant for both the SVM and the Fixed Weight system over the MST with chunking parser with 99% confidence, our previous baseline and best scoring base system from 2011 in terms of BLEU score. We examine our data versus MST with chunking instead of Charniak since we have preprocessed our gold data set with MST, allowing us a direct comparison in improvements. The fuzzy cluster system achieves a higher BLEU evaluation score than MST, but is not significant. In pairwise tests it wins approximately 78% of the time. This is the first dataset we have looked at where the BLEU score is higher for a component parser and not an ensemble system, although the NIST score is still higher for the ensemble systems.

	NIST	BLEU
2010	0.98	0.93
2011	0.98	0.94
2012	0.95	0.97

Table 2: Pearson correlation coefficients for each year and each metric when measured against UAS. Statistics are taken from the WMT results in Table 1. Overall NIST has the stronger correlation to UAS scores, however both NIST and BLEU show a strong relationship.

3.3.2 Human Manual Evaluation: SVM vs the Baseline System

We selected 200 sentences at random from our annotations and they were given to 7 native Czech speakers. 77 times the reviewers preferred the SVM system, 48 times they preferred the MST system, and 57 times they said there was no difference between the sentences. On average each reviewer looked at 26 sentences with a median of 30 sentences. Reviewers were allowed three options: sentence 1 is better, sentence 2 is better, both sentences are of equal quality. Sentences were displayed in a random order and the systems were randomly shuffled for each question and for each user.

	+	=	-
+	12	12	0
=		3	7
-			7

Table 3: Agreement for sentences with 2 or more annotators for our baseline and SVM systems. (-,-) all annotators agreed the baseline was better, (+,+) all annotators agreed the SVM system was better, (+,-) the annotators disagreed with each other

Table 3 indicates that the SVM system was preferred. When removing annotations marked as equal, we see that the SVM system was preferred 24 times to the Baseline's 14.

Although a small sample, this shows that using the ensemble parser will at worse give you equal results and at best a much improved result.

3.3.3 MT Results with Gold Data

In the perfect situation of having gold standard dependency trees, we obtained a NIST of 5.30 and a BLEU of 12.39. For our gold standard system run, the parsing component was removed and replaced with our hand annotated data. These are the highest NIST and BLEU scores we have obtained including using all base parsers or any combinations of parsers. This indicates that while an old problem which is a "solved" problem for some languages, Parsing is still worth researching and improving for its cascading effects down the NLP pipeline.

4 Conclusion

We have shown that ensemble parsing techniques have an influence on syntax-based machine translation both in manual and automatic evaluation. Furthermore we have shown a stronger correlation between parser accuracy and the NIST rather than the more commonly used BLEU metric. We have also introduced a gold set of English dependency trees based on the WMT 2012 machine translation task data, which shows a larger increase in both BLEU and NIST. While on some datasets it is inconclusive whether using an ensemble parser with better accuracy has a large enough effect, we do show that practically you will not do worse using one and in many cases do much better.

5 Acknowledgments

This research has received funding from the European Commission's 7th Framework Program (FP7) under grant agreement n° 238405 (CLARA). Additionally, this work has been using language resources developed and/or stored and/or distributed by the LINDAT-Clarin project of the Ministry of Education of the Czech Republic (project LM2010013).

References

Sabine Buchholz and Erwin Marsi. 2006. CoNLL-X Shared Task on Multilingual Dependency Parsing. In *Proceedings of the Tenth Conference on Computational Natural Language Learning*, CoNLL-X '06, pages 149–164, Stroudsburg, PA, USA. Association for Computational Linguistics.

Thomas G. Dietterich. 2000. Ensemble Methods in Machine Learning. In *Proceedings of the First International Workshop on Multiple Classifier Systems*, MCS '00, pages 1–15, London, UK. Springer-Verlag.

Jason Eisner. 1996. Three New Probabilistic Models for Dependency Parsing: An Exploration. In *Proceedings of the 16th International Conference on Computational Linguistics (COLING-96)*, pages 340–345, Copenhagen, August.

Richárd Farkas and Bernd Bohnet. 2012. Stacking of Dependency and Phrase Structure Parsers. In *Proceedings of COLING 2012*, pages 849–866, Mumbai, India, December. The COLING 2012 Organizing Committee.

Nathan Green and Zdeněk Žabokrtský. 2012. Hybrid Combination of Constituency and Dependency Trees into an Ensemble Dependency Parser. In *Proceedings of the EACL 2012 Workshop on Innovative hybrid approaches to the processing of textual data*, Avignon, France.

Nathan Green and Zdeněk Žabokrtský. 2012. Ensemble Parsing and its Effect on Machine Translation. Technical Report 48.

Nathan Green, Septina Dian Larasati, and Zdeněk Žabokrtský. 2012a. Indonesian Dependency Treebank: Annotation and Parsing. In *Proceedings of the 26th Pacific Asia Conference on Language, Information, and Computation*, pages 137–145, Bali,Indonesia, November. Faculty of Computer Science, Universitas Indonesia.

Nathan Green, Loganathan Ramasamy, and Zdeněk Žabokrtský. 2012b. Using an SVM Ensemble System for Improved Tamil Dependency Parsing. In *Proceedings of the ACL 2012 Joint Workshop on Statistical Parsing and Semantic Processing of Morphologically Rich Languages*, pages 72–77, Jeju, Republic of Korea, July 12. Association for Computational Linguistics.

Gholamreza Haffari, Marzieh Razavi, and Anoop Sarkar. 2011. An Ensemble Model that Combines Syntactic and Semantic Clustering for Discriminative Dependency Parsing. In *Proceedings of the 49th Annual Meeting of the Association for Computational Linguistics: Human Language Technologies*, pages 710–714, Portland, Oregon, USA, June. Association for Computational Linguistics.

Jan Hajič. 1998. Building a Syntactically Annotated Corpus: The Prague Dependency Treebank. In Eva Hajičová, editor, *Issues of Valency and Meaning. Studies in Honor of Jarmila Panevová*, pages 12–19. Prague Karolinum, Charles University Press.

Tomáš Holan and Zdeněk Žabokrtský. 2006. Combining Czech Dependency Parsers. In *Proceedings of the 9th international conference on Text, Speech and Dialogue*, TSD'06, pages 95–102, Berlin, Heidelberg. Springer-Verlag.

Richard Johansson and Pierre Nugues. 2007. Extended Constituent-to-dependency Conversion for English. In *Proceedings of NODALIDA 2007*, pages 105–112, Tartu, Estonia, May 25-26.

Dan Klein and Christopher D. Manning. 2003. Accurate unlexicalized parsing. In *Proceedings of the 41st Annual Meeting on Association for Computational Linguistics - Volume 1*, ACL '03, pages 423–430, Stroudsburg, PA, USA. Association for Computational Linguistics.

Ryan McDonald, Fernando Pereira, Kiril Ribarov, and Jan Hajič. 2005. Non-projective dependency parsing using spanning tree algorithms. In *Proceedings of the conference on Human Language Technology and Empirical Methods in Natural Language Processing*, HLT '05, pages 523–530, Morristown, NJ, USA. Association for Computational Linguistics.

Joakim Nivre and Ryan McDonald. 2008. Integrating Graph-Based and Transition-Based Dependency Parsers. In *Proceedings of ACL-08: HLT*, pages 950–958, Columbus, Ohio, June. Association for Computational Linguistics.

Joakim Nivre. 2003. An Efficient Algorithm for Projective Dependency Parsing. In *Proceedings of the 8th International Workshop on Parsing Technologies (IWPT*, pages 149–160.

Petr Pajas and Peter Fabian. 2011. TrEd 2.0 - newly refactored tree editor. http://ufal.mff.cuni.cz/tred/, Institute of Formal and Applied Linguistics, MFF UK.

Kishore Papineni, Salim Roukos, Todd Ward, and Wei-Jing Zhu. 2002. BLEU: A Method for Automatic Evaluation of Machine Translation. In *Proceedings of the 40th Annual Meeting on Association for Computational Linguistics*, ACL '02, pages 311–318, Morristown, NJ, USA. Association for Computational Linguistics.

Martin Popel and Zdeněk Žabokrtský. 2010. TectoMT: modular NLP framework. In *Proceedings of the 7th international conference on Advances in natural language processing*, IceTAL'10, pages 293–304, Berlin, Heidelberg. Springer-Verlag.

Martin Popel, David Mareček, Nathan Green, and Zdenek Zabokrtsky. 2011. Influence of parser choice on dependency-based mt. In *Proceedings of the Sixth Workshop on Statistical Machine Translation*, pages 433–439, Edinburgh, Scotland, July. Association for Computational Linguistics.

Chris Quirk and Simon Corston-Oliver. 2006. The impact of parse quality on syntactically-informed statistical machine translation. In *Proceedings of the 2006 Conference on Empirical Methods in Natural Language Processing*, EMNLP '06, pages 62–69, Stroudsburg, PA, USA. Association for Computational Linguistics.

Kenji Sagae and Alon Lavie. 2006. Parser Combination by Reparsing. In *Proceedings of the Human Language Technology Conference of the NAACL, Companion Volume: Short Papers*, pages 129–132, New York City, USA, June. Association for Computational Linguistics.

Kenji Sagae and Jun'ichi Tsujii. 2007. Dependency Parsing and Domain Adaptation with LR Models and Parser Ensembles. In *Proceedings of the CoNLL Shared Task Session of EMNLP-CoNLL 2007*, pages 1044–1050, Prague, Czech Republic, June. Association for Computational Linguistics.

Mihai Surdeanu and Christopher D. Manning. 2010. Ensemble models for dependency parsing: cheap and good? In *Human Language Technologies: The 2010 Annual Conference of the North American Chapter of the Association for Computational Linguistics*, HLT '10, pages 649–652, Stroudsburg, PA, USA. Association for Computational Linguistics.

Daniel Zeman and Zdeněk Žabokrtský. 2005. Improving Parsing Accuracy by Combining Diverse Dependency Parsers. In *In: Proceedings of the 9th International Workshop on Parsing Technologies.*

Yue Zhang and Stephen Clark. 2011. Syntactic Processing Using the Generalized Perceptron and Beam Search. *Computational Linguistics*, 37(1):105–151.

Using Unlabeled Dependency Parsing for Pre-reordering for Chinese-to-Japanese Statistical Machine Translation

Dan Han[1,2] **Pascual Martínez-Gómez**[2,3] **Yusuke Miyao**[1,2]
Katsuhito Sudoh[4] **Masaaki Nagata**[4]
[1]The Graduate University For Advanced Studies
[2]National Institute of Informatics, [3]The University of Tokyo
[4]NTT Communication Science Laboratories, NTT Corporation
{handan,pascual,yusuke}@nii.ac.jp
{sudoh.katsuhito,nagata.masaaki}@lab.ntt.co.jp

Abstract

Chinese and Japanese have a different sentence structure. Reordering methods are effective, but need reliable parsers to extract the syntactic structure of the source sentences. However, Chinese has a loose word order, and Chinese parsers that extract the phrase structure do not perform well. We propose a framework where only POS tags and unlabeled dependency parse trees are necessary, and linguistic knowledge on structural difference can be encoded in the form of reordering rules. We show significant improvements in translation quality of sentences from news domain, when compared to state-of-the-art reordering methods.

1 Introduction

Translation between Chinese and Japanese languages gains interest as their economic and political relationship intensifies. Despite their linguistic influences, these languages have different syntactic structures and phrase-based statistical machine translation (SMT) systems do not perform well. Current word alignment models (Och and Ney, 2003) account for local differences in word order between bilingual sentences, but fail at capturing long distance word alignments. One of the main problems in the search of the best word alignment is the combinatorial explosion of word orders, but linguistically-motivated heuristics can help to guide the search.

This work explores syntax-informed pre-reordering for Chinese; that is, we obtain syntactic structures of Chinese sentences, reorder the words to resemble the Japanese word order, and then translate the reordered sentences using a phrase-based SMT system. However, Chinese parsers have difficulties in extracting reliable syntactic information, mainly because Chinese has a loose word order and few syntactic clues such as inflection and function words.

On one hand, parsers implementing head-driven phrase structure grammars infer a detailed constituent structure, and such a rich syntactic structure can be exploited to design well informed reordering methods. However, inferring abundant syntactic information often implies introducing errors, and reordering methods that heavily rely on detailed information are sensitive to those parsing errors (Han et al., 2012).

On the other hand, dependency parsers are committed to the simpler task of finding dependency relations and dependency labels, which can also be useful to guide reordering (Xu et al., 2009). However, reordering methods that rely on those dependency labels will also be prone to errors, specially in the case of Chinese since it has a richer set of dependency labels when compared to other languages. Since improving parsers for Chinese is challenging, we thus aim at reducing the influence of parsing errors in the reordering procedure.

We present a hybrid approach that boosts the performance of phrase-based SMT systems by pre-reordering the source language using unlabeled parse trees augmented with constituent information derived from Part-of-Speech tags. Specifically, we propose a framework to pre-reorder a Subject-Verb-Object (SVO) language, in order to improve its translation to a Subject-Object-Verb (SOV) language, where the only required syntactic information are POS tags and unlabeled dependency parse trees. We test the performance of our pre-reordering method and compare it to state-of-the-art reordering methods in the news domain for Chinese.

In the next section, we describe similar work on pre-reordering methods for language pairs that involve either Chinese or Japanese, and explain how our method builds upon them. From a linguistic perspective, we describe in section 3 our observations of reordering issues between Chinese and Japanese and detail how our framework solves those issues. In section 4 we assess to what extent our pre-reordering method succeeds in reordering words in Chinese sentences to resemble the order of Japanese sentences, and measure its impact on translation quality. The last section is dedicated to discuss our findings and point to future directions.

2 Related Work

Although there are many works on pre-reordering methods for other languages to English translation or inverse (Xia and McCord, 2004; Xu et al., 2009; Habash, 2007; Wang et al., 2007; Li et al., 2007; Wu et al., 2011), reordering method for Chinese-to-Japanese translation, which is a representative of long distance language pairs, has received little attention.

The most related work to ours is in (Han et al., 2012), in which the authors introduced a refined reordering approach by importing an existing reordering method for English proposed in (Isozaki et al., 2010b). These reordering strategies are based on Head-driven phrase structure grammars (HPSG) (Pollard and Sag, 1994), in that the reordering decisions are made based on the head of phrases. Specifically, HPSG parsers (Miyao and Tsujii, 2008; Yu et al., 2011) are used to extract the structure of sentences in the form of binary trees, and head branches are swapped with their dependents according to certain heuristics to resemble the word order of the target language. However, those strategies are sensitive to parsing errors, and the binary structure of their parse trees impose hard constraints in sentences with loose word order. Moreover, as Han et al. (2012) noted, reordering strategies that are derived from the HPSG theory may not perform well when the head definition is inconsistent in the language pair under study. A typical example for the language pair of Chinese and Japanese that illustrates this phenomenon is the adverb "bu4", which is the dependent of its verb in Chinese but the head in Japanese.

The work in (Xu et al., 2009) used an English dependency parser and formulated handcrafted reordering rules with dependency labels, POS tags and weights as triplets and implemented them recursively into sentences. This design, however, limited the extensibility of their method. Our approach follows the idea of using dependency tree structures and POS tags, but we discard the information on dependency labels since we did not find them informative to guide our reordering strategies in our preliminary experiments, partly due to Chinese showing less dependencies and a larger label variability (Chang et al., 2009).

3 Methodology

In Subject-Verb-Object (SVO) languages, objects usually follow their verbs, while in Subject-Object-Verb (SOV) languages, objects precede them. Our objective is to reorder words in Chinese sentences (SVO) to resemble the word order of Japanese sentences (SOV). For that purpose, our method consists in moving verbs to the right-hand side of their objects. However, it is challenging to correctly identify the appropriate verbs and objects that trigger a reordering, and this section will be dedicated to that end.

More specifically, the first step of our method consists in identifying the appropriate verb (and certain words close to it) that need to be moved to the right-hand side of its object argument. Verbs (and those accompanying words) will move as a block, preserving the relative order among them. We will refer to them as *verbal blocks* (Vbs). The second step will consist in identifying the right-most argument object of the verb under consideration, and moving the verbal block to the right-hand side of it. Finally, certain invariable grammatical particles in the original vicinity of the verb will also be reordered, but their positions will be decided relative to their verb.

In what follows, we describe in detail how to identify verbal blocks, their objects and the invariable grammatical particles that will play a role in our reordering method. As mentioned earlier, the only information that will be used to perform this task will be the POS tags of the words and their unlabeled dependency structures.

3.1 Identifying verbal blocks (Vbs)

Verbal blocks are composed of a head (Vb-H) and possibly accompanying dependents (Vb-D). In the Chinese sentence "wo3 (I) chi1 le5 (ate) li2 (pear)."[1], "chi1" refers to the English verb "eat"

[1]In this paper, we represent a Chinese character by using Pinyin plus a tone number (there are 5 tones in Chinese). In the example, "chi1(eat)" is a verb and "le5(-ed)" is an aspect particle that adds preterit tense to the verb.

Vb-H	VV VE VC VA P
Vb-D	AD AS SP MSP CC VV VE VC VA
BEI	LB SB
RM-D	NN NR NT PN OD CD M FW CC ETC LC DEV DT JJ SP IJ ON
Oth-DEP	LB SB CS

Table 1: Lists of POS tags in Chinese used to identify blocks of words to reorder (Vb-H, Vb-D, BEI lists), the POS tags of their dependents (RM-D lists) which indicate the reordering position, and invariable grammatical particles (Oth-DEP) that need to be reordered.

and the aspect particle "le5" adds a preterit tense to the verb. The words "chi1 le5" are an example of verbal block that should be reordered as a block without altering its inner word order, i.e. "wo3 (I) li2 (pear) chi1 le5 (ate).", which matches the Japanese SOV order.

Possible heads of verbal blocks (Vb-H) are verbs (words with POS tags VV, VE, VC and VA), or prepositions (words with POS tag P). The Vb-H entry of Table 1 contains the list of POS tags for heads of verbal blocks. We use prepositions for Vb-H identification since they behave similarly to verbs in Chinese and should be moved to the right-most position in a prepositional phrase to resemble the Japanese word order. There are three conditions that a word should meet to be considered as a Vb-H:

i) Its POS tag is in the set of Vb-H in Table 1.
ii) It is a dependency head, which indicates that it may have an object as a dependent.
iii) It has no dependent whose POS tag is in the set of BEI in Table 1. BEI particles indicate that the verb is in passive voice and should not be reordered since it already resembles the Japanese order.

Chinese language does not have inflection, conjugation, or case markers (Li and Thompson, 1989). For that reason, some adverbs (AD), aspect particles (AS) or sentence-final particles (SP) are used to signal modality, indicate grammatical tense or add aspectual value to verbs. Words in this category preserve the order when translating to Japanese, and they will be candidates to be part of the verbal block (Vb-D) and accompany the verb when it is reordered. Other words in this category are coordinating conjunctions (CC) that connect multiple verbs, and both resultative "de5" (DER) and manner "de5" (DEV). The full list of POS tags used to identify Vb-Ds can be found in Table 1. To be a Vb-D, there are three necessary conditions as well:

i) Its POS tag is in the Vb-D entry in Table 1.
ii) It is a dependent of a word that is already in the Vb.
iii) It is next to its dependency head or only a coordination conjunction is in between.

To summarize, to build verbal blocks (Vbs) we first find the words that meet the three Vb-H conditions. Then, we test the Vb-D conditions on the words adjacent to the Vb-Hs and extend the verbal blocks to them if they meet the conditions. This process is iteratively applied to the adjacent words of a block until no more words can be added to the verbal block, possibly nesting other verbal blocks if necessary.

Figure 1a [2] shows an example of a dependency tree of a Chinese sentence that will be used to illustrate Vb identification. By observing the POS tags of the words in the sentence, only the words "bian1 ji4 (edit)" and "chu1 ban3 (publish)" have a POS tag (i.e. VV) in the Vb-H entry of Table 1. Moreover, both words are dependency heads and do not have any dependent whose POS tag is in the BEI entry of Table 1. Thus, "bian1 ji4 (edit)" and "chu1 ban3 (publish)" will be selected as Vb-Hs and form, by themselves, two separate incipient Vbs. We arbitrarily start building the Vb from the word "chu1 ban3 (publish)", by analyzing its adjacent words that are its dependents.

We observe that only "le5 (-ed)" is adjacent to "chu1 ban3 (publish)", it is its dependent, and its POS tag is in the Vb-D list. Since "le5 (-ed)" meets all three conditions stated above, "le5 (-ed)" will be included in the Vb originated by "chu1 ban3 (publish)". The current Vb thus consists of the sequence of tokens "chu1 ban3 (publish)" and "le5 (-ed)", and the three conditions for Vb-D are tested on the adjacent words of this block. Since the adjacent words (or words separated by a coordinating conjunction) do not meet the conditions, the block is not further extended. Figure 1b shows the dependency tree where the Vb block that consists of the words "chu1 ban3 (publish)" and "le5 (-ed)" is represented by a rectangular box.

By checking in the same way, there are three dependents that meet the requirements of being

[2] For all the dependency parsing trees in this paper, arrows are pointing from heads to their dependents.

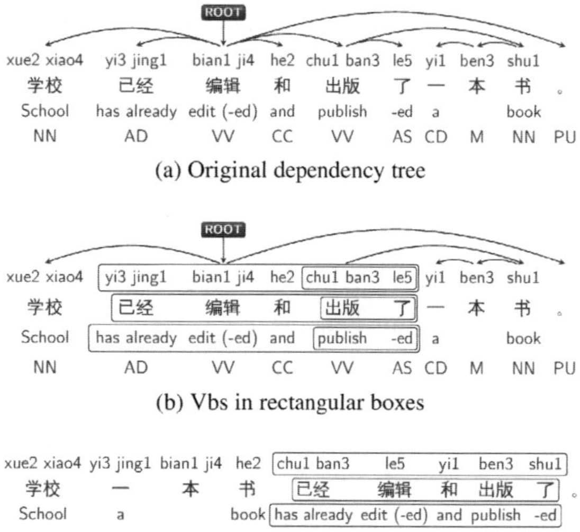

(a) Original dependency tree

(b) Vbs in rectangular boxes

(c) Merged and reordered Vb

Figure 1: An example that shows how to detect and reorder a Verbal block (Vb) in a sentence. In the first two figures 1a and 1b, Chinese Pinyin, Chinese tokens, word-to-word English translations, and POS tags of each Chinese token are listed in four lines. In Figure 1c, there are Chinese Pinyin, reordered Chinese sentence and its word-to-word English counterpart.

Vb-Ds for "bian1 ji4 (edit)": "yi3 jing1 (has already)", "he2 (and)" and "chu1 ban4 (publish)" and hence this Vb consists of three tokens and one Vb. The outer rectangular box in Figure 1b shows that the Vb "bian1 ji4 (edit)" as the Vb-H. Figure 1c shows an image of how this Vb will be reordered while the inner orders are kept. Note that the order of building Vbs from which Vb-Hs, "chu1 ban3 (publish)" or "bian1 ji4 (edit)" will not affect any change of the final result.

3.2 Identifying objects

In the most general form, objects are dependents of verbal blocks[3] that act as their arguments. While the simplest objects are nouns (N) or pronouns (PN), they can also be comprised of noun phrases or clauses (Downing and Locke, 2006) such as nominal groups, finite clauses (e.g. *that* clauses, *wh*-clauses) or non-finite clauses (e.g. *-ing* clauses), among others.

For every Vb in a verb phrase, clause, or sentence, we define the right-most object dependent (RM-D) as the word that:

[3]Dependents of verbal blocks are dependents of any word within the verbal block.

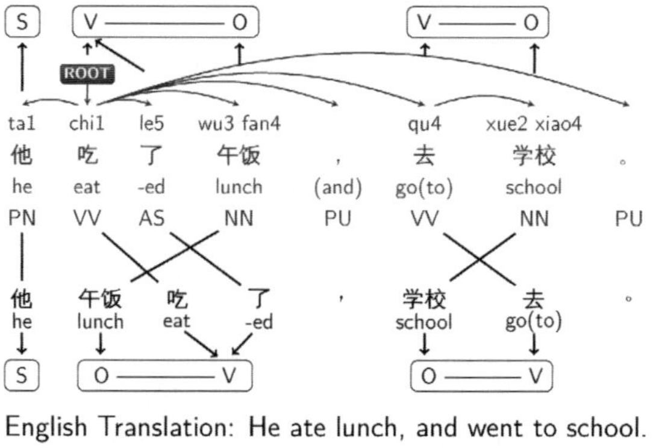

Figure 2: An example of a Chinese sentence with a coordination of verb phrases as predicate. Subject(S), verbs(V), and objects(O) are displayed for both verb phrases. Lines between the original Chinese sentence and the reordered Chinese sentence indicate the reordering trace of Verbal blocks(Vb).

i) its POS tag is in the RM-D entry of Table 1,
ii) its dependency head is inside of the verbal block, and
iii) is the right-most object among all objects of the verbal block.

All verbal blocks in the phrase, clause, or sentence will move to the right-hand side of their correspondent RM-Ds recursively. Figure 1b and Figure 1c show a basic example of object identification. The Chinese word corresponding to "shu1 (book)" is a dependent of a word within the verbal block and its POS tag is within the RM-D entry list of Table 1 (i.e. NN). For this reason, "shu1 (book)" is identified as the right-most dependent of the verbal block (Vb), and the Vb will move to the right-hand side of it to resemble the Japanese word order.

A slightly more complex example can be found in Figure 2. In this example, there is a coordination structure of verb phrases, and the dependency tree shows that the first verb, "chi1 (eat)", appears as the dependency head of the second verb, "qu4 (go)". The direct right-most object dependent (RM-D) of the first verb, "chi1 (eat)", is the word "wu3 fan4 (lunch)", and the verb "chi1 (eat)" will be moved to the right-hand side of its object dependent.

There are cases, however, where there is no coordination structure of verb phrases but a similar dependency relation occurs between two verbs. Figure 3 illustrates one of these cases, where the main verb "gu3 li4 (encourage)" has no direct de-

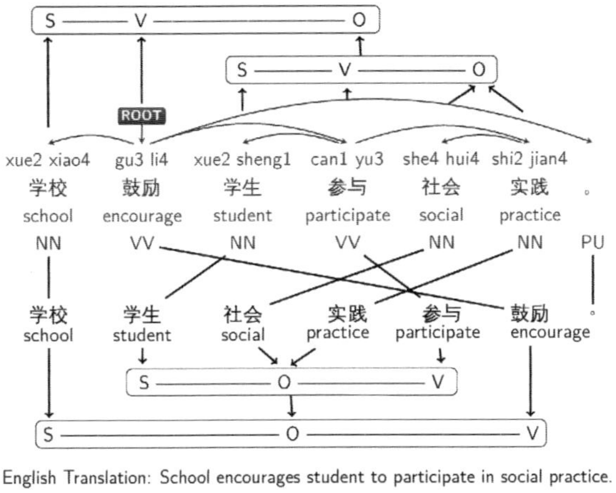

Figure 3: An example of a Chinese sentence in which an embedded clause appears as the object of the main verb. Subjects (S), verbs (V), and objects (O) are displayed for both the sentence and the clause. Lines between the original Chinese sentence and the reordered Chinese sentence indicate the reordering trace of Verbal blocks (Vb).

pendent that can be considered as an object since no direct dependent has a POS tag in the RM-D entry of Table 1. Instead, an embedded clause (SVO) appears as the object argument of the main verb, and the main verb "gu3 li4 (encourage)" appears as the dependency head of the verb "can1 yu2 (participate)".

In the news domain, reported speech is a frequent example that follows this pattern. In our method, if the main verb of the sentence (labeled as ROOT) has dependents but none of them is a direct object, we move the main verb to the end of the sentence. As for the embedded clause "xue2 sheng1 (student) can1 yu2 (participate) she4 hui4 (social) shi2 jian4 (practice)", the verbal block of the clause is the word "can1 yu2 (participate)" and its object is "shi2 jian4 (practice)". Applying our reordering method, the clause order results in "xue2 sheng1 (student) she4 hui4 (social) shi2 jian4 (practice) can1 yu2 (participate)". The result is an SOV sentence with an SOV clause, which resembles the Japanese word order.

3.3 Identifying invariable grammatical particles

In Chinese, certain invariable grammatical particles that accompany verbal heads have a different word order relative to their heads, when compared to Japanese. Those particles are typically "bei4" particle (POS tags LB and SB) and subordinating conjunctions (POS tag CS). Those particles appear on the left-hand side of their dependency heads in Chinese, and they should be moved to the right-hand side of their dependency heads for them to resemble the Japanese word order. Reordering invariable grammatical particles in our framework can be summarized as:

i) Find dependents of a verbal head (Vb-H) whose POS tags are in the Oth-DEP entry of Table 1.
ii) Move those particles to the right-hand side of their (possibly reordered) heads.
iii) If there is more than one such particle, move them keeping the relative order among them.

3.4 Summary of the reordering framework

Based on the definitions above, our dependency parsing based pre-reordering framework can be summarized in the following steps:

1. Obtain POS tags and an unlabeled dependency tree of a Chinese sentence.
2. Obtain reordering candidates: Vbs.
3. Obtain the object (RM-D) of each Vb.
4. Reorder each Vb in two exclusive cases by following the order:
   (a) If RM-D exists, reorder Vb to be the right-hand side of RM-D.
   (b) If Vb-H is ROOT and its RM-D does not exist, reorder Vb to the end of the sentence.
   (c) If none of above two conditions is met, no reordering happens.
5. Reorder grammatical particles (Oth-DEPs) to the right-hand side of their corresponding Vbs.

Note that, unlike other works in reordering distant languages (Isozaki et al., 2010b; Han et al., 2012; Xu et al., 2009), we do not prevent chunks from crossing punctuations or coordination structures. Thus, our method allows to achieve an authentic global reordering in reported speech, which is an important reordering issue in news domains.

In order to illustrate our method, a more complicated Chinese sentence example is given in Figure 4, which includes the unlabeled dependency

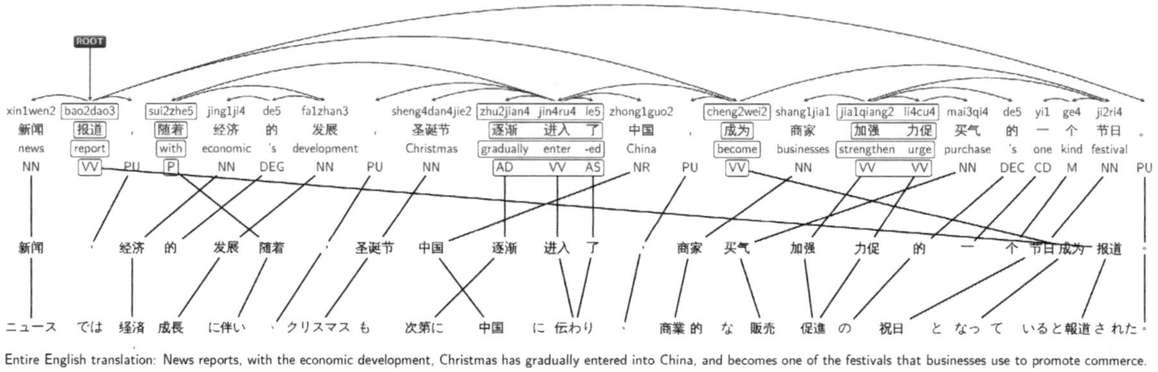

Figure 4: Dependency parse tree of a complex Chinese sentence example, and word alignments for reordered sentence with its Japanese counterpart. The first four lines are Chinese Pinyin, tokens, word-to-word English translations, and the POS tags of each Chinese token. The fifth line shows the reordered Chinese sentence while the sixth line is the segmented Japanese translation. The entire English translation for the sentence is showed in the last line.

parsing tree of the original Chinese sentence, and the word alignment between reordered Chinese sentence and its Japanese counterpart, etc.

Based on both POS tags and the unlabeled dependency tree, first step of our method is to obtain all Vbs. For all heads in the tree, according to the definition of Vb introduced in Section 3.1, there are six tokens which will be recognized as the candidates of Vb-Hs, that is "bao4 dao3 (report)", "sui2 zhe5 (with)", "jin4 ru4 (enter)", "cheng2 wei2 (become)", "jia1 qiang2 (strengthen)", and "li4 cu4 (urge)". Then, for each of the candidate, its direct dependents will be checked if they are Vb-Ds. For instance, for the verb of "jin4 ru4 (enter)", its dependents of "zhu2 jian4 (gradually)" and "le5 (-ed)" will be considered as the Vb-Ds. For the case of "jia1 qiang2 (strengthen)", instead of being a Vb-H, it will be recognized as Vb-D of the Vb "li4 cu4 (urge)" since it is one of the direct dependents of "li4 cu4 (urge)" with a qualified POS tag for Vb-D. Therefore, there are five Vbs in total, which are "bao4 dao3 (report)", "sui2 zhe5 (with)", "zhu2 jian4 (gradually) jin4 ru4 (enter) le5 (-ed)", "cheng2 wei2 (become)", and "jia1 qiang2 (strengthen) li4 cu4 (urge)".

The next step is to identify RM-D for each Vb, if there is one. By checking all conditions, four Vbs have their RM-Ds: "fa1 zhan3 (development)" is the RM-D of the Vb "sui2 zhe5 (with)"; "zhong1 guo2 (China)" is the RM-D of the Vb "zhu2 jian4 (gradually) jin4 ru4 (enter) le5 (-ed)"; "jie2 ri4 (festival)" is the RM-D of the Vb "cheng2 wei2 (become)"; "mai3 qi4 (purchase)" is the RM-D of the Vb "jia1 qiang2 (strengthen) li4 cu4 (urge)".

After obtaining all RM-Ds, we find those Vbs that have RM-Ds and move them to right of their RM-Ds. As for the case of "bao4 dao3 (report)", since it is the root and does not have any matched RM-D, it will be moved to the end of the sentence, before any final punctuation. Finally, since there is no any invariable grammatical particle in the sentence that need to be reordered, reordering has been finished. From the alignments between the reordered Chinese and its Japanese translation showed in the figure, an almost monotonic word alignment has been achieved.

For comparison purposes, particle seed words had been inserted into the reordered sentences in the same way as the Refined-HFC method, which is using the information of predicate argument structure output by Chinese Enju (Yu et al., 2011). We therefore can not entirely disclaim the use of the HPSG parser at the present stage in our method. However, we believe that dependency parser can provide enough information for inserting particles.

4 Experiments

We conducted experiments to assess how our proposed dependency-based pre-reordering for Chinese (DPC) impacts on translation quality, and compared it to a baseline phrase-based system and a Refined-HFC pre-reordering for Chinese to Japanese translation.

We used two Chinese-Japanese training data

	News		CWMT+News	
	BLEU	RIBES	BLEU	RIBES
Baseline	39.26	84.83	38.96	85.01
Ref-HFC	39.22	84.88	39.26	84.68
DPC	**39.93**	**85.23**	**39.94**	**85.22**

Table 3: Evaluation of translation quality of two test sets when CWMT, News and the combination of both corpora were used for training.

sets of parallel sentences, namely an in-house-collected Chinese-Japanese news corpus (News), and the News corpus augmented with the CWMT (Zhao et al., 2011) corpus. We extracted disjoint development and test sets from News corpus, containing 1,000 and 2,000 sentences respectively. Table 2 shows the corpora statistics.

We used MeCab [4] (Kudo and Matsumoto, 2000) and the Stanford Chinese segmenter [5] (Chang et al., 2008) to segment Japanese and Chinese sentences. POS tags of Chinese sentences were obtained using the Berkeley parser [6] (Petrov et al., 2006), while dependency trees were extracted using Corbit [7] (Hatori et al., 2011). Following the work in (Han et al., 2012), we re-implemented the Refined-HFC using the Chinese Enju to obtain HPSG parsing trees. For comparison purposes with the work in (Isozaki et al., 2010b), particle seed words were inserted at a preprocessing stage for Refined-HFC and our DPC method.

DPC and Refined-HFC pre-reordering strategies were followed in the pipeline by a standard Moses-based baseline system (Koehn et al., 2007), using a default distance reordering model and a lexicalized reordering model "msd-bidirectional-fe". A 5-gram language model was built using SRILM (Stolcke, 2002) on the target side of the corresponding training corpus. Word alignments were extracted using MGIZA++ (Gao and Vogel, 2008) and the parameters of the log-linear combination were tuned using MERT (Och, 2003).

Table 3 summarizes the results of the Baseline system (no pre-reordering nor particle word insertion), the Refined-HFC (Ref-HFC) and our DPC method, using the well-known BLEU score (Papineni et al., 2002) and a word order sensitive metric named RIBES (Isozaki et al., 2010a).

[4]http://mecab.googlecode.com/svn/trunk/mecab/doc/index.html

[5]http://nlp.stanford.edu/software/segmenter.shtml

[6]http://nlp.cs.berkeley.edu/Software.shtml

[7]http://triplet.cc/software/corbit

As it can be observed, our DPC method obtains around 0.7 BLEU points of improvement when compared to the second best system in both corpora. When measuring the translation quality in terms of RIBES, our method obtains an improvement of 0.3 and 0.2 points when compared to the second best system in News and CWMT + News corpora, respectively. We suspect that corpus diversity might be one of the reasons for Refined-HFC not to show any advantage in this setting.

We tested the significance of BLEU improvement for Refined-HFC and DPC when compared to the baseline phrase-based system. Refined-HFC tests obtained p-values 0.355 and 0.135 on News and CWMT + News corpora, while our proposed DPC method obtained p-values 0.002 and 0.0, which indicates significant improvements over the phrase-based system.

5 Conclusions

In the present paper, we have analyzed the differences in word order between Chinese and Japanese sentences. We captured the regularities of ordering differences between Chinese and Japanese sentences, and proposed a framework to reorder Chinese sentences to resemble the word order of Japanese.

Our framework consists in three steps. First, we identify verbal blocks, which consist of Chinese words that will move all together as a block without altering their relative inner order. Second, we identify the right-most object of the verbal block, and move the verbal block to the right of it. Finally, we identify invariable grammatical particles in the original vicinity of the verbal block and move them relative to their dependency heads.

Our framework only uses the unlabeled dependency structure of sentences and POS tag information of words. We compared our system to a baseline phrase-based SMT system and a refined head-finalization system. Our method obtained a Chinese word order that is more similar to Japanese word order, and we showed its positive impact on translation quality.

6 Discussion and future work

In the literature, there are mainly two types of parsers that have been used to extract sentence structure and guide reordering. The first type corresponds to parsers that extract phrase structures (i.e. HPSG parsers). These parsers infer a rich

		News		CWMT+News	
		Chinese	Japanese	Chinese	Japanese
Training	Sentences	342,050		621,610	
	Running words	7,414,749	9,361,867	9,822,535	12,499,112
	Vocabulary	145,133	73,909	214,085	98,333
News Devel.	Sentences	1,000		–	
	Running words	46,042	56,748	–	–
	Out of Vocab.	255	54	–	–
News Test	Sentences	2,000		–	
	Running words	51,534	65,721	–	–
	Out of Vocab.	529	286	–	–

Table 2: Basic statistics of our corpora. News Devel. and News Test were used to tune and test the systems trained with both training corpora. Data statistics were collected after tokenizing and filtering out sentences longer than 64 tokens.

annotation of the sentence in terms of semantic structure or phrase heads. Other reordering strategies use a different type of parsers, namely dependency parsers. These parsers extract dependency information among words in the sentence, often consisting in the dependency relation between two words and the type of relation (dependency label).

Reordering strategies that use syntactic information have proved successful, but they are likely to magnify parsing errors if their reordering rules heavily rely on abundant parse information. This is aggravated when reordering Chinese sentences, due to its loose word order and large variety of possible dependency labels.

In this work, we based our study of ordering differences between Chinese and Japanese solely on dependency relations and POS tags. This contrasts with the work in (Han et al., 2012) that requires phrase structures, phrase-head information and POS tags, and the work in (Xu et al., 2009) that requires dependency relations, dependency labels and POS tags.

In spite of the fact that our method uses less syntactic information, it succeeds at reordering sentences with reported speech even in presence of punctuation symbols. It is worth saying that reported speech is very common in the news domain, which might be one of the reasons of the superior translation quality achieved by our reordering method. Our method also accounted for ordering differences in serial verb constructions, complementizers and adverbial modifiers, which would have required an increase in the complexity of the reordering logic in other methods.

To the best of our knowledge, dependency parsers are more common than HPSG parsers across languages, and our method can potentially be applied to translate under-resourced languages into other languages with a very different sentence structure, as long as they count with dependency parsers and reliable POS taggers.

Implementing our method for other languages would first require a linguistic study on the reordering differences between the two distant language pairs. However, some word ordering differences might be consistent across SVO and SOV language pairs (such as verbs going before or after their objects), but other ordering differences may need special treatment for the language pair under consideration (i.e. Chinese "bei" particles).

There are two possible directions to extend the present work. The first one would be to refine the current method to reduce its sensitivity to POS tagging or dependency parse errors, and to extend our linguistic study on ordering differences between Chinese and Japanese languages. The second direction would be to manually or automatically find common patterns of ordering differences between SVO and SOV languages. The objective would be then to create a one-for-all reordering method that induces monotonic word alignments between sentences from distant language pairs, and that could also be easily extended to account for the unique characteristics of the source language of interest.

Acknowledgments

We would like to thank Dr. Takuya Matsuzaki for his precious advice on this work and Dr. Jun Hatori for his support on using Corbit.

References

Pi-Chuan Chang, Michel Galley, and Christopher D. Manning. 2008. Optimizing Chinese word segmentation for machine translation performance. In *Proc. of the 3rd Workshop on SMT*, pages 224–232.

Pi-Chuan Chang, Huihsin Tseng, Dan Jurafsky, and Christopher D Manning. 2009. Discriminative reordering with Chinese grammatical relations features. In *Proc. of the Third Workshop on Syntax and Structure in Statistical Translation*, pages 51–59.

Angela Downing and Philip Locke. 2006. *English grammar: a university course*. Routledge.

Qin Gao and Stephan Vogel. 2008. Parallel implementations of word alignment tool. In *Software Engineering, Testing, and Quality Assurance for Natural Language Processing*, pages 49–57.

Nizar Habash. 2007. Syntactic preprocessing for statistical machine translation. In *Proc. of Machine Translation Summit XI*, pages 215–222.

Dan Han, Katsuhito Sudoh, Xianchao Wu, Kevin Duh, Hajime Tsukada, and Masaaki Nagata. 2012. Head finalization reordering for Chinese-to-Japanese machine translation. In *Proc. of the Sixth Workshop on Syntax, Semantics and Structure in Statistical Translation*, pages 57–66.

Jun Hatori, Takuya Matsuzaki, Yusuke Miyao, and Junichi Tsujii. 2011. Incremental joint POS tagging and dependency parsing in Chinese. In *Proc. of 5th International Joint Conference on Natural Language Processing*, pages 1216–1224.

Hideki Isozaki, Tsutomu Hirao, Kevin Duh, Katsuhito Sudoh, and Hajime Tsukada. 2010a. Automatic evaluation of translation quality for distant language pairs. In *Proc. of EMNNLP*.

Hideki Isozaki, Katsuhito Sudoh, Hajime Tsukada, and Kevin Duh. 2010b. Head finalization: A simple reordering rule for SOV languages. In *Proc. of WMT-MetricsMATR*, pages 244–251.

Philipp Koehn, Hieu Hoang, Alexandra Birch, Chris Callison-Burch, Marcello Federico, Nicola Bertoldi, Brooke Cowan, Wade Shen, Christine Moran, Richard Zens, Chris Dyer, Ondřej Bojar, Alexandra Constantin, and Evan Herbst. 2007. Moses: open source toolkit for statistical machine translation. In *Proc. of ACL '07, Demonstration Sessions*, pages 177–180.

Taku Kudo and Yuji Matsumoto. 2000. Japanese dependency structure analysis based on support vector machines. In *Proc. of the EMNLP/VLC-2000*, pages 18–25.

Charles N Li and Sandra Annear Thompson. 1989. *Mandarin Chinese: A functional reference grammar*. Univ of California Press.

Chi-Ho Li, Minghui Li, Dongdong Zhang, Mu Li, Ming Zhou, and Yi Guan. 2007. A probabilistic approach to syntax-based reordering for statistical machine translation. In *Proc. of ACL*, page 720.

Yusuke Miyao and Jun'ichi Tsujii. 2008. Feature forest models for probabilistic HPSG parsing. *Computational Linguistics*, 34:35–80.

Franz Josef Och and Hermann Ney. 2003. A systematic comparison of various statistical alignment models. *Comput. Linguist.*, 29:19–51.

Franz J. Och. 2003. Minimum error rate training for statistical machine translation. In *Proc. of ACL*, pages 160–167.

Kishore Papineni, Salim Roukos, Todd Ward, and Wei-Jing Zhu. 2002. Bleu: A method for automatic evaluation of machine translation. In *Proc. of ACL*, pages 311–318.

Slav Petrov, Leon Barrett, Romain Thibaux, and Dan Klein. 2006. Learning accurate, compact, and interpretable tree annotation. In *Proc. of the 21st COLING and the 44th ACL*, pages 433–440.

Carl Jesse Pollard and Ivan A. Sag. 1994. *Head-driven phrase structure grammar*. The University of Chicago Press and CSLI Publications.

Andreas Stolcke. 2002. SRILM – an extensible language modeling toolkit. In *Proc. of the 7th international conference on Spoken Language Processing, 2002*, pages 901–904.

Chao Wang, Michael Collins, and Philipp Koehn. 2007. Chinese syntactic reordering for statistical machine translation. In *Proc. of the 2007 Joint Conference on EMNLP-CoNLL*, pages 737–745.

Xianchao Wu, Katsuhito Sudoh, Kevin Duh, Hajime Tsukada, and Masaaki Nagata. 2011. Extracting pre-ordering rules from predicate-argument structures. In *Proc. of 5th International Joint Conference on Natural Language Processing*, pages 29–37.

Fei Xia and Michael McCord. 2004. Improving a statistical MT system with automatically learned rewrite patterns. In *Proc. of the 20th international conference on Computational Linguistics*.

Peng Xu, Jaeho Kang, Michael Ringgaard, and Franz Och. 2009. Using a dependency parser to improve SMT for subject-object-verb languages. In *Proc. of HLT: NA-ACL 2009*, pages 245–253.

Kun Yu, Yusuke Miyao, Takuya Matsuzaki, Xiangli Wang, and Junichi Tsujii. 2011. Analysis of the difficulties in Chinese deep parsing. In *Proc. of the 12th International Conference on Parsing Technologies*, pages 48–57.

Hong-Mei Zhao, Ya-Juan Lv, Guo-Sheng Ben, Yun Huang, and Qun Liu. 2011. Evaluation report for the 7th China workshop on machine translation (CWMT2011). *The 7th China Workshop on Machine Translation (CWMT2011)*.

Reordering rules for English-Hindi SMT

Raj Nath Patel, Rohit Gupta, Prakash B. Pimpale and Sasikumar M
CDAC Mumbai, Gulmohar Cross Road No. 9,
Juhu, Mumbai-400049
India
{rajnathp,rohitg,prakash,sasi}@cdac.in

Abstract

Reordering is pre-processing stage for Statistical Machine Translation (SMT) system where the words of the source sentence are re-ordered as per the syntax of the target language. We are proposing a rich set of rules for better reordering. The idea is to facilitate the training process by better alignments and parallel phrase extraction for a phrase based SMT system. Reordering also helps the decoding process and hence improving the machine translation quality. We have observed significant improvements in the translation quality by using our approach over the baseline SMT. We have used BLEU, NIST, multi-reference word error rate, multi-reference position independent error rate for judging the improvements. We have exploited open source SMT toolkit MOSES to develop the system.

1 Introduction

This paper describes syntactic reordering rules to reorder English sentences as per the Hindi language structure. Generally in reordering approach, the source sentence is parsed(E) and syntactic reordering rules are applied to form reordered sentence(E\`). The training of SMT system is performed using parallel corpus having source side reordered(E\`) and target side. The decoding is done by supplying reordered source sentences. The source sentences prior to decoding are reordered using the same syntactic rules as applied for the training data. So, this process works as a preprocessing stage for the phrase-based SMT system. It has been observed that reordering as a pre-processing stage is beneficial for developing English-Hindi phrase based SMT system (Ramanathan et al., 2008; Rama et al., 2008). This paper describes a rich set of rules for the structural transformation of English sentence to Hindi language structure using Stanford (De et al., 2006) parse tree on source side. These rules are manually extracted based on analysis of source sentence tree and Hindi translation.

For the evaluation purpose we have trained and evaluated three different phrase based SMT systems using MOSES toolkit (Koehn et al. 2007) and GIZA++(Och and Ney, 2003). The first system was non-reordered baseline (Brown et al., 1990; Marcu and Wong, 2002; Koehn et al., 2003), second using limited reordering described in Ramanathan et al. (2008) and third using improved reordering technique proposed in the paper. Evaluation has been carried out for end to end English-Hindi translation outputs using BLEU score (Papineni et al., 2001), NIST score (Doddington, 2002), multi-reference position-independent word error rate (Tillmann et al., 1997), multi-reference word error rate (Nießen et al., 2000). We have observed improvement in each of these evaluation metrics used. Next section discusses related work. Section 3 describes our reordering approach followed by experiments and results in section 4 and conclusion in section 5.

2 Related Work

Various pre-processing approaches have been proposed for handling syntax within SMT systems. These proposed methods reconcile the word-order differences between the source and target language sentences by reordering the source prior to the SMT training and decoding stages. For English-Hindi statistical machine translation reordering approach is used by Ramanathan et al. (2008) and Rama et al. (2008). This approach (Ramanathan et al. 2008) has shown significant improvements over baseline (Brown et al., 1990; Marcu and Wong, 2002; Koehn et al., 2003). The BLEU score for the system has increased from 12.10 to 16.90 after reordering. The same reordering approach (Ramanathan et al., 2008) used by us has shown slight improvement in BLEU score of 0.64 over baseline i.e. BLEU score increased from 21.55 to

22.19 compare to +4.8 BLEU point increase in the previous case. The reason can be, when the system is able to get bigger chunks from the phrase table itself the local reordering (within phrase) is not needed and the long distance reordering employed in the earlier approach will be helpful for overall better translation. It may not be able to show significant improvements when local reordering is not captured by the translation model.

Other language pairs have also shown significant improvement when reordering is employed. Xia and Mc-Cord (2004) have observed improvement for French-English and Chao et al. (2007) for Chinese-English language pairs. Nießen and Ney (2004) have proposed sentence restructuring whereas Collins et al. (2005) have proposed clause restructuring to improve German-English SMT. Popovic and Ney (2006) have also reported the use of simple local transformation rules for Spanish-English and Serbian-English translation.

Recently, Khalilov and Fonollosa (2011) proposed a reordering technique using deterministic approach for long distance reordering and non-deterministic approach for short distance reordering exploiting morphological information. Some reordering approaches are also presented exploiting the SMT itself (Gupta et al., 2012; Dlougach and Galinskaya, 2012).

Various evaluation techniques are available for reordering and overall machine translation evaluation. Particularly for reordering Birch and Osborne (2010) have proposed LRScore, a language independent metric for evaluating the lexical and word reordering quality. The translation evaluation metrics include BLEU (Papineni et. al., 2002), Meteor (Lavie and Denkowski, 2009), NIST (Doddington, 2002), etc.

3 Reordering approach

Our reordering approach is based on syntactic transformation of the English sentence parse tree according to the target language (Hindi) structure. It is similar to Ramanathan et al. (2008) but the transformation rules are not restricted to "SVO to SOV" and "pre-modifier to post-modifier" transformations only.

The idea was to come up with generic syntactic transformation rules to match the target language grammatical structure. The motivation came from the fact that if words are already in a correct place with respect to other words in the sentence, system doesn't need to do the extra work of reordering at the decoding time. This problem becomes even more complicated when system doesn't able to get bigger phrases for translating a sentence. Assuming an 18 words sentence, if system is able to get only 2 word length phrases, there are 362880(9!) translations (permutations) possible (still ignoring the case where one phrase having more than one translation options) for a sentence.

The source and the target sentences are manually analyzed to derive the tree transformation rules. From the generated set of rules we have selected rules which seemed to be more generic. There are cases where we have found more than one possible correct transformations for an English sentence as the target language (Hindi) is a free word order language within certain limits. In such cases word order close to English structure is preferred over possible word orders with respect to Hindi.

We identified 5 categories which are most prominent candidates for reordering. These include VPs (verb phrases), NPs (noun phrases), ADJPs (adjective phrase), PPs (preposition phrase) and ADVPs (adverb phrase). In the following subsections, we have described rules for these in more detail.

Tag	Description(Penn tags)
dcP	*Any, parser generated phrase*
pp	*Prepositional Phrase(PP)*
whP	*WH Phrase(WHNP, WHADVP, WHADJP, WHPP)*
vp	*Verb Phrase(VP)*
sbar	*Subordinate clause(SBAR)*
np	*Noun phrase(NP)*
vpw	*Verb words(VBN, VBP, VB,VBG, MD, VBZ, VBD)*
prep	*Preposition words(IN, TO,VBN,VBG)*
adv	*Adverbial words(RB, RBR, RBS)*
adj	*Adjunct word(JJ,JJR,JJS)*
advP	*Adverb phrase(ADVP)*
punct	*Punctuation(,)*
adjP	*Adjective phrase(ADJP)*
OP	*advP, np and/or pp*
*Tag**	*One or more occurrences of Tag*
Tag?	*Zero or one occurrence of Tag*

Table 1: Tag description

The format for writing the rules is as follows:
Type_of_phrase(tag1 tag2 tag 3: tag2 tag1 tag3)

This means that *"tag1 tag2 tag3"*, structure has been transformed to *"tag2 tag1 tag3"* for the type_of_phrase. This type_of_phrase denotes our category (NP, VP, ADJP, ADVP, PP) in which rule fall. The table given above explains about various tags and corresponding Penn tags used in writing these rules.

The following subsections explain the reordering rules. The higher precedence rule is written prior to the lower precedence. In general the more specific rules have high precedence. Each rule is followed by an example with intermediate steps of parsing and transformation as per the Hindi sentence structure. "Partial Reordered" shows the effect of the particular rule whereas "Reordered" shows impact of the whole reordering approach. The Hindi (transliterated) sentence is also provided as a reference for the corresponding English sentence.

3.1 Noun Phrase Rules

NP (np1 PP[prep NP[np2 sbar]] : np2 prep np1 sbar) (1)

English: The time of the year when nature dawns all its colorful splendor, is beautiful.

Parse: *[NP (np1* the time*) [PP (prep* of*) [NP (np2* the year*) (sbar* when nature dawns all its colorful splendor*)]]]* , is beautiful .

Partial Reordered: *(np2* the year*) (prep* of*) (np1* the time*)* *(sbar* when nature dawns all its colorful splendor*)* , is beautiful .

Reordered: *(np2* the year*) (prep* of*) (np1* the time*) (sbar* when nature all its colorful splendor dawns*)* , beautiful is .

Hindi: *varsh ka samay jab prakriti apne sabhi rang-birange vabahv failati hai, sundar hai .*

NP(np SBAR[S[dcP]] :dcP np) (2)

English: September to march is **the best season to visit Udaipur**.

Parse: September to March is *[NP (np* the best season*) [SBAR [S (dcP* to visit Udaipur*)]]]* .

Partial Reordered: September to March is ***(dcP* to visit Udaipur*) (np* the best season*)*** .

Reordered: September to March *(dcP* Udaipur visit to*) (np* the best season*)* is .

Hindi: *september se march udaipur ghumane ka sabse achcha samay hai .*

NP(np punct advP : advP punct np) (3)

English: **The modern town of Mumbai, about 50 km south of Navi Mumbai** is Kharghar.

Parse: The modern town of *[NP (np* Mumbai*) (punct ,) (advP* about 50 km south of Navi Mumbai*)]* is Kharghar .

Partial Reordered: ***(advP* about 50 km south of Navi Mumbai*)) (punct ,) (dcP* The modern town of Mumbai*)*** is kharghar .

Reordered: *(advP* Navi Mumbai of about 50 km south*) (punct ,) (dcP* Mumbai of the modern town*)* kharghar is .

Hindi: *navi mumbai ke 50 km dakshin me mumbai ka adhunic sahar kharghar hai .*

NP(np vp : vp np) (4)

English: The main attraction is a **divine tree called as 'Kalptaru'**.

Parse: The main attraction is *[NP (np* a divine tree*) (vp* called as 'Kalptaru'*)]* .

Partial Reordered: The main attraction is ***(vp* ` called as 'Kalptaru'*) (np* a divine tree*)*** .

Reordered: The main attraction *(vp* ` Kalptaru ' as called*) (np* a divine tree*)* is .

Hindi: *iska mukhya akarshan kalptaru namak ek divya vriksh hai .*

3.2 Verb Phrase Rules

VP(vpw PP [prep NP[np punct? SBAR[whP dcP]]] : np prep vpw punct? whP dcP) (5)

English: The best time to visit **is in the afternoon** when the crowd thins out.

Parse: The best time to visit *[VP (vpw* is*) PP[(prep* in*) NP[(np* the afternoon*) [SBAR (whP* when*) (dcP* the crowd thins out*)]]]* .

Partial Reordered: The best time to visit ***(np* the afternoon*) (prep* in*) (vpw* is*)*** *(whP* when*) (dcP* the crowd thins out*)* .

Reordered: visit to The best time *(np* the afternoon*) (prep* in*) (vpw* is*) (whP* when*) (dcP* the crowd thins out*)* .

Hindi: *bhraman karane ka sabase achcha samay dopahar me hai jab bhid kam ho jati hai .*

VP(vpw NP[np punct? SBAR[whP dcP]] : np vpw punct? whP dcP) (6)

English: Jaswant Thada **is a white marble monument** which was built in 1899 in the memory of Maharaja Jaswant Singh II.

Parse: jaswant thada *[VP (vpw* is*) [NP (np* a white marble monument*) [SBAR (whP* which*) (dcP* was built in 1899 in the memory of Maharaja Jaswant Singh II*)]]* .

Partial Reordered: Jaswant Thada ***(np* a white marble monument*) (vpw* is*)*** *(whP* which*) (dcP* was built in 1899 in the memory of Maharaja Jaswant Singh II*)* .

Reordered: Jaswant Thada *(np* a white marble monument*) (vpw* is*) (whP* which*) (dcP* Maharaja Jaswant Singh II of the memory in 1899 in built was*)* .

Hindi: *jaswant thada ek safed sangmarmar ka smarak hai jo ki maharaja jaswant singh dwitiya ki yad me 1889 me banwaya gaya tha .*

VP(vpw OP sbar : OP vpw sbar) *(7)*

English: Temples in Bhubaneshwar are **built beautifully on a common plan** as prescribed by Hindu norms.

Parse: Temples in Bhubaneshwar are *[VP (vpw* built*) (advP* beautifully*) (pp* on a common plan*) (sbar* as prescribed by Hindu norms*)]* .

Partial Reordered: Bhubaneshwar in Temples are ***(advP* beautifully*) (pp* a common plan on*) (vpw* built*)*** *(sbar* as prescribed by Hindu norms) .

Reordered: Bhubaneshwar in Temples *(advP* beautifully*) (pp* a common plan on*) (vpw* built*)* are *(sbar* as Hindu norms by prescribed*)* .

Hindi: *bhubaneswar ke mandir hindu niyamon dwara nirdharit samanya yojana ke anusar banaye gaye hain .*

*VP(vpw pp1 pp*2: pp*2 pp1 vpw)* *(8)*

English: Avalanche is **located at a distance of 28 Kms from Ooty**.

Parse: Avalanche is *[VP (vpw* located*) (pp1* at a distance of 28 kms*) (pp2* from Ooty*)]* .

Partial Reordered: Avalanche is ***(pp2* from Ooty*) (pp1* at a distance of 28 kms*) (vpw* located*)* .**

Reordered: Avalanche *(pp2* Ooty from *) (pp1* 28 kms of a distance at*) (vpw* located*)* is .

Hindi: *avalanche ooty se 28 km ki duri par sthit hai .*

VP(vpw np pp : np pp vbw) *(9)*

English: Taxis and city buses available outside the station, **facilitate access to the city**.

Parse: Taxis and city buses available outside the station , *[VP (vpw* facilitate*) (np* access*) (pp* to the city*)]* .

Partial Reordered: Taxis and city buses available outside the station **, *(pp* to the city*) (np* access*) (vpw* facilitate*)*** .

Reordered: Taxis and city buses the station outside available , *(pp* the city to*) (np* access*) (vpw* facilitate*)* .

Hindi: *station ke baahar sahar jane ke liye taksi aur bus ki suvidha upalabdha hai .*

VP (prep dcP : dcP prep) *(10)*

English: A wall was built **to protect it**.

Parse: A wall was built *[VP (prep* to*) (dcP* protect it*)]* .

Partial Reordered: A wall was built **(protect it*) (prep* to*)*** .

Reordered: A wall *(dcP* it protect*) (prep* to*)* built was .

Hindi: *ek diwar ise surakshit karane ke liye banayi gayi thi .*

VP(adv vpw dcphrase: dcphrase adv vpw) *(11)*

English: Modern artist such as French sculptor Bartholdi is **best known by his famous work**.

Parse: Modern artists such as French sculptor Bartholdi is *[VP (adv* best*) (vpw* known*) (dcP* by his famous work*)]* .

Partial Reordered: Modern artists such as French sculptor Bartholdi is ***(dcP* by his famous work*) (adv* best*) (vpw* known*)*** .

Reordered: such as French sculptor Bartholdi Modern artists *(dcP* his famous work by*) (adv* best*) (vpw* known*)* is .

Hindi: *french shilpkar bartholdi jaise aadhunik kalakar apane prashidha kam ke liye vishesh rup se jane jate hain .*

VP(advP vpw dcP: advP dcP vpw) *(12)*

English: Bikaner, popularly **known as the camel county** is located in Rajasthan.

Parse: Bikaner , *[VP (advP* popularly*) (vpw* known*) (dcP* as the camel country*)]* is located in Rajsthan .

Partial Reordered: Bikaner **,** *(advP* popularly*)* ***(dcP* as the camel country*) (vpw* known*)*** is located in Rajsthan .

Reordered: Bikaner , *(advP* popularly*) (dcP* the camel country as*) (vpw* known*)* Rajsthan in located is .

Hindi: *bikaner , jo aam taur par unton ke desh ke naam se jana jata hai, rajasthan me sthit hai .*

VP(vpw adv? adjP? dcP: dcP adjP? adv? vpw) *(13)*

English: This palace has **been beautiful from many years**.

Parse: This palace has *[VP (vpw* been*) (adjP* beautiful*) (dcP* from many years*)]* .

Partial Reordered: This palace has ***(dcP* from many years*) (adjP* beautiful*) (vpw* been*)*** .

Reordered: This palace *(dcP* many years from*) (adjP* beautiful*) (vpw* been*)* has .

Hindi: *yah mahal kai varson se sunder raha hai .*

3.3 Adjective and Adverb Phrase Rules

ADJP(vpw pp : pp vpw) *(14)*

English: The temple is **decorated with paintings depicting incidents**.

Parse: The temple is *[ADJP (vpw* decorated*)* *(pp* with paintings depicting incidents *)]* .

Partial Reordered: The temple is ***(pp* with paintings depicting incidents*)* *(vpw* decorated*)*** .

Reordered: The temple *(pp* incidents depicting paintings with*)* *(vpw* decorated*)* is .

Hindi: *mandir ghatnao ko darshate hue chitron se sajaya gya hai .*

ADJP(adjP pp : pp adjP) *(15)*

English: As a resul, temperatures are now higher than ever before .

Parse: As a result , temperatures are now *[ADJP (adjP* higher*)* *(pp* than ever*)]* before .

Partial Reordered: As a result , temperatures are now *(pp* than ever*)* *(adj* higher*)* before .

Reordered: a result As , temperatures now before ***(pp* ever than*)* *(adj* higher*)*** are .

Hindi: *parinam swarup taapman ab pahle se bhi adhik hai .*

ADJP(adj dcP : dcP adj) *(16)*

English: The Kanha National park is **open to visitors**.

Parse: The Kanha National park is *[ADJP (adj* open*)* *(dcP* to visitors*)]* .

Partial Reordered: The Kanha National park *is* ***(pp to* visitors *)* *(adj* open*)*** .

Reordered: The Kanha National park *(pp* visitors to*)* *(adj* open*)* is .

Hindi: *kanha national park paryatakon ke liye khula hai .*

ADVP(adv dcP: dcP adv) *(17)*

English: The temple is most favored spot for tourists **apart from the pilgrims**.

Parse: The temple is most favored spot for tourists *[ADVP (adv* apart*)* *(dcP* from the pilgrims*)]* .

Partial Reordered: The temple is most favored spot for tourists ***(dcP* from the pilgrims *)* *(adv* apart*)*** .

Reordered: The temple most favored spot *(dcP* the pilgrims from*)* *(adv* apart*)* is .

Hindi: *mandir teerth yatriyon ke alawa paryatkon ke liye bhi lokpriya sthal hai .*

3.4 Preposition Phrase Rules

PP(adv prep? dcP : dcP prep? adv) *(18)*

English: Does kalajar occur **because of sun**?

Parse: Does kalajar occur *[PP (adv* because*)* *(prep?* of*)* *(dcP* sun*)]* ?

Partial Reordered: Does kalajar occur ***(dcp* sun*)* *(prep?* of*)* *(adv* because*)*** ?

Reordered: Does kalajar *(dcp* sun*)* *(prep?* of*)* *(adv* because*)* occur*?*

Hindi: *kya kalajar dhup ke karan hota hai ?*

input	Ahmedabad was named after the sultan Ahmed Shah, who built the city in 1411.
baseline	ahmedabad was named after the sultan ahmed shah, who built the city in 1411. अहमदाबाद के नाम पर रखा गया सुल्तान अहमद shah, वाले शहर 1411. *ahamdabad ke nam par rakha gaya sultan ahamad shah, wale shahar 1411.*
limited reordering	ahmedabad the sultan ahmed shah , who the city 1411 in built after named was . अहमदाबाद का नाम सुल्तान अहमदशाह के , जिसने १४११ में शहर बनवाया के नाम पर रखा गया था । *ahamdabad ka nam sultan ahamadshah ke , jisane 1411 me shahar banawaya ke nam par rakha gaya tha .*
our approach	ahmedabad the sultan ahmed shah after named was , who 1411 in the city built . अहमदाबाद का नाम सुल्तान अहमदशाह के नाम से पड़ा था जिसने १४११ में शहर बनवाया था । *ahamadabad ka nam sultan ahamadshah ke nam se pada tha jisane 1411 me shahar banawaya tha .*
reference	अहमदाबाद का नाम सुल्तान अहमदशाह के नाम पर पड़ा था, जिसने १४११ में शहर बनवाया था । *ahamadabad ka nam sultan ahamadshah ke nam par pada tha jisane 1411 me shahar banawaya tha .*

Table 2: Comparison of translation on a sentence from test corpus

4 Experiments and Results

The experiments were carried out on the corpus described in Table 3 below.

	#Sentences	#Words
Training	94926	1235163
Tuning	1446	23600
Test	500	9792

Table 3: Corpus distribution

The baseline system was setup by using the phrase-based model (Brown et al., 1990; Marcu and Wong, 2002; Koehn et al., 2003). For the language model, we carried out experiments and found on comparison that 5-gram model with modified Kneser-Ney smoothing (Chen and Goodman, 1998) to be the best performing. Target Hindi corpus from the training set was used for creating the language model. The KenLM (Heafield., 2011) toolkit was used for the language modeling experiments. The tuning corpus was used to set weights for the language models, distortion model, phrase translation model etc. using minimum error rate training (Och, 2003). Decoding was performed using the MOSES decoder. Stanford constituency parser (De et al., 2006) was used for parsing.

Table 2 above describes with the help of an example how the reordering and hence the translation quality has improved. From the example it can be seen that the translation by system using our approach is better than the other two systems. The output translation is structurally more correct in our approach and conveys the same meaning with respect to the reference translation.

phrase-length	**#phrases**			**#distinct-phrases(distinct on source)**		
	baseline	**limited re-ordering/ %IOBL/ IOBL**	**our approach/ %IOBL/ IOBL**	**baseline**	**limited re-ordering/ %IOBL/ IOBL**	**our approach/ %IOBL/ IOBL**
2	537017	579878/ 7.98/ 42861	579630/ 9.98/ **42613**	208988	249847/ 19.55/ 40859	254393/ ***21.72***/ **45405**
3	504810	590265/ 16.92/ 85455	616381/ 22.10/ **111571**	292183	384518/ 31.62/ 92335	408240/ ***39.72***/ **116057**
4	406069	493637/ 21.56/ 87568	531904/ 30.98/ **125835**	268431	372282/ 38.68/ 103851	409966/ ***52.72***/ **141535**
5	313368	391490/ 24.92/ 78122	431135/ 37.58/ **117766**	221228	313723/ 41.80/ 92495	354273/ ***60.13***/ **133045**
6	231146	292899/ 26.71/ 61753	327192/ 41.55/ **96046**	170852	244643/ 43.19/ 73791	279723/ ***63.72***/ **108871**
7	154800	196679/ 27.05/ 41879	220868/ 42.67/ **66068**	119628	170108/ 42.19/ 50480	194881/ ***62.90***/ **75253**

Table 4: Phrase count analysis

The Table 5 below lists four different evaluations of the systems under study. For BLEU and NIST higher score is considered as better and for mWER and mPER lower score is desirable. Table 5 shows the results of comparative evaluation of baseline, limited reordering and our approach with improved reordering. We find that addition of more reordering rules show substantial improvements over the baseline phrase based system and the limited reordering system (Ramanathan et al., 2008). The impact of improved syntactic reordering can be seen as the BLEU and NIST scores have increased whereas mWER and mPER scores have decreased.

	BLEU	NIST	mWER %	mPER %
baseline	21.55	5.72	68.08	45.54
limited reordering	22.19	5.74	66.44	44.70
our approach	**24.47**	**5.88**	**64.71**	**43.89**

Table 5: Evaluation scores

Table 4 above shows the count of overall phrases and distinct phrases (distinct on source) for baseline, limited reordering approach and our improved reordering approach. The table also shows increase over baseline (IOBL) and percentage increase over baseline(%IOBL) for limited reordering and improved reordering. We have observed that no. of distinct phrases extracted from the training corpus get increased. The %IOBL for bigger phrases is more compare to shorter phrases. This can be attributed to the better alignments resulting in extraction of more phrases (Koehn et al., 2003).

We have also observed that the overall increase is even lesser than the increase in no. of distinct phrases (distinct on source) for all the phrase-lengths in our approach (e.g. 42613 and 45405 for phrase-length 2) which shows that reordering makes word alignments more consistent and reduces multiple entries for the same source phrase. The training was done on maximum phrase-length 7(default).

5 Conclusion

It can be seen that addition of more reordering rules improve translation quality. As of now we have tried these rules only for English-Hindi pair, but the plan is to employ similar reordering rules in other English-Indian language pairs as most Indian languages are structurally similar to Hindi. Also plans are there to go for comparative study of improved reordering system and hierarchical model.

References

Alexandra Birch , Miles Osborne and Phil Blunsom. 2010. Metrics for MT evaluation: evaluating reordering. *Machine Translation* 24, no. 1: 15-26.

Peter F. Brown, John Cocke, Stephen A. Della Pietra, Vincent J. Della Pietra, Fredrick Jelinek, John D. Lafferty, Robert L. Mercer, and Paul S. Roossin. 1990. A statistical approach to machine translation. *Computational linguistics* 16(2): 79–85.

Wang Chao, Michael Collins, and Philipp Koehn. 2007. Chinese syntactic reordering for statistical machine translation. In *Proceedings of the 2007 Joint Conference on Empirical Methods in Natural Language Processing and Computational Natural Language Learning (EMNLP-CoNLL).*

Stanley F. Chen, Joshua Goodman. 1996. An empirical study of smoothing techniques for language modeling. In *Proceedings of the 34th annual meeting on Association for Computational Linguistics.* Association for Computational Linguistics.

Michael Collins, Philipp Koehn, and Ivona Kučerová. 2005. Clause restructuring for statistical machine translation. In *Proceedings of the 43rd Annual Meeting on Association for Computational Linguistics.*

Marneffe De, Marie-Catherine, Bill MacCartney, and Christopher D. Manning. 2006. Generating typed dependency parses from phrase structure parses. In *Proceedings of LREC*, vol. 6, pp. 449-454.

Jacob Dlougach and Irina Galinskaya. 2012. Building a reordering system using tree-to-string hierarchical model. In *Proceedings of the First Workshop on Reordering for Statistical Machine Translation at COLING*, Mumbai, India.

George Doddington. 2002. Automatic evaluation of machine translation quality using n-gram co-occurrence statistics. In *Proceedings of the second international conference on Human Language Technology Research.* Morgan Kaufmann Publishers Inc.

Rohit Gupta, Raj N. Patel and Ritesh Shah. 2012. Learning Improved Reordering Models for Urdu, Farsi and Italian using SMT. In *Proceedings of the first workshop on Reordering for Statistical Machine Translation, COLING 2012*, Mumbai, India.

Kenneth Heafield. 2011. KenLM: Faster and smaller language model queries. In *Proceedings of the Sixth Workshop on Statistical Machine Translation, Association for Computational Linguistics.*

Philipp Koehn, Franz Josef Och, and Daniel Marcu. 2003. Statistical phrase-based translation. In *Proceedings of the 2003 Conference of the North American Chapter of the Association for Computational Linguistics on Human Language Technology*-Volume 1.

Philipp Koehn, Hieu Hoang, Alexandra Birch, Chris Callison-Burch, Marcello Federico, Nicola Bertoldi, Brooke Cowan et al. 2007. Moses: Open source toolkit for statistical machine translation. In Proceedings of the 45th Annual Meeting of the ACL on Interactive Poster and Demonstration Sessions.

Daniel Marcu, and William Wong. 2002. A phrase-based, joint probability model for statistical machine translation. Proceedings of EMNLP.

Sonja Nießen, Franz J. Och, Gregor Leusch, and Hermann Ney. 2000. An Evaluation Tool for Machine Translation: Fast Evaluation for MT Research. International Conference on Language Resources and Evaluation.

Franz J. Och, and Hermann Ney. 2003. A systematic comparison of various statistical alignment models. *Computational linguistics*, Volume 29, number 1:19-51.

Franz Josef Och. 2003. Minimum error rate training in statistical machine translation. In *Proceedings of the 41st Annual Meeting on Association for Computational Linguistics*-Volume 1:pp. 160-167.

Kishore Papineni, Salim Roukos, Todd Ward, Wei-Jing Zhu. 2001. BLEU: a Method for Automatic Evaluation of Machine Translation. *IBM Research Report, Thomas J. Watson Research Center.*

Taraka Rama, Karthik Gali and Avinesh PVS. 2008. Does Syntactic Knowledge help English-Hindi SMT ?. *Proceedings of the NLP Tools contest, ICON.*

Ananthakrishnan Ramanathan, Pushpak Bhattacharyya, Jayprasad Hegde, Ritesh M. Shah, and M. Sasikumar. 2008. Simple syntactic and morphological processing can help English-Hindi statistical machine translation. *In International Joint Conference on NLP (IJCNLP08).*

Christoph Tillmann, Stephan Vogel, Hermann Ney, Alex Zubiaga, and Hassan Sawaf. 1997. Accelerated DP based search for statistical translation. *In European Conf. on Speech Communication and Technology.*

Fei Xia and Michael McCord. 2004. Improving a statistical MT system with automatically learned rewrite patterns. In *Proceedings of the 20th international conference on Computational Linguistics*, p. 508. Association for Computational Linguistics.

An English-to-Hungarian Morpheme-based Statistical Machine Translation System with Reordering Rules

László J. Laki, Attila Novák, Borbála Siklósi
MTA-PPKE Language Technology Research Group
Pázmány Péter Catholic University, Faculty of Information Technology
50/a Práter Street, 1083 Budapest, Hungary
{surname.firstname}@itk.ppke.hu

Abstract

Phrase-based statistical machine translation systems can generate translations of reasonable quality in the case of language pairs with similar structure and word order. However, if the languages are more distant from a grammatical point of view, the quality of translations is much behind the expectations, since the baseline translation system cannot cope with long distance reordering of words and the mapping of word internal grammatical structures. In our paper, we present a method that tries to overcome these problems in the case of English-Hungarian translation by applying reordering rules prior to the translation process and by creating morpheme-based and factored models. Although automatic evaluation scores do not reliably reflect the improvement in all cases, human evaluation of our systems shows that readability and accuracy of the translations were improved both by reordering and applying richer models.

1 Introduction

Phrase-based statistical machine translation systems rely on statistical observations derived from phrase alignments automatically extracted from parallel bilingual corpora. The main advantage of applying SMT is its language-independence. The phrase-based model works well for language pairs with similar syntactic structure and word order.

However, phrase-based models fail to handle great word-order differences adequately. We describe our attempt to improve performance by transforming source language (English) sentences to a structure similar to that of the corresponding target (Hungarian) sentence. We also describe our approach for handling data sparseness due to the inadequate coverage of linguistic structures by the limited training corpus. It is a common problem in the case of translation to agglutinating languages like Hungarian, where a much greater amount of training data would be necessary to provide adequate statistics than what is necessary for closely related language pairs involving only morphologically less complex languages.

2 Machine Translation from English to Hungarian

English and Hungarian are rather distant regarding morphological and syntactic structure and word order. Hungarian, like Finish or Turkish, is an agglutinating and compounding language, which morphological processes yield a huge number of different word forms. This, combined with free word order of main grammatical constituents and systematically different word order in NP's and PP's, results in poor performance of traditional phrase-based SMT systems. In order to have an SMT system produce correct translations of high quality, it is required to have a relevant statistical model acquired from bilingual corpora. Thus, even if a corpus of a substantial size were available (which is not the case), both the alignment phase of constructing a translation model and translation itself would be compromised by the high number of seldom or never seen word forms.

3 Related work

For language pairs having very different syntactic structure and word order, research has shifted towards using hierarchical models or the use of hybrid methods, such as augmenting purely statistical approaches by handmade rules as a preprocessing step. Such extensions have proved to improve results significantly in systems translating from English to German, Arabic or Turkish and several other languages (Yeniterzi and Oflazer, 2010; Gojun and Fraser, 2012; Collins et al., 2005). The hybrid models applied to English-Hungarian machine translation that we present in this paper belong to the latter line of research.

We applied both reordering and morphological segmentation in order to handle both word order problems and data sparseness caused by agglutination. Luong et al. (2010) applied only morphological analysis in the case of translation from English to Finnish. On the other hand, Yeniterzi and Oflazer (2010) described an approach for English to Turkish translation, in which they applied both syntactic source-side reordering and morphological segmentation. In their work, morphemes constructing a single word were joined during the translation process, but in our experiments, this method increased data sparseness in the training set, decreasing the quality of the final translation rather than improving it. Another difference between Yeniterzi and Oflazer (2010)'s and our work is that they applied the morphological generator integrated in the SMT system, while we used our computational morphology on SMT output as a word form generator, generating final word forms in cases, where the SMT system was not able to find it.

Relying on recent trends and results of research in the field of machine translation, we believe that neither a purely rule-based nor a statistical method by itself is an optimal way to handle the problem. Our work reflects this attitude by applying hand-made language-specific rules. Some works, such as (Jiang et al., 2010; Holmqvist et al., 2012; Genzel, 2010) have also tried deriving such reordering rules automatically.

A further method to apply would be using a hierarchical tree-based translation system, also augmented by reordering rules and morphological segmentation. Such a method is presented in (Gao et al., 2011), but focusing on a narrower problem and applying it to Chinese to English translation.

4 Hybrid morpheme-based machine translation system with reordering rules

In order to mitigate the aforementioned difficulties regarding word order and data sparseness, we created a hybrid system with different preprocessing and decoding solutions. First we applied reordering rules in order to transform the source sentence to a structure more appropriate for word alignment and phrase extraction. The problem of lexical granularity (i.e. the relatively substantial difference in the number of words in the corresponding sentences, see Table 1) was also to be solved. We explored two approaches: a) increasing the number of tokens on both sides using morphemes instead of words and b) decreasing the number of word tokens on the English side to approximate that of the corresponding Hungarian sentences.

		Test	Train
# of sentences		1000	1,026,836
Words	**en**	14.137	14.173
(AVG per sent.)	**hu**	11.672	11.764
Morphemes	**en**	16.764	16.768
(AVG per sent.)	**hu**	18.391	18.429

Table 1: Size of training and test datasets measured in the number of sentences, average number of words per sentences and the average number of morphemes per sentences on the English and Hungarian sides.

4.1 Reordering rules

In order to augment the phrase-based SMT system, we defined reordering rules as a preprocessing step. The goal of these transformations is to move words in the English source sentence to positions that correspond to their place in the Hungarian translation. Fig. 1 illustrates the transformation process on the phrase *the sons of the many merchants living in the city*. E.g., the subphrase *living in the city* is transformed to the order *the city in living* corresponding to the Hungarian translation *"a város+ban élő"* as shown in Fig. 1a. Our rules apply only to those word order differences, which are systematically present between the two grammars (e.g. prepositions vs. case endings/postpositions). We did not intend to handle free word order variations of Hungarian, where the same meaning can be expressed with several different orderings, since the actual word order in a sentence is not only determined by syntactic rules, but also by pragmatic factors.

Dependency structure: Reordering rules are guided by dependency relations. After generating a context-free parse, these relations are extracted by the Stanford parser (Marneffe et al., 2006) that we used in our experiments. The dependency structure of our example is shown in Fig. 1b.

Thus the example phrase *merchants living in the city* is transformed along the relations PART-

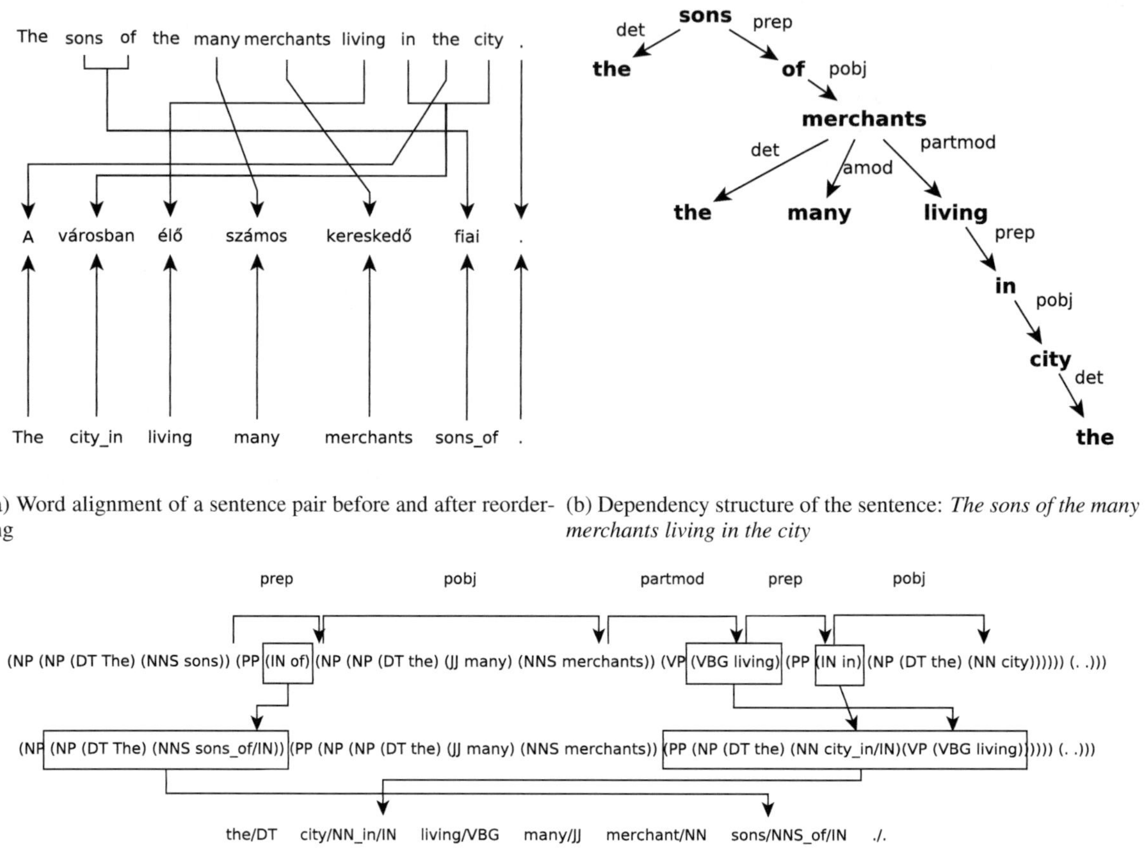

(a) Word alignment of a sentence pair before and after reordering

(b) Dependency structure of the sentence: *The sons of the many merchants living in the city*

(c) The process of reordering along dependency relations.

Figure 1: Word alignment, dependency relations and reordering

MOD(merchant, living)[1], PREP(living, in)[1] and POBJ(in, city)[1]. First the preposition is attached to the child of the POBJ relation, then they are positioned before the noun phrase preceding it as shown in Fig. 1c. The resulting word order *the city in living merchants* corresponds to the Hungarian structure *"a város+ban élő kereskedők"*.

Since these levels of analysis depend on each other, errors arising at each phase propagate and cumulate through the whole process having a significant effect on reordering. Even though we used the lexicalized version of the Stanford parser, which is reported to work more accurately, it still very often generates agrammatical parses with agreement errors and odd PoS sequences as shown in Table 2 (showing only the generated PoS tag sequences here).

[1]PARTMOD=participial modifier, PREP=prepositional modifier, POBJ=object of preposition. The full list of dependency relations can be found in `http://nlp.stanford.edu/software/dependencies_manual.pdf`

-/: 100/CD million/CD **sound/NN** good/JJ to/TO me/PRP ./.
For/IN airline/NN personnel/NNS ,/, we/PRP **cash/NN** personal/JJ **checks/VBZ** up/RP to/TO $/$ 100/CD ./.

Table 2: Examples of low level errors (verbs tagged as nouns and vice versa) that affect reordering and translation

Morpheme-based restructuring: Due to the agglutinating nature of Hungarian, many function words in English are expressed as suffixes in the Hungarian translation. In order to enable the phrase-based system to have them correspond to each other, we applied morphological analysis on the Hungarian sentences segmenting each word to their morphological constituents. To annotate the Hungarian side of the corpus, we used the PurePos automated morphological annotation system (Orosz and Novák, 2012). A simple example is a phrase like *in my house*, which is transformed to the form *house my in* corresponding to the single word *"házamban"* in Hungarian. The morphological segmentation of this word is *ház[N]+am[PxS1]+ban[Ine]*[1]. Defining and applying the rules for such short phrases is not particularly difficult. However, related words in longer sentences can be much further separated from each other and they may be involved in more than one relation, which often results in an interaction of word order constraints. In a similar manner, some rules insert morphological elements corresponding to those present in the Hungarian sentence, but not explicitly expressed in English, such as the accusative case suffix or subject agreement of verbs. These pieces of implicit structural information can be induced from the dependency relations. For example, in the English phrase *giving/VBG a/DT present/NN*, the word *present* is tagged as *acc* (based on its object role) corresponding to the Hungarian accusative *-t* suffix resulting in the reordered phrase of *giving a present+acc* now perfectly aligning to the Hungarian structure of *"adni egy ajándék+ot"*

4.2 Lexical granularity

The number of words is often rather different in a pair of Hungarian and English sentences enforcing the alignment module of the SMT system to create one-to-many or many-to-many alignments, or simply leave tokens unaligned. Such alignments often result in missing or 'hallucinated' words in the translation. Table 1 shows the differences in the average number of words and morphemes in our parallel corpus. The average number of words is smaller in Hungarian than in the English sentences. On the other hand, at least at the granularity of the morphological analysis we applied to our data, the number of morphemes is higher in Hungarian than in English. The number of tokens on both sides can be made more similar by either decreasing the number of words on the English side by joining function words corresponding to Hungarian suffixes or by increasing the number on both sides using morphemes as tokens.

As the difference is primarily due to the fact that some English function words are represented as suffixes in Hungarian, the relative difference between the number of morphemes in the corresponding sentences is lower than that of the words. So one possible approach to solving the lexical granularity difference problem is to use morphemes instead of words. One problem with morpheme-based translation is that it is often the case in longer sentences that instances of the same functional morpheme belong to more than one different word in the sentence. This causes indeterminacies in the alignment process (because the models implemented in the Giza++ word aligner cannot be forced to assume locally monotone alignment at the places where we in fact know that the alignment should be monotone), which often results in erroneous phrases being extracted from the training corpus. For example, if there are two nouns in a sentence and one of them is plural, then the [PL] tag corresponding to this feature might land at another noun.

The difficulty of aligning very frequent functional morphemes is illustrated by the fact that in the Giza++ alignments created from our training corpus, 39% of the nominal plural ([PL]) morphemes remained unaligned, 13% was not attached to the noun it should have been attached to, because the alignment was not monotone, while 1% was aligned to several (up to eight) instances of the corresponding morpheme. Alignment is not the only problem: some indivisible morpheme sequences (like noun+plural) should always stay together but we had concerns that, unless it is constrained to monotone decoding, the baseline distortion model of the decoder will often scatter suffixes throughout the sentence instead. A lexicalized reordering model can be expected to solve this problem, thus we used lexical reordering in our models but for comparison we also tested how each model performs when the decoder is constrained to monotone decoding.

Another approach we tested was fusing separate words on the English side that correspond to a single word in the Hungarian sentence (modeling English as an agglutinating language) to avoid the aligner connecting these morphemes to some other words on the Hungarian side and using a factored model to try to solve the data sparseness issues this move results in. For example, possessive determiners are attached to the head noun as suffixes in this model like the corresponding possessive suffixes in Hungarian : the phrase *my/PRP$ own/JJ mother/NN* is transformed to the form *own/JJ mother/NN_my/PRP$*, which corresponds to the Hungarian phrase *saját anyá_m*.

By applying either of the morpheme-token-

[1] *PxS1=Possessor:1Sg='my', Ine=Inessive='in'*

based or the factored morphosyntactic-feature-based solution, the translations generated by the SMT system contain sequences of lemmas and morphosyntactic tags, thus, in order to get the final form of the translated sentence, the surface form of the words have to be generated from the morpheme sequence. In our experiments, we applied the word form generator module of the Humor morphological analyzer to the output of the decoder (Novák, 2003; Prószéky and Kis, 1999).

4.3 Factored translation

The Moses SMT toolkit (Koehn et al., 2007), which we used in our experiments, is suitable for implementing factored translation models. Instead of relying on just the surface form of the words, further annotations such as morphological analysis can be used in the process of a factored translation. Translation factors might be the surface form of each word, its lemma, its main PoS tag and its morphosyntactic features. During factored translation, there is an opportunity to use multiple translation models, generation models or contextual language models. Since the system has the possibility to use any combination of these, in theory it is able to generate better translations using sparse linguistic data than a word-based baseline system. This feature is vital in cases where some abstraction is necessary, because some words in the sentence to be translated or generated are missing from the training set.

To see how well a factored model performs in the case of translation to an agglutinating language, we also trained a factored translation system combined with our reordering rules. The factors in our case were of the form: `lemma/PoS | PoS+morphtags`, where `PoS` is the main part-of-speech tag and `morphtags` are the rest of the morphological features and extra morphemes attached to the word as described in Section 4.2. Training the system with this combination of factors to handle data sparseness issues seems reasonable in theory; however, translation of lexical and grammatical factors is compromised by a serious weakness of the factored translation implementation in Moses. If the two factors are treated as connected at training time, then if a certain combination of a lemma and its morphology is not present in the translation models, which is very frequent in the case of an agglutinating language, then it can not be translated even if both the lemma and the morphological feature set are represented in the training corpus separately. In such cases none of the factors are translated and the source word is copied to the output untranslated.

Another method of training a factored model is to translate factors independently. This could indeed solve data sparseness problems, but, as we noted during our experiments, another problem arises in this case: at translation time, translations of morphological tags often land at wrong lemmas. This is due to the fact when translating a phrase, the system selects a translation having one word order, e.g. [Det N V], for one factor (the lemmas) and another, e.g. [V Det N] for the other (the morphosyntactic tags). This results in ill-formed structures, such as nominal morphosyntactic features landing on verbs and verbal morphosyntactic features landing on nouns etc., thus, although the translation might contain the relevant translations regarding both lemmas and morphological features, the final sentence will be an inconsistent mixture of them, making generation of the right word forms impossible. Due to word order variations in Hungarian, this situation turned out to be rather frequent, affecting 21% of our 1000 test sentences.

In order to improve translations compromised by inconsistent mapping of lemmas and morphology, we introduced a postprocessing step extracting and restoring the proper positions of the morphological tags in the result of factored translations. Relying on the alignment information, the proper position of each morphological tag in the sequence can be found. At translation time, Moses can output which source words each target phrase was translated from. We introduced two auxiliary factors to the phrase table that represent alignments of our two main factors. If the alignments in the two factors mismatch, we can realign them using the auxiliary alignment factors (using the word order in the lemma factor as pivot). Once having the factors rematched, the two factors of the target translation are unified and the morphological generator can be applied to generate the final word forms. As it is evident from the evaluation data presented in Section 5, the realignment of factors consistently improved the quality of translations produced by all factored models.

5 Experiments and results

We performed experiments on word-based, morpheme-based and factored translations from English to Hungarian with and without applying our reordering rules as a preprocessing step. We also contrasted the performance of our experimental systems with that of some commercial systems: the rule-based MetaMorpho (Novák et al., 2008; Novák, 2009) and the major commercial translation services, Google Translate and Bing Translator, which apply their language independent statistical systems trained on huge parallel corpora. Low BLEU scores of translations generated by these systems (compared to those usually obtained for other languages) indicate that machine translation to Hungarian is indeed a difficult task.

In all of our experiments, the Moses (Koehn et al., 2007) toolkit was used for building the translation models and performing the translation task itself, using IRSTLM (Federico et al., 2008) to build language models. Wherever it was necessary, PurePos (Orosz and Novák, 2012) was used for morphological analysis and generation, and the Stanford Parser (Marneffe et al., 2006) for constituent and dependency parsing.

5.1 Datasets

As training data, we used the Hunglish (Varga et al., 2005) corpus, created by BME MOKK[2] and the Research Institute for Linguistics of the Hungarian Academy of Sciences. This corpus contains parallel texts from the following domains: literature and magazines, legal texts and movie subtitles. There is a great degree of variation in the quality of different parts of the corpus. We automatically eliminated sentence pairs from the corpus that caused technical problems, but overall translation quality was not checked.

The corpus we used for training the system consists of 1,026,836 parallel sentences with 14,553,765 words on the English side and 12,079,557 on the Hungarian side. For testing purposes, a 1000-sentence-long portion was selected from the same corpus with one reference translation. Automatic evaluation was performed on this set using the BLEU evaluation metric. Results for each system are listed in Table 3.

[2]MOKK Centre for Media Research and Education at the Department of Sociology and Communication, Budapest University of Technology and Economics

5.2 Baseline systems

We built a word-based, a morpheme-based, and a factored baseline system (featured as *w*, *m* and *f* in Table 3), not using the reordering rules described in Section 4.1, each trained using Moses.

For the word-based baseline model *w*, the only preprocessing we applied was standard tokenization and lowercasing. A phrase table with a phrase length limit of 7 was extracted, and a 5-gram language model was built. A lexicalized reordering model with a distortion limit of 6 was used in this baseline model (and all other models with non-monotone decoding).

We evaluated this system using two automatic metrics: the usual word-based BLEU (w-BLEU) and, in order to have a relevant base of comparison to the other systems, a morpheme-based score (mm-BLEU), which in the case of the word-based baseline was computed applying morphological analysis to the translations. mm-BLEU is based on counts of identical abstract morpheme sequences in the generated and the reference translations instead of identical word sequences. Note that this differs from m-BLEU as used in e.g. (Clifton and Sarkar, 2011), which is BLEU applied to pseudo-morphs generated by an unsupervised segmenter. mm-BLEU measures the ability of the system to generate the correct morphemes in the translations.

The second baseline system *m* was trained on morphologically segmented sentences, thus the output of the decoder is a sequence of morphemes. A BLEU score computed on the output of the decoder in this case is mm-BLEU. The morphological generator was applied to the output of the Moses decoder in order to acquire the final word forms. The morpheme-based system *m* performed better in terms of mm-BLEU, although it got a lower w-BLEU score.

The third, factored baseline model *f* was outperformed by the two other models both in terms of w-BLEU and mm-BLEU, even when the problem caused by a different word order in the factors was fixed as described in Section 4.3 (the system *fx*).

5.3 Reordered models

Based on considerations described in Sections 4.1 and 4.2, we performed reordering as a preprocessing step both at training and translation time. Models using this configuration were also evaluated applying the same w-BLEU and mm-BLEU

ID	w-BLEU	mm-BLEU
w-based baseline (*w*)	14.57%	59.32%
m-based baseline mon. (*mm*)	11.69%	63.18%
m-based baseline (*m*)	12.19%	63.87%
factored baseline monotone (*fm*)	9.70%	56.00%
factored baseline mon. fixed (*fmx*)	9.84%	57.09%
w-based reord. (*wre*)	**14.83%**	58.06%
w-based reord. joined (*wre_*)	13.05%	57.21%
m-based reord. mon. (*mrem*)	12.01%	64.24%
m-based reord. (*mre*)	12.22%	**64.94%**
fact. reord. mon. (*frem*)	10.50%	59.56%
fact. reord. mon. fixed (*fremx*)	10.64%	60.28%
fact. reord. (*fre*)	10.78%	59.97%
fact. reord. fixed (*frex*)	10.88%	60.83%
Google Translate (*goo*)	***15.68%***	*55.86%*
Bing Translator (*bing*)	*12.16%*	*53.05%*
MetaMorpho (*mmo*)	*6.86%*	*50.97%*

Table 3: Automatic evaluation scores for systems tested in the experiments.

metrics. We implemented various morpheme-based, factored and word-based reordered models. The two word-based setups performed the same transformations moving function words, the difference between the two was only whether the moved words were kept as distinct words (*wre*) or joined to the target word as suffixes to form a single word form (*wre_*). The models allowed further reordering during decoding using a lexicalized reordering model.

The morpheme-based (*mre*) and the factored models (*fre* and *frex*, the latter with factor misalignment fixed) were contrasted with alternative setups where the decoder was constrained to monotone decoding (*mrem, frem, fremx*). We had concerns that in the case of the morpheme-based model the decoder might move suffixes to incorrect positions. However, using a lexicalized reordering model prevented these problems and the systems with reordering during decoding performed consistently better. Monotone decoding blocked the decoder from fixing word order in the preverbal field of the comment part of Hungarian sentences, where strict word order constraints apply in contrast to the free word order of the topic and the postverbal part of the comment. While our reordering rules did not capture these constraints depending on various subtle features of the actually selected translation that cannot be reliably inferred from the English original, the lexically constrained reordering performed by the decoder did manage to generate translations that conformed to them at least to some extent.

The results presented in Table 3 show that the reordered *wre, mre* and *frex* models obtained consistently higher BLEU scores than the corresponding baseline models (the only exception being the mm-BLEU score of the *wre* model). Although the BLEU scores do not show this clearly, the translations generated by the *wre_* model are far worse than the output of any other system due to a high number of untranslated "agglutinating English" words with function words attached to content words as suffixes.

Figure 4 shows the translation results of our different systems. As it can be seen, *mre* performed the best, regarding fluency and reflecting the original meaning.

6 Human evaluation

It has been shown that system rankings based on single reference BLEU scores often do not correspond to how humans evaluate the translations. For this reason, automatic evaluation has for a long time not been used to officially rank systems at Workshops on Statistical Machine Translation (WMT) (Callison-Burch et al., 2007). In our work, we presented results of automated evaluation using a single reference BLEU metrics, but we also investigated translations generated by each system using human evaluation, applying the ranking scheme used at WMT workshops to officially rank systems.

300 sentences were randomly chosen from the test set for the purpose of human evaluation. Five annotators evaluated translations generated by each of the above described systems plus the reference translation in the corpus with regard to translation quality (considering both adequacy and fluency in a single quality ranking). The order of translations was randomized for each sentence and a balanced number of comparisons was performed for each system pair. The systems were ranked based on a score that was defined as the number of times the output of a system was deemed not worse than that of the other in pairwise comparisons divided by the number of pairwise comparisons. The aggregate results of human evaluation are listed in Table 5.

Manual investigation of the translation outputs revealed that the system incorporating morphological and syntactic information are better at capturing grammatical relations in the original text and rendering them in the translation by generating the

original English	After you were picked up at sea , our listening post in Malta intercepted that fax .
reordered English	after/[IN] you/[PRP] be/[VB] [Past] pick/[VB] [PPart] up/[RP] at/[IN] sea/[NN] ,/[,] our/[PRP$] listen/[VB] [ING] post/[NN] in/[IN] malta/[NNP] intercept/[VB] [PPart] that/[DT] fax/[NN] ./[.]
morpheme based translation	miután/[KOT] felvesz/[IGE] [Past] [t3] [Def] maga/[FN_NM] [e3] [ACC] a/[DET] tenger/[FN] [SUP] ,/[PUNCT] hallgat/[IGE] [Past] [e3] [Def] a/[DET] hely/[FN] [PSt1] ,/[PUNCT] hogy/[KOT] málta/[FN] [INE] áll/[IGE] [Past] [e3] [Def] ez/[FN_NM] [ACC] a/[DET] fax/[FN] [ACC] ./[PUNCT]
final translation back-translation	Miután felvették magát a tengeren , hallgatta a helyünk , hogy málta állta ezt a faxot . After you were picked up at sea, our listening post caught the fax in Malta.
baseline translation back-translation	Azután , hogy felvette a tengeren , a máltai hallgatta az emelkedő , hogy fax . After you, he picked it up at the sea, and that Malta were caught, that it is a fax.
Hungarian reference back-translation	Miután önt kihalászták , ezt fogták el egy máltai postán . After you were fished out, this was caught at a post in Malta.

Table 4: Translation results of our systems with hand made backtranslations for comparison with the reference.

ref	mmo	goo	bing	**mre**	frex	m	fx	w	wre	wre_
88.33	76.30	72.80	61.66	**55.60**	55.42	54.28	52.03	51.33	50.89	37.57

Table 5: Human evaluation ranking of systems measured as percentage of generating a translation not worse than the other in pairwise comparisons

appropriate inflected forms. Rule-based reordering also improved quality when using linguistically rich models. The only ones that performed worse than the baseline were the word-based reordered solutions, especially the one based on "agglutinating English", the poor performance of which came as no surprise. BLEU scores do not correspond well to human judgments. Of our models, the *wre* system had the highest BLEU score, however, human evaluation ranked that worse than any of the morpheme-based systems. Moreover, MetaMorpho, the commercial system having highest rank had by far the lowest BLEU score.

Considering all the systems in the ranking procedure, it can be observed that the reference translation used also for measuring BLEU score does not always represent the best translation either according to our evaluators. It is worth noting though that there was a rather significant variance in the ranking of reference translations due to some evaluators ranking them much less favourably than others (75.29% vs. 92.98%).

7 Conclusion

We performed several experiments on English-Hungarian machine translation. Automatic evaluation consistently scored models including rule-based reordering higher than systems not including it. Human evaluation confirmed that applying reordering and morphological segmentation does improve translation quality in the case of translating to an agglutinating language like Hungarian.

Our models are not yet on par with commercial systems. The rather limited amount of training corpus that also has serious quality problems is certainly one factor playing a role in this. Our future plans include enlarging and improving our training corpus, improving alignment and components of the syntactic annotation and reordering chain as well as experimenting with combination of morpheme-based and factored models.

Acknowledgement

This work was partially supported by TÁMOP – 4.2.1.B – 11/2/KMR-2011-0002 and TÁMOP – 4.2.2./B – 10/1-2010-0014.

References

Chris Callison-Burch, Cameron Fordyce, Philipp Koehn, Christof Monz, and Josh Schroeder. 2007. (Meta-)evaluation of machine translation. In *Proceedings of the Second Workshop on Statistical Machine Translation*, StatMT '07, pages 136–158, Stroudsburg, PA, USA. Association for Computational Linguistics.

Ann Clifton and Anoop Sarkar. 2011. Combining morpheme-based machine translation with post-processing morpheme prediction. In *Proceedings of the 49th Annual Meeting of the Association for Computational Linguistics: Human Language Technologies - Volume 1*, HLT '11, pages 32–42, Stroudsburg,

PA, USA. Association for Computational Linguistics.

Michael Collins, Philipp Koehn, and Ivona Kučerová. 2005. Clause restructuring for statistical machine translation. In *Proceedings of the 43rd Annual Meeting on Association for Computational Linguistics*, ACL '05, pages 531–540, Stroudsburg, PA, USA. Association for Computational Linguistics.

Marcello Federico, Nicola Bertoldi, and Mauro Cettolo. 2008. Irstlm: an open source toolkit for handling large scale language models. In *INTERSPEECH*, pages 1618–1621.

Yang Gao, Philipp Koehn, and Alexandra Birch. 2011. Soft dependency constraints for reordering in hierarchical Phrase-Based translation. In *Proceedings of the 2011 Conference on Empirical Methods in Natural Language Processing*, pages 857–868, Edinburgh, Scotland, UK., jul. Association for Computational Linguistics.

Dmitriy Genzel. 2010. Automatically learning source-side reordering rules for large scale machine translation. In *COLING*, pages 376–384.

Anita Gojun and Alexander Fraser. 2012. Determining the placement of German verbs in English-to-German SMT. In Walter Daelemans, Mirella Lapata, and Llus Mrquez, editors, *EACL*, pages 726–735. The Association for Computer Linguistics.

Hieu Hoang. 2007. Factored translation models. In *In Proceedings of the 2007 Joint Conference on Empirical Methods in Natural Language Processing and Computational Natural Language Learning (EMNLP-CoNLL*, pages 868–876.

Maria Holmqvist, Sara Stymne, Lars Ahrenberg, and Magnus Merkel. 2012. Alignment-based reordering for SMT. In Nicoletta Calzolari (Conference Chair) et al., editor, *Proceedings of the Eight International Conference on Language Resources and Evaluation (LREC'12)*, Istanbul, Turkey, may. European Language Resources Association (ELRA).

Jie Jiang, Jinhua Du, and Andy Way. 2010. Source-side syntactic reordering patterns with functional words for improved phrase-based SMT. In *Proceedings of SSST-4, Fourth Workshop on Syntax and Structure in Statistical Translation*, pages 19–27, Beijing.

P. Koehn, H. Hoang, A. Birch, C. Callison-Burch, M. Federico, N. Bertoldi, B. Cowan, W. Shen, C. Moran, R. Zens, C. Dyer, O. Bojar, A. Constantin, and E. Herbst. 2007. Moses: Open Source Toolkit for Statistical Machine Translation. In *Proceedings of the ACL 2007 Demo and Poster Sessions*, pages 177–180, Prague. Association for Computational Linguistics.

Minh-Thang Luong, Preslav Nakov, and Min-Yen Kan. 2010. A hybrid morpheme-word representation for machine translation of morphologically rich languages. In *Proceedings of the 2010 Conference on Empirical Methods in Natural Language Processing*, EMNLP '10, pages 148–157, Stroudsburg, PA, USA. Association for Computational Linguistics.

Marie-Catherine De Marneffe, Bill Maccartney, and Christopher D. Manning. 2006. Generating typed dependency parses from phrase structure parses. In *In LREC 2006*.

Attila Novák, László Tihanyi, and Gábor Prószéky. 2008. The MetaMorpho translation system. In *Proceedings of the Third Workshop on Statistical Machine Translation*, StatMT '08, pages 111–114, Stroudsburg, PA, USA. Association for Computational Linguistics.

Attila Novák. 2003. What is good Humor like? In *I. Magyar Számtógépes Nyelvészeti Konferencia*, pages 138–144, Szeged. SZTE.

Attila Novák. 2009. MorphoLogic's submission for the WMT 2009 Shared Task. In *Proceedings of the Fourth Workshop on Statistical Machine Translation at EACL 2009*, Athens, Greece.

György Orosz and Attila Novák. 2012. PurePos – an open source morphological disambiguator. In *Proceedings of the 9th International Workshop on Natural Language Processing and Cognitive Science.*, Wroclaw, Poland.

Kishore Papineni, Salim Roukos, Todd Ward, and Wei-Jing Zhu. 2002. BLEU: a method for automatic evaluation of machine translation. In *Proceedings of the 40th Annual Meeting on Association for Computational Linguistics*, ACL '02, pages 311–318, Stroudsburg, PA, USA. Association for Computational Linguistics.

Gábor Prószéky and Balázs Kis. 1999. A unification-based approach to morpho-syntactic parsing of agglutinative and other (highly) inflectional languages. In *Proceedings of the 37th annual meeting of the Association for Computational Linguistics on Computational Linguistics*, ACL '99, pages 261–268, Stroudsburg, PA, USA. Association for Computational Linguistics.

D. Varga, L. Németh, P. Halácsy, A. Kornai, V. Trón, and V. Nagy. 2005. Parallel corpora for medium density languages. In *Recent Advances in Natural Language Processing (RANLP 2005)*, pages 590–596.

Reyyan Yeniterzi and Kemal Oflazer. 2010. Syntax-to-morphology mapping in factored phrase-based statistical machine translation from English to Turkish. In *Proceedings of the 48th Annual Meeting of the Association for Computational Linguistics*, ACL '10, pages 454–464, Stroudsburg, PA, USA. Association for Computational Linguistics.

Controlled Ascent: Imbuing Statistical MT with Linguistic Knowledge

William D. Lewis and Chris Quirk
Microsoft Research
One Microsoft Way
Redmond, WA 98052
{wilewis,chrisq}@microsoft.com

Abstract

We explore the intersection of rule-based and statistical approaches in machine translation, with a particular focus on past and current work here at Microsoft Research. Until about ten years ago, the only machine translation systems worth using were rule-based and linguistically-informed. Along came statistical approaches, which use large corpora to directly guide translations toward expressions people would actually say. Rather than making local decisions when writing and conditioning rules, goodness of translation was modeled numerically and free parameters were selected to optimize that goodness. This led to huge improvements in translation quality as more and more data was consumed. By necessity, the pendulum is swinging towards the inclusion of linguistic features in MT systems. We describe some of our statistical and non-statistical attempts to incorporate linguistic insights into machine translation systems, showing what is currently working well, and what isn't. We also look at trade-offs in using linguistic knowledge ("rules") in pre- or post-processing by language pair, with a particular eye on the return on investment as training data increases in size.

1 Introduction

Machine translation has undergone several paradigm shifts since its original conception. Early work considered the problem as cryptography, imagining that a word replacement cipher could find the word correspondences between two languages. Clearly Weaver was decades ahead of his time in terms of both computational power and availability of data: only now is this approach gaining some traction (Knight, 2013)[1] At the time, however, this direction did not appear promising, and work turned toward rule-based approaches.

Effective translation needs to handle a broad range of phenomena. Word substitution ciphers may address lexical selection, but there are many additional complexities: morphological normalization in the source language, morphological inflection in the target language, word order differences, and sentence structure differences, to name a few. Many of these could be captured, at least to a first degree of approximation, by rule-based approaches. A single rule might capture the fact that English word order is predominantly SVO and Japanese word order is predominantly SOV. While many exceptions exist, such rules handle many of the largest differences between languages rather effectively. Therefore, rule-based systems that did a reasonable job of addressing morphological and syntactic differences between source and target dominated the marketplace for decades.

With the broader usage of computers, greater amounts of electronic data became available to systems. Example-based machine translation systems, which learn corpus-specific translations based on data, began to show substantial improvements in the core problem of lexical selection. This task was always quite difficult for rule-based approaches: finding the correct translation in context requires a large amount of knowledge. In practice, nearby words are effective disambiguators once a large amount of data has been captured.

Phrasal statistical machine translation systems formalized many of the intuitions in example-based machine translation approaches, replacing heuristic selection functions with robust statistical estimators. Effective search techniques developed originally for speech recognition were strong starting influences in the complicated realm of MT decoding. Finally, large quantities of parallel data and even larger quantities of monolingual data allowed such phrasal methods to shine even in broad domain translation.

Translations were still far from perfect, though. Phrasal systems capture local context and local reordering well, but struggle with global reordering. Over the past decade, statistical machine translation has begun to be influenced by linguistic information once again. Syntactic models have shown some of the most compelling gains. Many systems leverage the syntactic structure of either the

[1] For the original 1949 *Translation* memorandum by Weaver see (Weaver, 1955).

source or the target sentences to make better decisions about reordering and lexical selection.

Our machine translation group has been an active participant in many of these latest developments. The first MSR MT system used deep linguistic features, often with great positive effect. Inspired by the successes and failures of this system, we invested heavily in syntax-based SMT. However, our current statistical systems are still linguistically impoverished in comparison.

This paper attempts to document important lessons learned, highlight current best practices, and identify promising future directions for improving machine translation. A brief review of our earlier generation of machine translation technology sets the stage; this older system remains relevant given renewed interest in semantics (*e.g.*, http://amr.isi.edu/). Next we describe some of our statistical and non-statistical attempts to incorporate linguistic insights into machine translation systems, showing what is currently working well, and what is not. We also look at trade-offs in using linguistic knowledge ("rules") in pre- or post-processing by language pair, with a particular eye on the return on investment as training data increases in size. Systems built on different architectures, particularly those incorporating some linguistic information, may have different learning curves on data. The advent of social media and big data presents new challenges; we review some effective research in this area. We conclude by exploring promising directions for improving translation quality, especially focusing on areas that stand to benefit from linguistic information.

2 Logical Form Translation

Machine translation research at Microsoft Research began in 1999. Analysis components had been developed to parse surface sentences into deep *logical forms*: predicate-argument structures that normalized away many morphological and syntactic differences. This deep representation was originally intended for information mining and question answering, allowing facts to reinforce one another, and simplifying question and answer matching. These same normalizations helped make information more consistent across languages: machine translation was a clear potential application. Consider the deep representations of the sentence pairs in Figure 1: many of the surface differences, such as word order and morphological inflection, are normalized away, potentially easing the translation process.

```
To please reviewers is difficult.
be1 (+Pres +Proposition)
 \Tobj——difficult1 (+Proposition +F0)
          \Tsub——please1 (+Inf +Psych)
                  \Tsub——_X1
                   \Tind——reviewer1 (+Plur)
Reviewers are difficult to please.
be1 (+Pres +Proposition)
 \Tobj——difficult1 (+Proposition +B3)
          \Tsub——please1 (+Inf +Psych)
                  \Tsub——_X1
                   \Tind——reviewer1 (+Plur)
Pleasing reviewers is difficult.
be1 (+Pres +Proposition)
 \Tobj——difficult1 (+Proposition +F0)
          \Tsub——please1 (+Verbnoun +Psych)
                  \Tsub——_X1
                   \Tind——reviewer1 (+Plur)
```

Figure 1: Example logical forms for three distinct inputs, demonstrating how differences in syntactic structure may be normalized away. In each case, the logical form is a graph of nodes such as "be" and "difficult", and relations such as "Tobj" (typical object) and "Tsub" (typical subject). In addition, nodes are marked with binary features called bits, prefixed with a + symbol in the notation, that capture unstructured pieces of information such as tense and number.

Substantial differences remained, however. Many words and phrases have non-compositional contextually-influenced translations. Commercial systems of the time relied on complex, hand-curated dictionaries to make this mapping. Yet example-based and statistical systems had already begun to show promise, especially in the case of domain-specific translations. Microsoft in particular had large internal demand for "technical" translations. With increasing language coverage and continuing updates to product documentation and support articles came increasing translation costs. Producing translations tailored to this domain would have been an expensive task for a rule-based system; a corpus-based approach was pursed.

This was truly a hybrid system. Source and target language surface sentences were parsed into deep logical forms using rule-based analyzers.[2]

[2]These parsers were developed with a strong focus on corpora, though. George Heidorn, Karen Jensen, and the NLP research group developed a toolchain for quickly parsing a large bank of test sentences and comparing against the last best result. The improvements and regressions resulting from a change to the grammar could be manually evaluated, and the changes refined until the end result. The end result was a

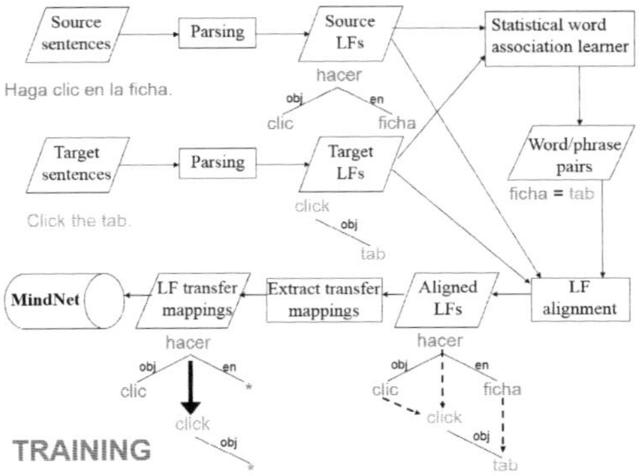

Figure 2: The process of learning translation information from parallel data in the LF system.

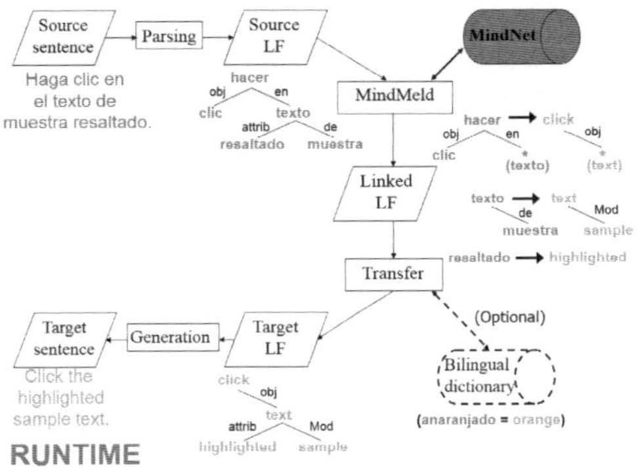

Figure 3: The process of translating a new sentence in the LF system.

Likewise a rule-based target language generation component could find a surface realization of a deep logical form. However, the mapping from source language logical form fragments to target language logical form fragments was learned from parallel data.

2.1 Details of the LF-based system

Training started with a parallel corpus. First, the source and target language sentences were parsed. Then the logical forms of the source and target were aligned (Menezes and Richardson, 2001). These aligned logical forms were partitioned into minimal non-compositional units, each consisting of some non-empty subset of the source and target language nodes and relations. Much like in example-based or phrasal systems, both minimal and composed versions of these units were then stored as possible translations. A schematic of the this data flow is presented in Figure 2.

At runtime, an input sentence was first parsed into a logical form. Units whose source sides matched the logical form were gathered. A heuristic search found a set of fragments that: (a) covered every input node at least once, and (b) were consistent in their translation selections. If some node or relation was not uncovered, it was copied from source to target. The resulting target language logical form was then fed into a generation component, which produced the final string. A schematic diagram is presented in Figure 3.

This overview sweeps many fine details under the rug. Many morphological and syntactic distinctions were represented as binary features ("bits") in the LF; mapping bits was difficult. The logical form was a graph rather than a tree – in "John ate and drank", *John* is the DSUB (deep subject) of both *eat* and *drink* – which led to complications in transferring structure. Many such complications were often handled through rules; these rules grew more complex over time. Corpus-based approaches efficiently learned many non-compositional and domain specific issues.

2.2 Results and lessons learned

The system was quite successful at the time. MSR used human evaluation heavily, performing both absolute and relative quality evaluations. In the absolute case, human judges gave each translation a score between 1 (terrible translation) and 4 (perfect). For relative evaluations, judges were presented with two translations in randomized order, and were asked whether they preferred system A, system B, or neither. In its training domain, the LF-based system was able to show substantial improvements over rule-based systems that dominated the market at the time.

Much of these gains were due to domain- and context-sensitivity of the system. Consider the Spanish verb "activar". A fair gloss into English is "activate", but the most appropriate translation in context varies ("signal", "flag", etc.). The example-based approach was able to capture those contexts very effectively, leading to automatic domain customization given only translation memories. This was a huge improvement over rule-based systems of the time.

During this same era, however, statistical approaches (Och and Ney, 2004) were showing great promise. Therefore, we ran a comparison between the LF-based system and a statistical system

data driven but not statistical approach to parser development.

(a) Effecitve LF translation. Note how the LF system is able to translate "se lleveban a cabo" even though that particular surface form was not present in the training data.

SRC: La tabla muestra además dónde se llevaban a cabo esas tareas en Windows NT versión 4.0.
REF: The table also shows where these tasks were performed in Windows NT version 4.0.
LF: The table shows where, in addition, those tasks were conducted on Windows NT version 4.0.
STAT: The table also shows where llevaban to Windows NT version 4.0.

(b) Parsing errors may degrade translation quality; the parser interprted '/' as coordination.

SRC: La sintaxis del operador / tiene las siguientes partes:
REF: The / operator syntax has these parts:
LF: The operator syntax it has the parts:
STAT: The / operator syntax has these parts:

(c) Graph-like structures for situations such as coordination are difficult to transfer (see the parenthesized group in particular); selecting the correct form at generation time is difficult in the absence of a target language model.

SRC: Debe ser una consulta de selección (no una consulta de tabla de referencias cruzadas ni una consulta de acción).
REF: Must be a select query (not a crosstab query or action query).
LF: You must not be a select query neither not a query in table in cross-references nor not an action query.
STAT: Must be a select query (not a crosstab query or an action query).

Figure 4: Example source Spanish sentences, English reference translations of those sentences, translations from the LF system, and translations from a statistical translation system without linguistic features.

without linguistic information. Both systems were trained and tuned on the same data, and translated the same unseen test set. The linguistic system had the additional knowledge sources at its disposal: morphological, lexical, syntactic, and semantic information. Regardless, the systems performed nearly equally well on average. Each had distinct strengths and weaknesses, though.

Often the success or failure of the LF-system was tied to the accuracy of its deep analysis. When these representations were accurate, they could lead to effective generalizations and better translations of rare phenomena. Since surface words were lemmatized and syntactic differences normalized, unseen surface forms could still be translated as long as their lemma was known (see Figure 4(a)). Yet mistakes in identifying the correct logical form could lead to major translation errors, as in Figure 4(b).

Likewise the lack of statistics in the components could cause problems. Statistical approaches found great benefits from the target language model. Using a rule-based generation component made it difficult to leverage a target language model. Often, even if a particular translation was presented tens, hundreds, or thousands of times in the data, the LF-based system could not produce it because the rule-based generation component would not propose the common surface form, as in Figure 4(c).

We drew several lessons from this system when developing our next generation of machine translation systems. It was clear to us that syntactic representations can help translation, especially in reordering and lexical selection: appropriate representations allows better generalization. However, over-generalization can lead to translation error, as can parsing errors.

3 The Next Generation MSR MT Systems

Research in machine translation at Microsoft has been strongly influenced by this prior experience with the LF system. First we must notice that there is a huge space of possible translations. Consider human reference translations: unless tied to a specific domain or area, they seldom agree completely on lexical selection and word order. If our system is to produce reasonable output, it should consider a broad range of translation options, preferring outputs most similar to language used by humans. Why do we say "order of magnitude" rather than "magnitude order", or "master of ceremonies" rather than "ceremonies master"? Many choices in language are fundamentally arbitrary, but we need to conform to those arbitrary decisions if we are to produce fluent and understandable output. Second, while there is leverage to be gained from deep features, seldom do we have a component that identifies these features with perfect accuracy. In practice it seems that the error rate increases as the depth of component analysis increases. Finally, we need a representation of "good translations" that is understandable by a computer. When forced to choose between two translations, the system needs to make a choice: an ordering.

Therefore, our data-driven systems crucially rely on several components. First, we must efficiently search a broad range of translations. Second, we must rank according to both our linguistic intuitions and the patterns that emerge from data.

We use a number of different systems based on the availability of linguistic resources. So-called *phrasal* statistic machine translation systems, which model translations using no more than sequences of contiguous words, perform surprisingly well and require nothing but tokenization in both languages. In language pairs for which we have a source language parser, a parse of the input sentence is used to guide reordering and help select relevant non-contiguous units; this is the *treelet* system (Quirk and Menezes, 2006). Regardless of which system we use, however, target language models score the fluency of the output, and have a huge positive impact on translation quality.

We are interested in means of incorporating linguistic intuition deeper into such a system. As in the case of the treelet system, this may define the broad structure of the system. However, there are also more accessible ways of influencing existing systems. For instance, linguists may author features that identify promising or problematic translations. We describe one such attempt in the following system.

3.1 Like and DontLike

Even in our linguistically-informed treelet system (Quirk and Menezes, 2006), which uses syntax in its translation system, many of the individual mappings are clearly bad, at least to a human. When working with linguistic experts, one gut response is to write rules that inspect the translation mappings and discard those translation mappings that appear dangerous. Perhaps they seem to delete a verb, perhaps they use a speculative reordering rule – something makes them look bad to a linguist. However, even if we are successful in removing a poor translation choice, the remaining possibilities may be even worse – or perhaps no translation whatsoever remains.

Instead, we can soften this notion. Imagine that a linguist is able to say that this mapping is not preferred because of some property. Likewise, a skilled linguist might be able to identify mappings that look particularly promising, and prefer those mappings to others; see Figure 5 for an example.

This begs the question: how much should we weight such influence? Our answer is a corpus driven one. Each of these linguistic preferences should be noted, and the weight of these preferences should be tuned with all others to optimize the goodness of translation. Already our statistical system has a number of signals that attempt to gauge translation quality: the translation models attempt to capture fidelity of translation; language models focus on fluency; etc. We use techniques such as MERT (Och, 2003) and PRO (Hopkins and May, 2011) to tune the relative weight of these signals. Why not tune indicators from linguists in the same manner?

When our linguists mark a mapping as +Like or +DontLike, we track that throughout the search. Each final translation incorporates a count of Like mappings and a count of DontLike mappings, just as it accumulates a language model score, translation model scores, word penalties, and so on. These weights are tuned to optimize some approximate evaluation metric. In Figure 6, the weight of Like and DontLike is shown for a number of systems, demonstrating how optimization may be used to tune the effect of hand-written rules. Removing these features degrades the performance of an MT system by at least 0.5 BLEU points, though the degradations are often even more visible to humans.

This mechanism has been used to capture a number of effects in translation commonly missed by statistical methods. It is crucial yet challenging to maintain negation during translation, especially in language pairs where negation is expressed differently: some languages use a free morpheme (Chinese tends to have a separate word), others use a bound morpheme (English may use prefixes), others require two separated morphemes (French has negation agreement); getting any of these wrong can lead to poor translations. Rules that look at potentially distant words can help screen away negation errors. Likewise rules can help ensure that meaning is preserved, by preventing main verbs mapping to punctuation, or screen-

```
// don't allow verb to be lost
if (forany(NodeList(rMapping),[Cat=="Verb" & ^Aux(SynNode(InputNode))])) {
    list {segrec} bad_target=sublist(keeplist,
        [forall(NodeList,[pure_punk(Lemma) | coord_conjunction(foreign_language,Lemma)])]);
    if (bad_target) {
        segrec rec;
        foreach (rec; bad_target) {
            +DontLike(rec);
        }
    }
}
```

Figure 5: An example rule for marking mappings as "DontLike". In this case, the rule searches for source verbs that are not auxiliaries and that are translated into lemmas or punctuation. Such translations are marked as DontLike.

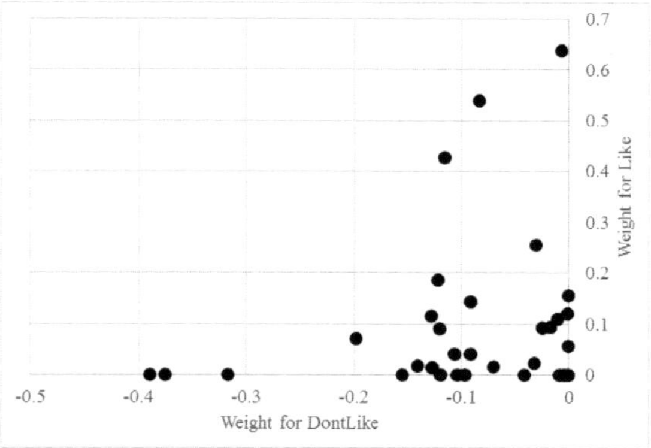

Figure 6: A plot of the weights +Like mapping count and +DontLike mapping count weights across language pairs. Generally Like is assigned a positive weight (sometimes quite positive), and DontLike is assigned a negative weight. In our system, weights are L1 normalized (the sum of the absolute values of the weights is equal to one), so feature weights greater than 0.1 are very influential.

ing out mappings that seem unlikely, especially when those mappings involve unusual tokens.

These two features are a rather coarse means of introducing linguistic feedback. As our parameter estimation techniques scale to larger features more effectively, we are considering using finer-grained feedback from linguists to say not only that they like or don't like a particular mapping, but why. The relative impact of each type of feedback can be weighted: perhaps it is critical to preserve verbs, but not so important to handle definiteness. Given recent successes in scaling parameter estimation to larger and larger values, this area shows great promise.

3.2 Linguistic component accuracy

Another crucial issue is the quality of the linguistic components. We would certainly hope that better quality of linguistic analysis should lead to better quality translations. Indeed, in certain circumstances it appears that this correlation holds.

In the case of the treelet system, we hope to derive benefit from linguistic features via a dependency tree. To investigate the impact of the parse quality, we can degrade a Treebank-trained parser by limiting the amount of training data made available. As this decreases, the parser quality should degrade. If we hold all other information in the MT system fixed (parallel and monolingual training data, training regimen, etc.), then all differences should be due to the changes in parse quality. Table 1 presents the results of an experiment of this form (Quirk and Corston-Oliver, 2006). As the amount of training data increase, we see a substantial increase in parse quality.

Another way to mitigate parser error is to maintain syntactic ambiguity through the translation process. For syntax directed translation systems, this can be achieved by translating forests rather than single trees, ideally including the score of

System	English-German	English-Japanese
Phrasal	31.7	32.9
Right branching	31.4	28.0
250 instances	32.8	34.1
2,500 instances	33.0	34.6
25,000 instances	33.7	35.7
39,082 instances	33.8	36.0

Table 1: Comparison of BLEU scores as linguistic information is varied. A phrasal system provides a baseline free of linguistic information. Next we consider a treelet system with a very weak baseline: a right branching tree is always proposed. This baseline is much worse than a simple phrasal system. The final four rows evaluate the impact of a parser trained on increasing amounts of sentences from the English Penn Treebank. Even with a tiny amount of training data, the system gets some benefit from syntactic information, and the returns appear to increase with more training data.

parse as part of the translation derivation. In unpublished results, we found that this made a substantial improvement in translation quality; the effect was corroborated in other syntax directed translation systems (Mi et al., 2008). Alternatively, allowing a neighborhood of trees similar to some predicted tree can handle ambiguity even when the original parser does not maintain a forest. This also allows translation to handle phenomena that are systematically mis-parsed, as well as cases where the parser specification is not ideal for the translation task. Recent work in this area has show substantial improvements (Zhang et al., 2011).

4 Evaluation

4.1 Fact or Fiction: BLEU is Biased Against Rule-Based or Linguistically-Informed Systems?

It has generally been accepted as common wisdom that BLEU favors statistical MT systems and disfavors those that are linguistically informed or rule-based. Surprisingly, the literature on the topic is rather sparse, with some notable exceptions (Riezler and Maxwell, 2005; Farrús et al., 2012; Carpuat and Simard, 2012). We too have made this assumption, and had a few years ago coined the term *treelet penalty* to indicate the degree by which BLEU favored our phrasal systems over our treelet systems. We had noted on a few occasions that treelet systems had lower BLEU scores than our phrasal systems over the same data (the "penalty"), but when compared against one another in human evaluation, there was little difference, or often, treelet was favored. A notable case was on German-English, where we noted a three-point difference in BLEU between equivalent treelet and phrasal systems (favoring phrasal), and a ship/no-ship decision was dependent on the resulting human eval. The general consensus of the team was that the phrasal system was markedly better, based on the BLEU result, and treelet system should be pulled. However, after a human eval was conducted, we discovered that the treelet system was significantly better than the phrasal. From that point forward, we talked about the *treelet penalty* for German being three points, a "fact" that has lived in the lore of our team ever since.

What was really missing, however, was systematic experimental evidence showing the differences between treelet and phrasal systems. We talked about the treelet penalty as a given, but there was slow rumble of counter evidence suggesting that maybe the assumptions behind the "penalty" were actually unfounded, or minimally, misinformed.

One piece of evidence was from experiments done by Xiaodong He and an intern that showed an interaction in quality differences between treelet and phrasal gated by the length of the sentence. Xiaodong was able to show that phrasal systems tended to do better on longer sentences and treelet on shorter: for Spanish-English, he showed a difference in BLEU of 1.29 on "short" content on a general domain test set, and 1.77 for short content on newswire content (the NIST08 test set). The BLEU difference diminished as the length of the content increased, until there was very little difference (less than 1/2 point) for longer content.[3] An interaction between decoder type and sentence length means that there might also be an interac-

[3]These results were not published, but were provided to the authors in a personal conversation with Xiaodong. In a related paper (He et al., 2008), He and colleagues showed significant improvements in BLEU on a system combination system, but no diffs in human eval. Upon analysis, the researchers were able to show that the biggest benefit to BLEU was in short content, but the same preference was not exhibited on the same content by the human evaluators. In other words, the improvements observed in the short content that BLEU favored had little impact on the overall impressions of the human evaluators.

tion between decoder type and test set, especially if particular test sets contain a lot of long-ish sentences, *e.g.,* WMT and Europarl). To the contrary, most IT text, which is quite common in Microsoft-specific localization content, tends to be shorter.

The other was based on general impressions between treelet and phrasal systems. Because treelet systems are informed by dependency parses built over the source sentences (a parse can help constrain a search space of possible translations, and prune undesirable mappings *e.g.,* constrain to nominal types when the source is a noun), and, as noted earlier, because the parses allow linguists to pre- or post-process content based on observations in the parse, we have tended to see more "fluent" output in treelet than phrasal. However, as the sizes of data have grown steadily over the years, the quality of translations in our phrasal systems have grown proportionally with the increase in data. The question arose: is there also an interaction between the size of our training data and decoder type? In effect, does the quality of phrasal systems catch-up to the quality of treelet systems when trained over very large sets of data?

4.2 Treelet Penalty Experiments

We ran a set of experiments to measure the differences between treelet and phrasal systems over varying sizes of data, in order to measure the size of the treelet penalty and its interaction with training data size. Our assumption was that a such a penalty existed, and that the penalty decreased as training data size increased, perhaps converging on zero for very large systems. Likewise, we wanted to test the interaction between decoder type and sentence length.

We chose two languages to run these experiments on, Spanish and German, which we ran in both directions, that is, English-to-target (EX) and target-to-English (XE). We chose Spanish and German for several reasons, first among them being that we have high-quality parsers for both languages, as we do for English. Further, we have done significant development work on pre- and post-processing for both languages over the past several years. Both of these facts combined meant that the treelet systems stood a real chance of being strong contenders in the experiments against the equivalent phrasal systems. Further, although the languages are typologically close neighbors of English, the word order differences and high distortion rates from English to or from German might favor a parser-based approach.

We had four baseline systems that were built over very large sets of data. For Spanish ⇄ English, the baseline systems were trained on over 22M sentence pairs; for German ⇄ English, the baseline systems were trained on over 36M sentence pairs.[4] We then created five samples of the baseline data for each language pair, consisting of 100K, 500K, 1M, 2M, and 5M sentence pairs (the same samples were used for both EX and XE for the respective pairs). We then trained both treelet and phrasal systems in both directions (EX and XE) over each sample of data. Language models were trained on all systems over the target-side data.

For dev data, we used development data from the 2010 WMT competition (Callison-Burch et al., 2010), and we used MERT (Och, 2003) to tune each system. We tested each system against three different test sets: two were from the WMT competitions of 2009 and 2010, and the other was one locally constructed from 5000 sentences of content translated by users of our production service (http://bing.com/translator), which we subsequently had manually translated into the target languages. The former two test sets are somewhat news focused; the latter is a random sample of miscellaneous translations, and is more generally focused.

The results of the experiments are shown in Tables 2 and 3, with the relevant graphs in Figures 9 - 10. The reader will note that in *all* cases—Spanish and German, EX and XE—the treelet systems scored higher than the related phrasal systems. This result surprised us, since we thought that treelet systems would score *less* than phrasal systems, especially at lower data sizes. That said, in the Spanish systems, there is a clear convergence as data sizes increased: on the WMT09 test set for English-Spanish, for instance, the diff starts at 1.46 BLEU (treelet minus phrasal) for the 100K sentence system, with a steady convergence to near zero (0.12) for the full-data baseline. The other test sets show the same steady convergence, although they do not approach zero quite as closely. (One might ask whether they would converge to zero with more training data.) The

[4] A sizable portion of the data for each were scraped from the Web, but there were other sources used as well, such as Europarl, data from TAUS, MS internal localization data, UN content, WMT news content, etc.

other direction is even more dramatic: on all test sets the diffs converge on negative values, indicating that phrasal systems surpass the quality of the associated treelet systems at the largest data points. This is a nice result since it shows, at least in the case of Spanish, that there is an interaction between decoder type and the amount of data: treelet clearly does better at lower data amounts, but phrasal catches up with, and can even pass, the quality of equivalent treelet given sufficient data. With larger data, phrasal may, in fact, be favored over treelet.

The German systems do not tell quite as nice a story. While it is still true that treelet has higher BLEU scores than phrasal throughout, and that systems trained using both decoders improve in quality as more data is added (and the trajectory is similar), there is no observable convergence as data size increases. For German, then, we can only say that more data helps either decoder, but we cannot say that phrasal benefits from larger data more than treelet. Why the difference between Spanish and German? We suspect there may be an interaction with the parsers, in that two separate teams developed them. Thus, it could be the fact that the strength of the respective parsers affected how "linguistically informed" particular systems are. There could also be an interaction with the number of word types vs. tokens in the German data—given German's rampant compounding—which increases data sparsity, dampening effects until much larger amounts of data are used. We are still in the process of running additional experiments to see if there are observable effects in German with much larger data sizes, or at least, to determine why German does not show the same effects as Spanish.

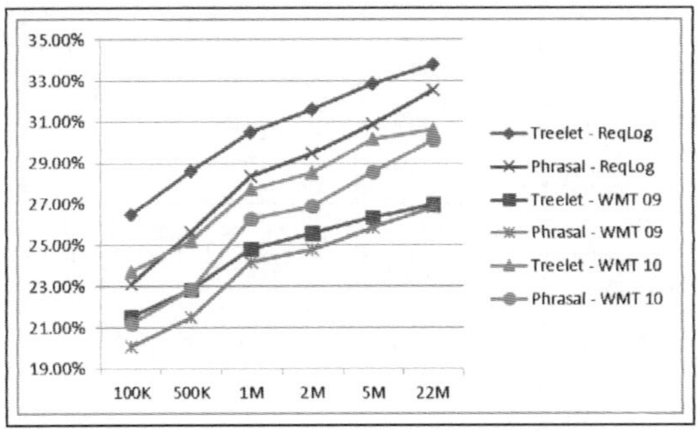

Figure 7: English-Spanish BLEU graph across different data sizes, Treelet vs. Phrasal.

Since human evaluation is the gold standard we

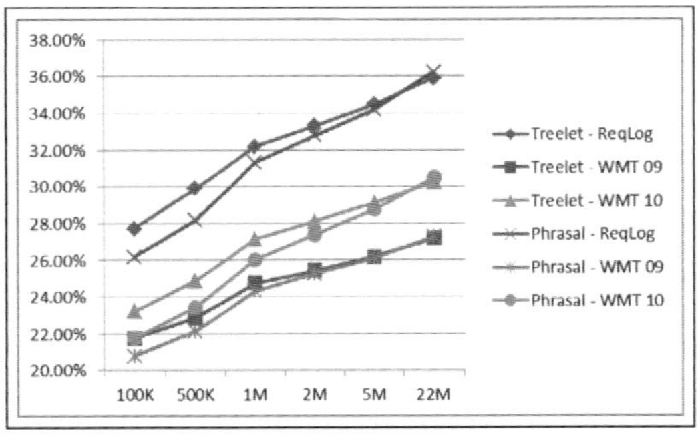

Figure 8: Spanish-English BLEU graph across different data sizes, Treelet vs. Phrasal.

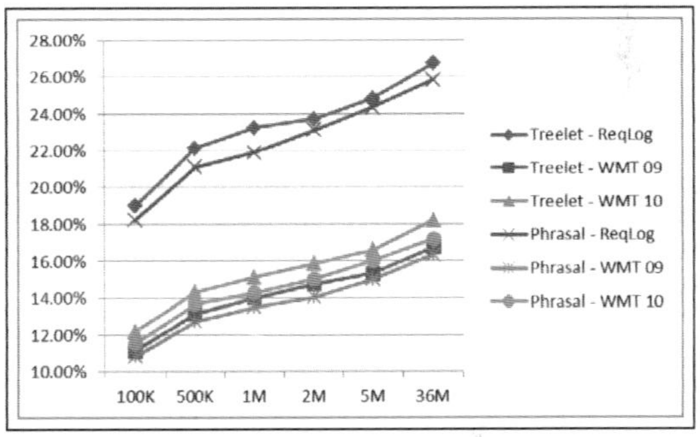

Figure 9: English-German BLEU graph across different data sizes, Treelet vs. Phrasal.

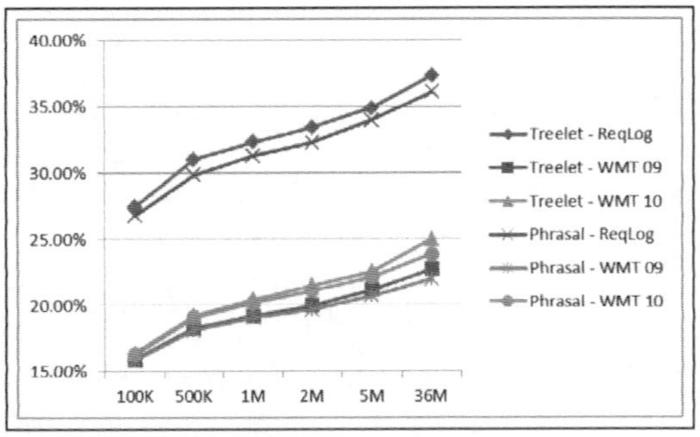

Figure 10: German-English BLEU graph across different data sizes, Treelet vs. Phrasal.

EX		Treelet			Phrasal			Diff - T-P	
	Req Log	WMT 2009	WMT 2010	Req Log	WMT 2009	WMT 2010	Req Log	WMT 2009	WMT 2010
100K	26.49	21.52	23.69	23.10	20.06	21.19	3.39	1.46	2.50
500K	28.61	22.85	25.20	25.64	21.47	22.86	2.97	1.38	2.34
1M	30.52	24.82	27.74	28.36	24.17	26.28	2.16	0.65	1.46
2M	31.61	25.59	28.54	29.48	24.76	26.91	2.13	0.83	1.63
5M	32.86	26.37	30.14	30.89	25.84	28.56	1.97	0.53	1.58
22M	33.80	27.01	30.61	32.55	26.89	30.12	1.25	0.12	0.49
XE									
100K	27.72	21.76	23.21	26.18	20.80	21.78	1.54	0.96	1.43
500K	29.89	22.86	24.89	28.16	22.15	23.44	1.73	0.71	1.45
1M	32.18	24.76	27.14	31.32	24.32	26.02	0.86	0.44	1.12
2M	33.31	25.44	28.09	32.77	25.26	27.38	0.54	0.18	0.71
5M	34.47	26.17	29.10	34.18	26.10	28.74	0.29	0.07	0.36
22M	35.88	27.16	30.20	36.21	27.26	30.48	-0.33	-0.10	-0.28

Table 2: BLEU Score results for the Spanish Treelet Penalty experiments

EX		Treelet			Phrasal			Diff (T-P)	
	Req Log	WMT 2009	WMT 2010	Req Log	WMT 2009	WMT 2010	Req Log	WMT 2009	WMT 2010
100K	18.98	11.13	12.19	18.22	10.81	11.53	0.76	0.32	0.66
500K	22.13	13.18	14.33	21.09	12.74	13.68	1.04	0.44	0.65
1M	23.23	13.98	15.12	21.89	13.51	14.27	1.34	0.47	0.85
2M	23.72	14.77	15.87	23.11	14.04	15.03	0.61	0.73	0.84
5M	24.82	15.31	16.58	24.35	15.00	16.01	0.47	0.31	0.57
36M	26.72	16.72	18.20	25.83	16.33	17.18	0.89	0.39	1.02
XE									
100K	27.42	15.91	16.37	26.75	15.83	16.28	0.67	0.08	0.09
500K	30.98	18.25	19.16	29.80	18.11	19.09	1.18	0.14	0.07
1M	32.30	19.16	20.40	31.26	19.06	20.18	1.04	0.10	0.22
2M	33.40	19.95	21.48	32.25	19.65	21.06	1.15	0.30	0.42
5M	34.86	21.14	22.55	33.91	20.67	22.13	0.95	0.47	0.42
36M	37.31	22.72	24.97	36.08	21.99	23.85	1.23	0.73	1.12

Table 3: BLEU Score results for the German Treelet Penalty experiments

seek to achieve with our quality measures, and since BLEU is only weakly correlated with human eval (Coughlin, 2003), we ran human evals against both the English-Spanish and English-German output. Performing human evaluation gives us two additional perspectives on the data: (1) do humans perceive a qualitative difference between treelet and phrasal, as we see with BLEU, and (2), if the difference is perceptible, what is its magnitude relative to BLEU. If the magnitude of the difference is much larger than that of BLEU, and especially does not show convergence in the Spanish cases, then we still have a strong case for the Treelet Penalty. In fact, if human evaluators perceive a difference Spanish cases on the full data systems, the case where we show convergence, then the resulting differences could be described as the penalty value.

Unfortunately, our human evaluation data on the Treelet Penalty effect was inconclusive. Our evaluations show a strong correlation between BLEU and human evaluation, something that is attested to in the literature (*e.g.,* , the first paper on BLEU (Papineni et al., 2002), and a deeper exploration in (Coughlin, 2003)). However, the effect we were looking for – that is, a difference between human evaluations across decoders – was not evident. In fact, the human evaluations followed the differences we saw in BLEU between the two decoders very closely. Figure 11 shows data points for each data size for each decoder, plotting BLEU against human evaluation. When we fit a regression line against the data points for each decoder, we see complete overlap.[5]

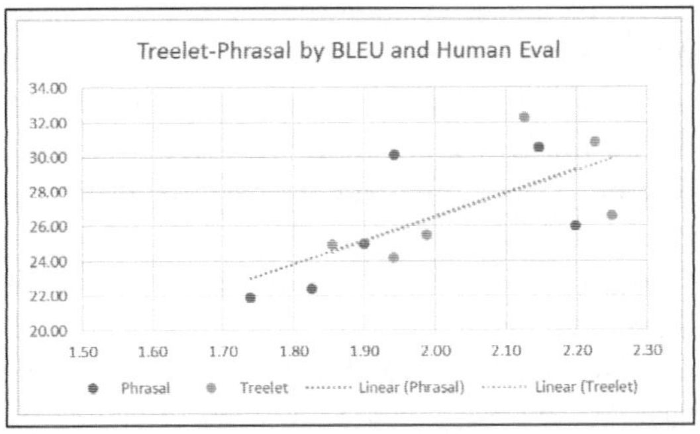

Figure 11: Scatterplot showing Treelet vs Phrasal systems across different data sizes, plotting BLEU (Y) against Human Eval scores (X)

[5]Clearly, the sample is *very* small, so the regression line should be taken with a grain of salt. We would need a lot more data to be able to draw any strong conclusions.

In summary, we show a strong effect of treelet systems performing better than phrasal systems trained on the same data. That difference, however, generally diminishes as data sizes increase, and in the case of Spanish (both directions), there is a convergence in very large data sizes. These results are not completely surprising, but still are a nice systematic confirmation that linguistically informed systems really do better in lower-data environments. Without enough data, statistical systems cannot learn the generalizations that might otherwise be provided by a parse, or codified in rules. What we failed to show, at least with Spanish and German, is a confirmation of the existence of the Treelet Penalty. Given the small number of samples, a larger study which includes many more language pairs and data sizes, may once and for all confirm the Penalty. Thus far, human evaluations do not show qualitative differences between the two decoders—at least, not divergent from BLEU.

4.3 Interaction Between Decoder Type and Sentence Length

When comparing the differences between decoders, another area to pay special attention to is systematic differences in behavior as input content is varied. For example, we may expect a phrasal decoder to do better on noisier, less grammatical data than a parser-informed decoder, since in the latter case the parser may fail to parse; the failure could ripple through subsequent processes, and thus lessen the quality of the output. Likewise, a parser-informed decoder may do better on content that is short and easy to parse. If we were to do a coarse-grained separation of data into length buckets, making the very gross assumption that short equals easy-to-parse and long not, then we may see some qualitative differences between the decoders across these buckets.

To see length-based effects across decoder types, we designed a set of experiments on German and Spanish in both directions, where we separated the WMT 2010 test data into length-based word-count buckets: 0-10, 10-20, 20-30, 30-40, and 40+ words. We then calculated the BLEU scores on each of these buckets, the results for which are shown in Figures 12.

Treelet does better than phrasal in almost all conditions (except one). That is not surprising, given the results we observed in Section 4.2. What is interesting is to see how much stronger treelet

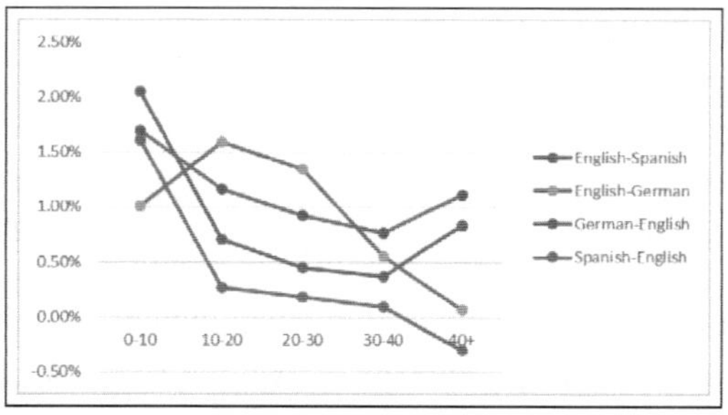

Figure 12: Treelet-Phrasal BLEU differences by bucket across language pair

performs on short content than phrasal: treelet does the best on the shortest content, with quality dropping off anywhere between 10-30 words.

One conclusion that can be drawn from these data is that treelet performs best on short content precisely because the parser can easily parse the content, and the parse is effective in informing subsequent processes. The most sustained benefit is observable in English-German, with a bump up at 10-20, and a slow tapering off thereafter. Processing the structural divergence between the two languages, especially when it comes to word order, may benefit more from a parse. In other words, the parser can help inform alignment where there are long-distance distortion effects; a phrasal system's view is too local to catch them. However, at longer sentence sizes, the absence of good parses lessen the treelet advantage. In fact, in English-German (and in Spanish-English) at 40+, there is no observable benefit of treelet over phrasal.[6]

5 The Data Gap

All Statistical Machine Translation work relies on data, and the manipulation of the data as a preprocess can often have significant effects downstream. "Data munging", as we like to call it, is every team's "secret sauce", something that can often lead to multi-point differences in BLEU. For most teams, the heuristics that are applied are fairly ad hoc, and highly dependent on the kind of data being consumed. Since data sources are often quite noisy, *e.g.,* the Web, noise reduction is a key component of many of the heuristics. Here is a list of common heuristics applied to data. Some of these are drawn from our own pre-processing, some are mentioned explicitly in other literature, in particular, (Denkowski et al., 2012).

- Remove lines containing escape characters, invalid Unicode, and other non-linguistic noise.
- Remove content that where the ratio of certain content passes some threshold, *e.g.,* alphabetic/numeric ratio, script ratio (percentage of characters in wrong form passes some threshold, triggering removal).
- Normalize space, hyphens, quotes, etc. to standard forms.
- Normalize Unicode characters to canonical forms, *e.g.,* Form C, Form KC.
- In parallel data, measure the degree of ratio of length imbalance (*e.g.,* character or word count) between source and target, as a test for misalignments. Remove sentence pairs that pass some threshold.
- Remove content where character count for any token, or token count across a sentence, exceeds some threshold (the assumption being that really long content is of little benefit due to complications it causes in downstream processing).

The point of *data cleaning* heuristics is to increase the value of training data. Each data point that is noisy increases the chance of learning something that could be distracting or harmful. Likewise, each data point that is cleaned reduces the level of data sparsity (*e.g.,* through normalizations or substitutions) and improves the chances that the models will be more robust. Although it has been shown that increasing the amount of training data for SMT improves results (Brants et al., 2007), not all data is beneficial, and clean data is best of all.

Crucially, most data munging is done through heuristics, or rules, although thresholds or constraints can be tuned by data. A more sophisticated example of data cleaning is described in (Denkowski et al., 2012) where the authors used machine learning methods for measuring quality estimation to select the "best" portions of a corpus. So, rather than training their SMT on an entire corpus, they trained an estimator that selected

[6]The bump up at 40+ on English-Spanish and German-English is inexplicable, but may be attributable to the difficulty that either decoder has in processing such long content. There is also likely an interaction with statistical noise cause by such small sample sizes.

the best portions, and used only those. In their entry in the 2012 WMT competition, they used only 60% of the English-French Gigaword corpus[7] and came in first in the shared translation task for the pair.

Another important aspect of data as it relates to SMT is task-dependence: what domain or genre of data will an SMT engine be applied to? For instance, will an SMT engine be used to translate IT content, news content, subtitles, or Europarl proceedings? If the engine itself is trained on data that is dissimilar to the desired goal, then results may be less than satisfying. This is a common problem in the field, and a cottage industry has been built around customization and domain-adaptation, *e.g.,* (Moore and Lewis, 2010; Axelrod et al., 2011; Wang et al., 2012). In general, the solution is to adapt an SMT engine to the desired domain using a set of seed data in that domain.

A more difficult problem is when there is very little parallel data in the desired domain, which is a problem we will look at in the next section.

5.1 Preprocessing Data to Make it Match

A little over a year ago, Facebook activated a translation feature in their service, which directly called Bing Translator. This feature has allowed users to translate pages or posts not in their native language with a *See Translation* option. An example is shown in Figure 13.

The real problem with translating "FB-speak", or content from virtually any kind of social media, is the paucity of parallel data in the domain. This flies in the face of the usual way problems are tackled in SMT, that is, locate (lots of) relevant parallel data, and then train up a decoder. Outside of a few slang dictionaries, there is almost no FB-like parallel content available.

Given the relatively formal nature of the text that most of our engines are trained on, the mismatch between FB content and our translation engines often led to very poor translations. Yet, given the absence of in-domain parallel data, it was not possible for us to train-up FB-specific SMT engines. We realized that our only option was to somehow manipulate the input to make it look more like the content we trained our engines on. Effectively, if we treated "FB-speak" as a dialect of the source language, we could use distributional queues of dialect-specific content to find the counterparts in the majority dialect.

Regex	Output
frnd[sz]	friends
plz+	please
yess*	yes
be?c[uo][sz]	because
nuff	enough
wo?u?lda	would have
srr+y	sorry

Table 5: Some example regexes to "fix" FaceBook content

Table 4 gives some examples of FB content on the left, and the more formal representation of the same on the right. The reader will note some systematic characteristics of the FB content as compared to the formal content (see also (Hassan and Menezes, 2013)). Given the absence of parallel training data, we could "correct" the FB content to make it look more like English, and then translate the "corrected" English through our engines.

Our first inclination was to examine the logs of the most frequent words being translated by FB users and use string substitutions or regexes (regular expressions) to effect repairs. We arrived very quickly at a large set of simple repairs like those shown in Table 5. We were able to achieve greater than 97% precision using a large table of substitutions for the most common translations (against a held-out set of FB content). However, there were two problems with the approach: (1) recall was relatively low, at 52.03%, and (2) the solution was not easily scalable to additional languages and scenarios.

To address these two deficiencies, we sought a more data-driven approach. But we had to be creative since our standard "hammer" of parallel data did not exist. Our intuition was that there were distributional regularities in the FB content that could help discover a mapping for a given target word, *e.g.,* the distribution of *plzzz* in the FB content would allow us to discover that it distributes similarly to *please* in our non-FB content. Hany Hassan developed a TextCorrector tool that is, as he put it (Hassan and Menezes, 2013), "based on constructing a lattice from possible normalization candidates and finding the best normalization sequence according to an n-gram language model using a Viterbi decoder", where he developed an

[7] The English-French Gigaword corpus is described in (Callison-Burch et al., 2009)

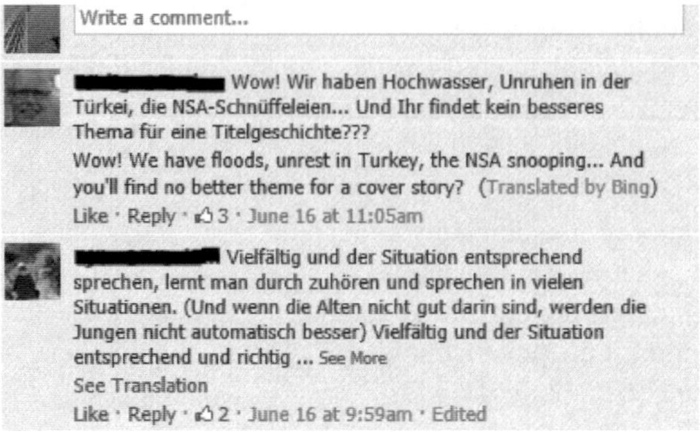

Figure 13: Two Facebook posts: the first translated, the second showing the *See Translation* option

FB Speak	English Translation	Comment
goooood morniiing	good morning	Extended characters for emphasis or dramatic effect
wuz up bro	What's up brother	"Phonetic" spelling to reflect local dialect or usage
cm to c my luv	Come to see my love	Remove vowels in common words, sound-alike sequences
4get, 2morrow	forget, tomorrow	Sound-alike number substitution
r u 4 real?	Are you for real?	Sound-alike letter and number substitutions
LMS	Like my status	Single 'word' abbreviations for
IDK	I don't know	multi-word expressions
ROFL	Rolling on the floor laughing	

Table 4: FB Speak with English references

"unsupervised approach to learn the normalization candidates from unlabeled text data." He then used a Random Walk strategy to walk a contextual similarity graph. The two principal benefits of this approach is that it did not require parallel training data—two large monolingual corpora are required, one for the "noisy" data (*i.e.,* FB content) and one for the clean data (*i.e.,* our large supply of language model training data)—nor did it require labeled data (*i.e.,* , the algorithm is unsupervised). After several iterations over very large corpora (tens of millions of sentences) he arrived at a solution that had comparable precision to the regex method but had much higher recall. The best iteration achieved 96.51% precision (the regex approach achieve 97.07% precision) and 72.38% recall (regex: 52.03%).[8] Crucially, as the size of the data increases, the TextCorrector continues to show improvement.

The end result was a much better User Experience for FB users. Rather than badly mangled translations, or worse, no translations at all, users get translations generated by our standard, very large statistical engines (for English source, notably, our *treelet* engines). An example English source string is shown in Table 6, with translations shown for both the corrected and uncorrected source.

[8]For a complete description of TextCorrector, please see (Hassan and Menezes, 2013).

6 Conclusions and Future Directions

A crucial lesson from the work on the FB corrections described in Section 5.1 is its analog to Machine Learning as a whole: rule-based approaches often achieve very high precision, but often at the sacrifice of recall. The same is true in Machine Translation: rule-based MT is often more accurate when it was accurate, resulting in more precise and grammatical translations. However, it tends to be somewhat brittle and does not do as well on cases not explicitly coded for. SMT, on the other hand, tends to be more malleable and adaptable, but often less precise. Tapping rule-based approaches in a statistical framework can really give us the best of both worlds, giving us higher precision *and* higher recall.

Finding an appropriate mix is difficult, though. As in the case of parsing, we can see how errors can substantially degrade translation quality, especially if we only consider the single best analysis. By making our analysis components as robust as possible, quantifying our degree of certainty with scoring mechanisms, and preserving ambiguity of the analysis, we can achieve a better return on in-

Language	Unrepaired	Repaired
Original English	i'l do cuz ma parnts r ma lyf	I'll do because my parents are my life
To Italian	i ' l fare cuz ma parnts r ma lyf	lo far perch i miei genitori sono la mia vita
To German	i ' l tun Cuz Ma Parnts R Ma lyf	Ich werde tun, weil meine Eltern mein Leben sind
To Spanish	traer hacer cuz ma parnts r ma lyf	voy a hacer porque mis padres son mi vida

Table 6: One English FB sentence with and without normalizations, translated to various languages

vestment. Making this linguistic information be included *softly* as features is a powerful way of surfacing linguistic generalizations to the system while not forcing its hand.

Some of the greatest successes in mixing linguistic and statistical methods have been in syntax. There is much ground to cover still. Morphology is integrated weakly into current SMT systems, mostly as broad features (Jeong et al., 2010) though sometimes with more sophistication (Chahuneau et al., 2013). Better integration of morphological features could have great effect, especially in agglutinative languages such as Finnish and Turkish.

Deeper models of semantics present a rich challenge to the field. As we proceed into deeper models, picking the correct representation is a significant issue. Humans can generally agree on words, mostly on morphology, and somewhat on syntax. But semantics touches on issues of meaning representation: how should we best represent semantic information? Should we attempt to faithfully represent all the information in the source language, or gather only a simple model that suffices to disambiguate information? Others are focusing on lexical semantics using continuous space representations (Mikolov et al., 2013), a softer means of representing meaning.

Regardless of the details, one point is very clear: future work in MT will require dealing with data. Systems, whether statistical or rule-based, will need to work with and learn from the increasing volumes of information available to computers. Effective hybrid systems will be no exception – tempering the keen insights of experts with the noisy wisdom of big data from the crowd holds great promise.

References

Amittai Axelrod, Xiaodong He, and Jianfeng Gao. 2011. Domain adaptation via pseudo in-domain data selection. In *Proceedings of EMNLP*, pages 355–362.

Thorsten Brants, Ashok C. Popat, Peng Xu, Franz J. Och, and Jeffrey Dean. 2007. Large language models in machine translation. In *Proceedings of the 2007 Joint Conference on Empirical Methods in Natural Language Processing and Computational Natural Language Learning (EMNLP-CoNLL)*, pages 858–867, Prague, Czech Republic, June. Association for Computational Linguistics.

Chris Callison-Burch, Philipp Koehn, Christof Monz, and Josh Schroeder. 2009. Findings of the 2009 Workshop on Statistical Machine Translation. In *Proceedings of the Fourth Workshop on Statistical Machine Translation*, pages 1–28, Athens, Greece, March. Association for Computational Linguistics.

Chris Callison-Burch, Philipp Koehn, Christof Monz, Kay Peterson, Mark Przybocki, and Omar Zaidan. 2010. Findings of the 2010 joint workshop on statistical machine translation and metrics for machine translation. In *Proceedings of the Joint Fifth Workshop on Statistical Machine Translation and MetricsMATR*, pages 17–53, Uppsala, Sweden, July. Association for Computational Linguistics.

Marine Carpuat and Michel Simard. 2012. The trouble with smt consistency. In *Proceedings of the Seventh Workshop on Statistical Machine Translation*, pages 442–449, Montréal, Canada, June. Association for Computational Linguistics.

Victor Chahuneau, Noah A. Smith, and Chris Dyer. 2013. Knowledge-rich morphological priors for bayesian language models. In *Proceedings of the 2013 Conference of the North American Chapter of the Association for Computational Linguistics: Human Language Technologies*, pages 1206–1215, Atlanta, Georgia, June. Association for Computational Linguistics.

Deborah A. Coughlin. 2003. Correlating automated and human assessments of machine translation quality. In *Proceedings of MT Summit IX*, New Orleans, Louisiana, USA, September. The Association for Machine Translation in the Americas (AMTA).

Michael Denkowski, Greg Hanneman, and Alon Lavie. 2012. The CMU-Avenue French-English Translation System. In *Proceedings of the NAACL 2012 Workshop on Statistical Machine Translation*.

Mireia Farrús, Marta R. Costa-jussá, and Maja Popovic. 2012. Study and correlation analysis of linguistic, perceptual and automatic machine translation evaluations. *Journal of the American Society for Information Science and Technology*, 63(1):174–184, January.

Hany Hassan and Arul Menezes. 2013. Social text normalization using contextual graph random walks. In *Proceedings of the 51st Annual Meeting of the Association for Computational Linguistics*, Sofia, Bulgaria, August. Association for Computational Linguistics.

Xiaodong He, Mei Yang, Jianfeng Gao, Patrick Nguyen, and Robert Moore. 2008. Indirect-hmm-based hypothesis alignment for combining outputs from machine translation systems. In *Proceedings of EMNLP*.

Mark Hopkins and Jonathan May. 2011. Tuning as ranking. In *Proceedings of the 2011 Conference on Empirical Methods in Natural Language Processing*, pages 1352–1362, Edinburgh, Scotland, UK., July. Association for Computational Linguistics.

Minwoo Jeong, Kristina Toutanova, Hisami Suzuki, and Chris Quirk. 2010. A discriminative lexicon model for complex morphology. In *The Ninth Conference of the Association for Machine Translation in the Americas (AMTA-2010)*.

Kevin Knight. 2013. Tutorial on decipherment. In *ACL 2013*, Sofia, Bulgaria, August.

Arul Menezes and Stephen D. Richardson. 2001. A best-first alignment algorithm for automatic extraction of transfer mappings from bilingual corpora. In *Association for Computational Linguistics*.

Haitao Mi, Liang Huang, and Qun Liu. 2008. Forest-based translation. In *Proceedings of ACL-08: HLT*, pages 192–199, Columbus, Ohio, June. Association for Computational Linguistics.

Tomas Mikolov, Wen-tau Yih, and Geoffrey Zweig. 2013. Linguistic regularities in continuous space word representations. In *Proceedings of the 2013 Conference of the North American Chapter of the Association for Computational Linguistics: Human Language Technologies*, pages 746–751, Atlanta, Georgia, June. Association for Computational Linguistics.

Robert C. Moore and William D. Lewis. 2010. Intelligent Selection of Language Model Training Data. In *Proceedings of the ACL 2010 Conference Short Papers*, Uppsala, Sweden, July.

Franz Josef Och and Hermann Ney. 2004. The Alignment Template Approach to Statistical Machine Translation. *Computational Linguisitics*, 30(4):417–449, September.

Franz Josef Och. 2003. Minimum error rate training in statistical machine translation. In *Proceedings of the 41st ACL*, Sapporo, Japan.

Kishore Papineni, Salim Roukos, Todd Ward, and Wei-Jing Zhu. 2002. BLEU: a method for automatic evaluation of machine translation. In *Proceedings of the 40th ACL*, Philadelphia, PA.

Chris Quirk and Simon Corston-Oliver. 2006. The impact of parse quality on syntactically-informed statistical machine translation. In *Proceedings of the 2006 Conference on Empirical Methods in Natural Language Processing*, pages 62–69, Sydney, Australia, July. Association for Computational Linguistics.

Chris Quirk and Arul Menezes. 2006. Dependency Treelet Translation: The convergence of statistical and example-based Machine Translation? *Machine Translation*, 20:43–65.

Stefan Riezler and John T. Maxwell. 2005. On some pitfalls in automatic evaluation and significance testing for MT. In *Proceedings of the ACL Workshop on Intrinsic and Extrinsic Evaluation Measures for Machine Translation and/or Summarization*, pages 57–64, Ann Arbor, Michigan, June. Association for Computational Linguistics.

Wei Wang, Klaus Macherey, Wolfgang Macherey, Franz Och, and Peng Xu. 2012. Improved domain adaptation for statistical machine translation. In *Proceedings of AMTA*.

Warren Weaver. 1955. Translation. In William N. Locke and A. Donald Booth, editors, *Machine Translation of Languages*, pages 15–23. MIT Press, Massachussets.

Hao Zhang, Licheng Fang, Peng Xu, and Xiaoyun Wu. 2011. Binarized forest to string translation. In *Proceedings of the 49th Annual Meeting of the Association for Computational Linguistics: Human Language Technologies*, pages 835–845, Portland, Oregon, USA, June. Association for Computational Linguistics.

Unsupervised Transduction Grammar Induction via Minimum Description Length

Markus Saers and **Karteek Addanki** and **Dekai Wu**
Human Language Technology Center
Dept. of Computer Science and Engineering
Hong Kong University of Science and Technology
{masaers|vskaddanki|dekai}@cs.ust.hk

Abstract

We present a minimalist, unsupervised learning model that induces relatively clean phrasal inversion transduction grammars by employing the minimum description length principle to drive search over a space defined by two opposing extreme types of ITGs. In comparison to most current SMT approaches, the model learns a very parsimonious phrase translation lexicons that provide an obvious basis for generalization to abstract translation schemas. To do this, the model maintains internal consistency by avoiding use of mismatched or unrelated models, such as word alignments or probabilities from IBM models. The model introduces a novel strategy for avoiding the pitfalls of premature pruning in chunking approaches, by incrementally splitting an ITG while using a second ITG to guide this search.

1 Introduction

We introduce an unsupervised approach to inducing parsimonious, relatively clean phrasal inversion transduction grammars or ITGs (Wu, 1997) that employs a theoretically well-founded minimum description length (MDL) objective to explicitly drive two opposing, extreme ITGs towards one minimal ITG. This represents a new attack on the problem suffered by most current SMT approaches of learning phrase translations that require enormous amounts of run-time memory, contain a high degree of redundancy, and fails to provide an obvious basis for generalization to abstract translation schemas. In particular, phrasal SMT models such as Koehn *et al.* (2003) and Chiang (2005) often search for candidate translation segments and transduction rules by committing to a word alignment based on very different assumptions (Brown *et al.*, 1993; Vogel *et al.*, 1996), and heuristically derive lexical segment translations (Och and Ney, 2003). In fact, it is possible to improve the performance by tossing away most of the learned segmental translations (Johnson *et al.*, 2007). In addition to preventing such wastefulness, our work aims to also provide an obvious basis for generalization to abstract translation schemas by driving the search for phrasal rules by simultaneously using two opposing types of ITG constraints that have both individually been empirically proven to match phrase reordering patterns across translations well.

We adopt a more "pure" methodology for evaluating transduction grammar induction than typical system building papers. Instead of embedding our learned ITG in the midst of many other heuristic components for the sake of a short term boost in BLEU, we focus on scientifically understanding the behavior of pure MDL-based search for phrasal translations, divorced from the effect of other variables, even though BLEU is naturally much lower this way. The common practice of plugging some aspect of a learned ITG into either (a) a long pipeline of training heuristics and/or (b) an existing decoder that has been patched up to compensate for earlier modeling mistakes, as we and others have done before—see for example Cherry and Lin (2007); Zhang *et al.* (2008); Blunsom *et al.* (2008, 2009); Haghighi *et al.* (2009); Saers and Wu (2009, 2011); Blunsom and Cohn (2010); Burkett *et al.* (2010); Riesa and Marcu (2010); Saers *et al.* (2010); Neubig *et al.* (2011, 2012)—obscures the specific traits of the induced grammar. Instead, we directly use our learned ITG in translation mode (any transduction grammar also represents a decoder when parsing with the input sentence as a hard constraint) which allows us to see exactly which aspects of correct translation the transduction rules have captured.

When the structure of an ITG is induced without supervision, it has so far been assumed that smaller rules get clumped together into larger rules. This is a natural way to search, since maximum likelihood (ML) tends to improve with longer rules, which is typically balanced with Bayesian priors (Zhang *et al.*, 2008). Bayesian priors are also used in Gibbs sampling (Blunsom *et al.*, 2008, 2009; Blunsom and Cohn, 2010), as well as other non-parametric learning methods (Neubig *et al.*, 2011, 2012). All of the above evaluate their models by feeding them into mismatched decoders, making it hard to evaluate how accurate the learned models themselves were. In this work we take a radically different approach, and start with the longest rules possible and attempt to segment them into shorter rules iteratively. This makes ML useless, since our initial model maximizes it. Instead, we balance the ML objective with a minimum description length (MDL) objective, which let us escape the initial ML optimum by rewarding *model parsimony*.

Transduction grammars can also be induced with supervision from treebanks, which cuts down the search space by enforcing external constraints (Galley *et al.*, 2006). This complicates the learning process by adding external constraints that are bound to match the translation model poorly. It does, however, constitute a way to borrow nonterminal categories that help the translation model.

MDL has been used before in monolingual grammar induction (Grünwald, 1996; Stolcke and Omohundro, 1994), as well as to interpret visual scenes (Si *et al.*, 2011). Our work is markedly different in that we (a) induce an ITG rather than a monolingual grammar, and (b) focus on learning the terminal segments rather than the nonterminal categories. Iterative segmentation has also been used before, but only to derive a word alignment as part of a larger pipeline (Vilar and Vidal, 2005).

The paper is structured as follows: we start by describing the MDL principle (Section 2). We then describe the initial ITGs (Section 3), followed by the algorithm that induces an MDL-optimal ITG from them (Section 4). After that we describe the experiments (Section 5), and the results (Section 6). Finally, we offer some conclusions (Section 7).

2 Minimum description length

The minimum description length principle is about finding the optimal balance between the size of a model and the size of some data given the model (Solomonoff, 1959; Rissanen, 1983). Consider the information theoretical problem of encoding some data with a model, and then sending both the encoded data *and* the information needed to decode the data (the model) over a channel; the minimum description length is the minimum number of bits sent over the channel. The encoded data can be interpreted as carrying the information necessary to disambiguate the uncertainties that the model has about the data. The model can *grow in size* and become *more certain* about the data, and it can *shrink in size* and become *more uncertain* about the data. Formally, description length (DL) is:

$$\mathrm{DL}(\Phi, D) = \mathrm{DL}(D|\Phi) + \mathrm{DL}(\Phi)$$

where Φ is the model and D is the data.

In practice, we rarely have complete data to train on, so we need our models to generalize to unseen data. A model that is very certain about the training data runs the risk of not being able to generalize to new data: it is over-fitting. It is bad enough when estimating the parameters of a transduction grammar, and catastrophic when inducing the structure.

The information-theoretic view of the problem gives a hint at the operationalization of description length of a corpus given a grammar. Shannon (1948) stipulates that we can get a lower bound on the number of bits required to encode a specific outcome of a random variable. We thus define description length of the corpus given the grammar to be: $\mathrm{DL}(D|\Phi) = -\mathrm{lg}P(D|\Phi)$

Information theory is also useful for the description length of the grammar: if we can find a way to serialize the grammar into a sequence of tokens, we can figure out how that sequence can be optimally encoded. To serialize an ITG, we first need to determine the alphabet that the message will be written in. We need one symbol for every nonterminal, L_0- and L_1-terminal. We will also make the assumption that all these symbols are used in at least one rule, so that it is sufficient to serialize the rules in order to express the entire ITG. We serialize a rule with a type marker, followed by the left-hand side nonterminal, followed by all the right-hand side symbols. The type marker is either $[]$ denoting the start of a straight rule, or $\langle\rangle$ denoting the start of an inverted rule. Unary rules are considered to be straight. We serialize the ITG by concatenating the serialized form of all the rules, assuming that each symbol can be serialized into $-\mathrm{lg}c$ bits where c is the symbol's relative frequency in the serialized form of the ITG.

3 Initial ITGs

To tackle the exponential problem of searching for an ITG that minimizes description length, it is useful to contrast two extreme forms of ITGs. Description length has two components, model length and data length. We call an ITG that minimizes the data at the expense of the model a **long ITG**; we call an ITG that minimizes the model at the expense of the data a **short ITG**.[1] The long ITG simply has all the sentence pairs as biterminals:

$$\begin{aligned} S &\rightarrow A \\ A &\rightarrow e_{0..T_0}/f_{0..V_0} \\ A &\rightarrow e_{0..T_1}/f_{0..V_1} \\ &\cdots \\ A &\rightarrow e_{0..T_N}/f_{0..V_N} \end{aligned}$$

where S is the start symbol, A is the nonterminal, N is the number of sentence pairs, T_i is the length of the ith output sentence (making $e_{0..T_i}$ the ith output sentence), and V_i is the length of the ith input sentence (making $f_{0..V_i}$ the ith input sentence). The short ITG is a token-based bracketing ITG:

$$S \rightarrow A, \quad A \rightarrow [AA], \quad A \rightarrow \langle AA \rangle,$$
$$A \rightarrow e/f, \quad A \rightarrow e/\epsilon, \quad A \rightarrow \epsilon/f$$

where, S is the start symbol, A is the nonterminal symbol, e is an L_0-token, f is an L_1-token, and ϵ is the empty sequence of tokens.

4 Shortening the long ITG

To shorten the long ITG, we will identify good split candidates in the terminal rules by parsing them with the short ITG, and commit to split candidates that give a net gain. A split candidate is an existing long terminal rule, information about where to split its right-hand side, and whether to invert the resulting two rules or not. Consider the terminal rule $A \rightarrow e_{s..t}/f_{u..v}$; it can be split at any point S in L_0 and any point U in L_1, giving the three rules $A \rightarrow [AA]$, $A \rightarrow e_{s..S}/f_{u..U}$ and $A \rightarrow e_{S..t}/f_{U..v}$ when it is split in straight order, and the three rules $A \rightarrow \langle AA \rangle$, $A \rightarrow e_{s..S}/f_{U..v}$ and $A \rightarrow e_{S..t}/f_{u..U}$ when it is split in inverted order. We will refer to the original long rule as r_0, and the resulting three rules as r_1, r_2 and r_3.

To identify the split candidates and to figure out how the probability mass of r_0 is to be distributed

[1] Long and short ITGs correspond well to *ad-hoc* and promiscuous grammars in Grünwald (1996).

Algorithm 1 Rule shortening.

```
G_l                                          ▷ The long ITG
G_s                                          ▷ The short ITG
repeat
  cands ← collect_candidates(G_l, G_s)
  δ ← 0
  removed ← {}
  repeat
    score(cands)
    sort_by_delta(cands)
    for all c ∈ cands do
      r ← original_rule(c)
      if r ∉ removed and δ_c ≤ 0 then
        G_l ← update_grammar(G_l, c)
        removed ← {r} ∪ removed
        δ ← δ + δ_c
      end if
    end for
  until δ ≥ 0
until δ ≥ 0
return G_l
```

to the new rules, we use the short ITG to biparse the right-hand side of r_0. The distribution is derived from the inside probability of the bispans that the new rules are covering in the chart, and we refer to them as λ_1, λ_2 and λ_3, where the index indicates which new rule they apply to. This has the effect of preferring to split a rule into parts that are roughly equally probable, as the size of the data is minimized when the weights are equal.

To choose which split candidates to commit to, we need a way to estimate their impact on the total MDL score of the model. This breaks down into two parts: the difference in description length of the grammar: $\text{DL}(\Phi') - \text{DL}(\Phi)$ (where Φ' is Φ after committing to the split candidate), and the difference in description length of the corpus given the grammar: $\text{DL}(D|\Phi') - \text{DL}(D|\Phi)$. The two are added up to get the total change in description length.The difference in grammar length is calculated as described in Section 2. The difference in description length of the corpus given the grammar can be calculated by biparsing the corpus, since $\text{DL}(D|\Phi') = -\lg P(D|p')$ and $\text{DL}(D|\Phi) = -\lg P(D|p)$ where p' and p are the rule probability functions of Φ' and Φ respectively. Biparsing is, however, a very costly process that we do not want to carry out for every candidate. Instead, we assume that we have the original corpus probability (through biparsing when generating the can-

Table 1: The results of decoding. NIST and BLEU are the translation scores at each iteration, followed by the number of rules in the grammar, followed by the average (as measured by mean and mode) number of English tokens in the rules.

Iteration	NIST	BLEU	Rules	Mean	Mode
1	2.7015	11.97	43,704	7.20	6
2	4.0116	14.04	42,823	6.30	6
3	4.1654	16.58	41,867	5.68	2
4	**4.3723**	17.43	40,953	5.23	1
5	4.2032	**18.78**	40,217	4.97	1
6	4.1329	17.28	39,799	4.84	1
7	4.0710	17.31	39,587	4.79	1
8	4.0437	17.10	39,470	4.75	1

didates), and estimate the new corpus probability from it (in closed form). The new rule probability function p' is identical to p, except that:

$$\begin{aligned} p'(r_0) &= 0 \\ p'(r_1) &= p(r_1) + \lambda_1 p(r_0) \\ p'(r_2) &= p(r_2) + \lambda_2 p(r_0) \\ p'(r_3) &= p(r_3) + \lambda_3 p(r_0) \end{aligned}$$

We assume the probability of the corpus given this new rule probability function to be:

$$P(D|p') = P(D|p) \frac{p'(r_1)\, p'(r_2)\, p'(r_3)}{p(r_0)}$$

This gives the following description length difference:

$$\text{DL}(D|\Phi') - \text{DL}(D|\Phi) = -\lg \frac{p'(r_1) p'(r_2) p'(r_3)}{p(r_0)}$$

We will commit to all split candidates that are estimated to lower the DL, restricting it so that any original rule is split only in the best way (Algorithm 1).

5 Experimental setup

To test whether minimum description length is a good driver for unsupervised inversion transduction induction, we implemented and executed the method described above. We start by initializing one long and one short ITG. The parameters of the long ITG cannot be adjusted to fit the data better, but the parameters of the short ITG can be tuned to the right-hand sides of the long ITG. We do so with an implementation of the cubic time algorithm described in Saers *et al.* (2009), with a beam width of 100. We then run the introduced algorithm.

As training data, we use the IWSLT07 Chinese–English data set (Fordyce, 2007), which contains 46,867 sentence pairs of training data, and 489 Chinese sentences with 6 English reference translations each as test data; all the sentences are taken from the traveling domain. Since the Chinese is written without whitespace, we use a tool that tries to clump characters together into more "word like" sequences (Wu, 1999).

After each iteration, we use the long ITG to translate the held out test set with our in-house ITG decoder. The decoder uses a CKY-style parsing algorithm (Cocke, 1969; Kasami, 1965; Younger, 1967) and cube pruning (Chiang, 2007) to integrate the language model scores. The decoder builds an efficient hypergraph structure which is scored using both the induced grammar and a language model. We use SRILM (Stolcke, 2002) for training a trigram language model on the English side of the training corpus. To evaluate the resulting translations, we use BLEU (Papineni *et al.*, 2002) and NIST (Doddington, 2002).

We also perform a combination experiment, where the grammar at different stages of the learning process (iterations) are interpolated with each other. This is a straight-forward linear interpolation, where the probabilities of the rules are added up and the grammar is renormalized. Although it makes little sense from an MDL point of view to increase the size of the grammar so indiscriminately, it does make sense from an engineering point of view, since more rules typically means better coverage, which in turn typically means better translations of unknown data.

6 Results

As discussed at the outset, rather than burying our learned ITG in many layers of unrelated heuristics just to push up the BLEU score, we think it is more

Table 2: The results of decoding with combined grammars. NIST and BLEU are the translation scores for each combination, followed by the number of rules in the grammar, followed by the average (as measured by mean and mode) number of English tokens in the rules.

Combination	NIST	BLEU	Rules	Mean	Mode
1–2 (2 grammars)	4.2426	15.28	74,969	6.69	6
3–4 (2 grammars)	4.5087	18.75	54,533	5.41	3
5–6 (2 grammars)	4.1897	18.19	44,264	4.86	1
7–8 (2 grammars)	4.0953	17.40	40,785	4.79	1
1–4 (4 grammars)	**4.9234**	19.98	109,183	6.19	5
5–8 (4 grammars)	4.1089	17.86	47,504	4.84	1
1–8 (8 grammars)	4.8649	**20.41**	124,423	5.92	3

important to illuminate scientific understanding of the behavior of pure MDL-driven rule induction without interference from other variables. Directly evaluating solely the ITG in translation mode—instead of (a) deriving word alignments from it by committing to only the one-best parse, but then discarding any trace of structure and/or (b) evaluating it through a decoder that has been patched up to compensate for deficiencies in disparate aspects of translation—allows us to see exactly how accurate the learned transduction rules are.

The results from the individual iterations (Table 1) show that we learn very parsimonious models that far outperforms the only other result we are aware of where an ITG is tested exactly as it was learned without altering the model itself: Saers *et al.* (2012) induce a pure ITG by iteratively chunking rules, but they report significantly lower translation quality (8.30 BLEU and 0.8554 NIST) despite a significantly larger ITG (251,947 rules). The average rule length also decreases as smaller reusable spans are found. The English side of the training data has a mean of 8.45 and a mode of 7 tokens per sentence, and these averages drop steadily during training. It is very encouraging to see the mode drop to one so quickly, as this indicates that the learning algorithm finds translations of individual English words. Not only are the rules getting fewer, but they are also getting shorter.

The results from the combination experiments (Table 2) corroborate the engineering intuition that more rules give better translations at the expense of a larger model. Using all eight grammars gives a BLEU score of 20.41, at the expense of approximately tripling the size of the grammar. All individual iterations benefit from being combined with other iterations—but for the very best iterations more additional data is needed to get this improvement; the fifth iteration, which excelled at BLEU score needs to be combined with all other iterations to see an improvement, whereas the first and second iterations only need each other to see an improvement.

7 Conclusions

We have presented a minimalist, unsupervised learning model that induces relatively clean phrasal ITGs by iteratively splitting existing rules into smaller rules using a theoretically well-founded minimum description length objective. The resulting translation model is very parsimonious and provide an obvious foundation for generalization to more abstract transduction grammars with informative nonterminals.

8 Acknowledgements

This material is based upon work supported in part by the Defense Advanced Research Projects Agency (DARPA) under BOLT contract no. HR0011-12-C-0016, and GALE contract nos. HR0011-06-C-0022 and HR0011-06-C-0023; by the European Union under the FP7 grant agreement no. 287658; and by the Hong Kong Research Grants Council (RGC) research grants GRF620811, GRF621008, and GRF612806. Any opinions, findings and conclusions or recommendations expressed in this material are those of the authors and do not necessarily reflect the views of DARPA, the EU, or RGC.

References

Phil Blunsom and Trevor Cohn. Inducing synchronous grammars with slice sampling. In *HLT/NAACL2010*, pages 238–241, Los Angeles, California, June 2010.

Phil Blunsom, Trevor Cohn, and Miles Osborne. Bayesian synchronous grammar induction. In *Proceedings of NIPS 21*, Vancouver, Canada, December 2008.

Phil Blunsom, Trevor Cohn, Chris Dyer, and Miles Osborne. A gibbs sampler for phrasal synchronous grammar induction. In *Proceedings of the Joint Conference of the 47th Annual Meeting of the ACL and the 4th International Joint Conference on Natural Language Processing of the AFNLP*, pages 782–790, Suntec, Singapore, August 2009.

Peter F. Brown, Stephen A. Della Pietra, Vincent J. Della Pietra, and Robert L. Mercer. The Mathematics of Machine Translation: Parameter estimation. *Computational Linguistics*, 19(2):263–311, 1993.

David Burkett, John Blitzer, and Dan Klein. Joint parsing and alignment with weakly synchronized grammars. In *HLT/NAACL'10*, pages 127–135, Los Angeles, California, June 2010.

Colin Cherry and Dekang Lin. Inversion transduction grammar for joint phrasal translation modeling. In *Proceedings of SSST'07*, pages 17–24, Rochester, New York, April 2007.

David Chiang. A hierarchical phrase-based model for statistical machine translation. In *Proceedings of ACL'05*, pages 263–270, Ann Arbor, Michigan, June 2005.

David Chiang. Hierarchical phrase-based translation. *Computational Linguistics*, 33(2):201–228, 2007.

John Cocke. *Programming languages and their compilers: Preliminary notes*. Courant Institute of Mathematical Sciences, New York University, 1969.

George Doddington. Automatic evaluation of machine translation quality using n-gram cooccurrence statistics. In *Proceedings of HLT'02*, pages 138–145, San Diego, California, 2002.

C. S. Fordyce. Overview of the IWSLT 2007 evaluation campaign. In *Proceedings IWSLT'07*, pages 1–12, 2007.

Michel Galley, Jonathan Graehl, Kevin Knight, Daniel Marcu, Steve DeNeefe, Wei Wang, and Ignacio Thayer. Scalable inference and training of context-rich syntactic translation models. In *Proceedings COLING/ACL'06*, pages 961–968, Sydney, Australia, July 2006.

Peter Grünwald. A minimum description length approach to grammar inference in symbolic. *Lecture Notes in Artificial Intelligence*, (1040):203–216, 1996.

Aria Haghighi, John Blitzer, John DeNero, and Dan Klein. Better word alignments with supervised itg models. In *Proceedings of ACL/IJCNLP'09*, pages 923–931, Suntec, Singapore, August 2009.

Howard Johnson, Joel Martin, George Foster, and Roland Kuhn. Improving translation quality by discarding most of the phrasetable. In *Proceedings EMNLP/CoNLL'07*, pages 967–975, Prague, Czech Republic, June 2007.

Tadao Kasami. An efficient recognition and syntax analysis algorithm for context-free languages. Technical Report AFCRL-65-00143, Air Force Cambridge Research Laboratory, 1965.

Philipp Koehn, Franz Joseph Och, and Daniel Marcu. Statistical Phrase-Based Translation. In *Proceedings of HLT/NAACL'03*, volume 1, pages 48–54, Edmonton, Canada, May/June 2003.

Graham Neubig, Taro Watanabe, Eiichiro Sumita, Shinsuke Mori, and Tatsuya Kawahara. An unsupervised model for joint phrase alignment and extraction. In *Proceedings of ACL/HLT'11*, pages 632–641, Portland, Oregon, June 2011.

Graham Neubig, Taro Watanabe, Shinsuke Mori, and Tatsuya Kawahara. Machine translation without words through substring alignment. In *Proceedings of ACL'12*, pages 165–174, Jeju Island, Korea, July 2012.

Franz Josef Och and Hermann Ney. A Systematic Comparison of Various Statistical Alignment Models. *Computational Linguistics*, 29(1):19–51, 2003.

Kishore Papineni, Salim Roukos, Todd Ward, and Wei-Jing Zhu. BLEU: a method for automatic evaluation of machine translation. In *Proceedings of ACL'02*, pages 311–318, Philadelphia, Pennsylvania, July 2002.

Jason Riesa and Daniel Marcu. Hierarchical search for word alignment. In *Proceedings of ACL'10*, pages 157–166, Uppsala, Sweden, July 2010.

Jorma Rissanen. A universal prior for integers and estimation by minimum description length. *The Annals of Statistics*, 11(2):416–431, June 1983.

Markus Saers and Dekai Wu. Improving phrase-based translation via word alignments from Stochastic Inversion Transduction Grammars. In *Proceedings of SSST'09*, pages 28–36, Boulder, Colorado, June 2009.

Markus Saers and Dekai Wu. Principled induction of phrasal bilexica. In *Proceedings of EAMT'11*, pages 313–320, Leuven, Belgium, May 2011.

Markus Saers, Joakim Nivre, and Dekai Wu. Learning stochastic bracketing inversion transduction grammars with a cubic time biparsing algorithm. In *Proceedings of IWPT'09*, pages 29–32, Paris, France, October 2009.

Markus Saers, Joakim Nivre, and Dekai Wu. Word alignment with stochastic bracketing linear inversion transduction grammar. In *Proceedings of HLT/NAACL'10*, pages 341–344, Los Angeles, California, June 2010.

Markus Saers, Karteek Addanki, and Dekai Wu. From finite-state to inversion transductions: Toward unsupervised bilingual grammar induction. In *Proceedings of COLING 2012: Technical Papers*, pages 2325–2340, Mumbai, India, December 2012.

Claude Elwood Shannon. A mathematical theory of communication. *The Bell System Technical Journal*, 27:379–423, 623–656, July, October 1948.

Zhangzhang Si, Mingtao Pei, Benjamin Yao, and Song-Chun Zhu. Unsupervised learning of event and-or grammar and semantics from video. In *Proceedings of the 2011 IEEE ICCV*, pages 41–48, November 2011.

Ray J. Solomonoff. A new method for discovering the grammars of phrase structure languages. In *IFIP Congress*, pages 285–289, 1959.

Andreas Stolcke and Stephen Omohundro. Inducing probabilistic grammars by bayesian model merging. In R. C. Carrasco and J. Oncina, editors, *Grammatical Inference and Applications*, pages 106–118. Springer, 1994.

Andreas Stolcke. SRILM – an extensible language modeling toolkit. In *Proceedings of the International Conference on Spoken Language Processing*, pages 901–904, Denver, Colorado, September 2002.

Juan Miguel Vilar and Enrique Vidal. A recursive statistical translation model. In *ACL-2005 Workshop on Building and Using Parallel Texts*, pages 199–207, Ann Arbor, Jun 2005.

Stephan Vogel, Hermann Ney, and Christoph Tillmann. HMM-based Word Alignment in Statistical Translation. In *Proceedings of COLING-96*, volume 2, pages 836–841, 1996.

Dekai Wu. Stochastic Inversion Transduction Grammars and Bilingual Parsing of Parallel Corpora. *Computational Linguistics*, 23(3):377–403, 1997.

Zhibiao Wu. LDC Chinese segmenter, 1999.

Daniel H. Younger. Recognition and parsing of context-free languages in time n^3. *Information and Control*, 10(2):189–208, 1967.

Hao Zhang, Chris Quirk, Robert C. Moore, and Daniel Gildea. Bayesian learning of non-compositional phrases with synchronous parsing. In *Proceedings of ACL/HLT'08*, pages 97–105, Columbus, Ohio, June 2008.

Integrating morpho-syntactic features in English-Arabic statistical machine translation

Ines Turki Khemakhem
MIRACL Laboratory,
ISIM Sfax,
pôle Technologique,
Route de Tunis Km 10, B.P.
242 Sfax 3021, Tunisie
Ines_turki@yahoo.fr

Salma Jamoussi
MIRACL Laboratory,
ISIM Sfax,
pôle Technologique,
Route de Tunis Km 10, B.P.
242 Sfax 3021, Tunisie
Salma.jammoussi@isimsf.rnu.tn

Abdelmajid Ben Hamadou
MIRACL Laboratory,
ISIM Sfax,
pôle Technologique,
Route de Tunis Km 10, B.P.
242 Sfax 3021, Tunisie
abdelmajid.benh--amadou@isimsf.rnu.tn

Abstract

This paper presents a hybrid approach to the enhancement of English to Arabic statistical machine translation quality. Machine Translation has been defined as the process that utilizes computer software to translate text from one natural language to another. Arabic, as a morphologically rich language, is a highly flexional language, in that the same root can lead to various forms according to its context. Statistical machine translation (SMT) engines often show poor syntax processing especially when the language used is morphologically rich such as Arabic. In this paper, to overcome these shortcomings, we describe our hybrid approach which integrates knowledge of the Arabic language into statistical machine translation. In this framework, we propose the use of a featured language model SFLM (Smaïli et al., 2004) to be able to integrate syntactic and grammatical knowledge about each word. In this paper, we first discuss some challenges in translating from English to Arabic and we explore various techniques to improve performance on this task. We apply a morphological segmentation step for Arabic words and we present our hybrid approach by identifying morpho-syntactic class of each segmented word to build up our statistical feature language model. We propose the scheme for recombining the segmented Arabic word, and describe their effect on translation.

1 Introduction

Arabic is characterized by complex morphology and rich vocabulary. It is a derivational, flexional language. In addition, Arabic is an agglutinative language. In fact, most Arabic words are made up by the concatenation of certain morphemes together. An Arabic corpus will therefore have more surface forms than an English corpus of the same size.

On the other hand, many Arabic words are homographic: they have the same orthographic form, but they have not the same meaning. This property can reduce the size of the translation vocabulary and has an important implication for statistical modeling of the Arabic language. These factors affect the performance of English-Arabic Statistical Machine Translation (SMT).

To overcome these weaknesses of SMT, we propose a hybrid approach that seeks to integrate the linguistic information and enrich the lexical and syntactic resources in the statistical machine translation.

Arabic language translation has been widely studied recently. Most of the time, the rich morphology of Arabic language is seen as a serious problem that must be resolved to build up an efficient translation system. It has been proven that pre-processing Arabic data and integrating its morpho-syntactic features is useful to improve machine translation results. The use of similar techniques for English-to-Arabic SMT requires recombination of the target side into valid surface forms, which is not a trivial task.

In this paper, we describe an initial set of experiments on English-to-Arabic machine translation: we apply a morphological segmentation step for Arabic words and we present our hybrid approach by identifying morpho-syntactic class of each segmented word to build up our statistical feature language model. We propose the scheme for recombining the segmented Arabic, and describe their effect on translation.

This paper is organized as follows: section 2 gives a brief description of some related works using hybrid approach to Machine Translation to introduce morpho-syntactic features in a machine translation process. Section 3 describes the baseline system. Then, section 4 presents the used morphological analyzer MORPH2 for Arabic texts, able to recognize word composition and to provide more specific morphological information about it. Next, we give information about Arabic syntax and morphology in section 5; in the remainder of this section, we discuss the complexity of the Arabic morphology and the challenge of recombining the translated and segmented Arabic words in to their surface forms. The Statistical Feature Language Model (SFLM) is explained in section 6, when used it aims to integrate morpho-syntactic knowledge about word in the language model. We propose in section 7 a scheme for recombining the translated and segmented Arabic words in to their surface forms. Section 8 gives a short overview of the data and tools used to build up our SMT system and shows the experimental details of our system using SFLM and the morphological analyzer MORPH2. Section 9 discusses the obtained results and, finally, section 10 presents some conclusions.

2 Related work

Arabic language translation has been widely studied recently. Most of the time, the rich morphology of Arabic language is seen as a serious problem that must be resolved to build up an efficient translation system. Research into machine translation hybridization has increased over the last few years particulary with the statistical approach for machine translation. Habash et al. (Habash et al., 2006) boost generation-heavy machine translation (GHMT) with statistical machine translation components. They use hybridization approach from the opposite direction by incorporating SMT components into rule-based systems. In (Sawaf, 2010), authors described a novel approach on how to deal with Arabic noisy and dialectal data. They normalize the input text to a commun form to be able to process it.

In recent years, the overall quality of machine translation output has been improved greatly. Still, SMT engines often show poor results in their syntactic forms. Hybrid approach try to overcome these typical errors by integrating knowledge of Arabic language. It has been proven that pre-processing Arabic data and integrating its features such as morphological information and syntactic structure is useful to improve machine translation results.

In the next, we review this body of research. Our own research differs in that how to integrate information into SMT components systems.

Most of the related work is on Arabic-to-English SMT. In prior work (Lee, 2004) (Habash and Sadat, 2006), it has been shown that morphological segmentation of the Arabic source benefits the performance of Arabic-to-English SMT. In (Lee, 2004), the author uses a trigram language model to segment Arabic words. He then proceeds to deleting or merging some of the segmented morphemes in order to make the segmented Arabic source align better with the English target. Habash and Sadat (Habash and Sadat, 2006) compared the use of the BAMA (Buckwalter, 2002.) and MADA (Habash and Rambow, 2005) toolkits to segment the Arabic source as well as simple pattern matching to do morphological analysis for Arabic-English SMT, and were able to improve translation for tasks with out-of-domain training corpora. Sadat and Habash (Sadat and Habash. 2006) also showed that it was possible to combine the use of several variations of morphological analysis both while decoding (combining multiple phrase tables) and rescoring the combined outputs of distinct systems.

Introducing morphological analyzers in Arabic machine translation process is very present in the literature. The recent work (Besacier et al., 2008) conducted in depth a study of the influence of Arabic segmenters on the translation quality of an Arabic to English phrase-based system using the Moses decoder. In this work, authors demonstrate that the use of the morphology information in the SMT has a great impact in improving results. They believe that simultaneously using multiple segmentations is a promising way to improve machine translation of Arabic.

Arabic is an inflected language with several homonyms words, consequently linguistic features are very useful to reduce statistical machine translation errors due to this phenomena. Some research works have been conducted in this area (Bilmes and Kirchhoff, 2003) (Schwenk and Déchelotte, 2007). The factored language model (FLM) approach of Bilmes and Kirchhoff (Bilmes and Kirchhoff, 2003) is a more linguistically-informed modeling approach than the n-gram one. FLM are an extension of standard language model where the prediction is based upon a set of features (and not only on previous occurrences of the predicted word). FLM addresses the problems of data-sparsity in morphologically complex languages by representing words as bundles of features, thus one can easily capture dependencies between subword parts of adjacent words. Some other works have been proposed to integrate linguistic information such as part-of-speech, morphology and shallow syntax in conventional phrase-based statistical translation (Koehn and Hoang. 2007). These translation models allow integrating multiple levels of information into the translation process instead of incorporating linguistic markers in either preprocessing or postprocessing steps. For example, in morphologically rich languages it may be preferable to translate lemma, part-of-speech and morphological information separately and combine the information on the target side to generate the output surface words. In this model the translation process is broken up into three steps. Translate input lemmas into output lemmas in a first step. Then, translate morphological and POS factors in a second step. Finally, generate surface forms given the lemma and the linguistic factors. These factored translation models have been used to improve the word level translation accuracy by incorporating the factors in phrase-based translation. In (Schwenk and Déchelotte. 2007), authors focus on incorporating morpho-syntactic features in the translation model for the English-Spanish machine translation process. In this work, authors propose the use of augmented units in the translation model instead of simple words. These units are composed by surface word forms combined with their morpho-syntactic categories. This method allows lexical disambiguation of words using their roles and their grammatical contexts.

Previous works on English-to-Arabic SMT using factored models were proposed in (Sarikaya and Deng. 2007) and (Badr et al., 2008). The first uses shallow segmentation, and does not make use of contextual information. In this work authors use Joint Morphological-Lexical Language Models to rerank the output. The second work shows that morphological decomposition of the Arabic text is beneficial, especially for smaller-size corpora, and investigates different recombination techniques. In this work, authors propose the use of factored translation models for English to Arabic translation. The factors on the English side are POS tags and the surface word. On the Arabic side, they use the surface word, the stem and the POS tag concatenated to the segmented clitics.

In (Kholy and Habash. 2010), authors emphasized on the sparsity problem of English-Arabic translation. They considered the tokenization and normalization of Arabic data to improve English-to-Arabic SMT.

3 Phrase-Based Machine Translation

Statistical machine translation methods have evolved from using the simple word based models (Brown et al., 1993) to phrase based models (Marcu and Wong, 2002; Och and Ney. 2003).

The SMT has been formulated as a noisy channel model in which the target language sentence, s is seen as distorted by the channel into the foreign language t. In that, we try to find the sentence t which maximizes the $P(t|s)$ probability:

$$\mathrm{argmax}_t P(t|s) = \mathrm{argmax}_t P(s|t)P(t) \quad (1)$$

Where P(t) is the language model and P(s|t) is the translation model. We can get the language model from a monolingual corpus (in the target language). The translation model is obtained by using an aligned bilingual corpus.

The translation model is combined together with the following six additional feature models: the target language model, the word and the phrase bonus and the source-to-target and target-to-source lexicon model and the reordering model. These models are optimized by the decoder[1]. In our case, we use the open source Moses decoder described in (Koehn et al., 2007).

4 Segmentation for Arabic translation

Arabic is a morphologically complex language. Compared with English, an Arabic word can sometimes correspond to a whole English sentence (Example: the Arabic word "أتتذكروننا" corresponds in English to: "Do you remember us").

The aim of a morphological analysis step is to recognize word composition and to provide specific morphological information about it. For

[1] http://www.statmt.org/moses/

Example: the word "يعرفون" (in English: they know) is the result of the concatenation of the prefix "ي" indicating the present and suffix "ون" indicating the plural masculine of the verb "عرف" (in English: to know). The morphological analyzer determines for each word the list of all its possible morphological features.

In Arabic language, some conjugated verbs or inflected nouns can have the same orthographic form due to absence of vowels (Example: non-voweled Arabic word "فصل" can be a verb in the past "فَصَلَ" (He dismissed), or a masculine noun "فَصْلٌ" (chapter / season), or a concatenation of the coordinating conjunction " فَ" (then) with the verb "صل": imperative of the verb (bind)).

In order to handle the morphological ambiguities, we decide to use MORPH2, an Arabic morphological analyzer developed at the Miracl laboratory[2]. MORPH2 is based on a knowledge-based computational method. It accepts as input an Arabic text, a sentence or a word. Its morphological disambiguation and analysis method is based on five steps:

- A tokenization process is applied in a first step. It consists of two sub-steps. First, the text is divided into sentences, using the system Star (Belguith et al., 2005), an Arabic text tokenizer based on contextual exploration of punctuation marks and conjunctions of coordination. The second sub-step detects the different words in each sentence.
- A morphological preprocessing step which aims to extract clitics agglutinated to the word. A filtering process is then applied to check out if the remaining word is a particle, a number, a date, or a proper noun.
- An affixal analysis is then applied to determine all possible affixes and roots. It aims to identify basic elements belonging to the constitution of a word (the root and affixes i.e. prefix, infix and suffix).
- The morphological analysis step consists of determining for each word, all its possible morpho-syntactic features (i.e, part of speech, gender, number, time, person, etc.). Morpho-syntactic features detection is made up on three stages. The first stage identifies the part-of-speech of the word (i.e. verb "فعل", noun "اسم", particle "أداة" and proper noun "اسم علم"). The second stage extracts for each part-of-speech a list of its morpho-syntactic features. A filtering of these feature lists is made in the third stage.
- Vocalization and validation step: each handled word is fully vocalized according to its morpho-syntactic features determined in the previous step.

[2] http://www.miracl.rnu.tn

5 Challenges on English-Arabic SMT

In this section, we briefly explore the challenges that prevent the construction of successful SMT. The divergence of Arabic and English puts a rocky barrier in building a prosperous machine translation system. Morphological and syntactic preprocessing is important in order to converge the two languages.

Arabic is a highly agglutinative language with a rich set of suffixes. Inflectional and derivational productions introduce a big growth in the number of possible word forms. In Arabic, articles, prepositions, pronouns, etc. can be affixed to adjectives, nouns, verbs and particles to which they are related. The richness in morphology introduces many challenges to the translation problem both to and from Arabic.

In general, ambiguities in Arabic word are mainly caused by the absence of the short vowels. Thus, a word can have different meanings. There are also the usual homographs of uninflected words with/without the same pronunciation, which have different meanings and usually different POS's. For example: the word "ذهب", can correspond in English to: "gold" or to: "go". In Arabic there are four categories of words: noun, proper noun, verbs and particles. The absence of short vowels can cause ambiguities within the same category or cross different categories. For example: the word "بعد" corresponds to many categories (table 1).

meanings of a word "بعد"	Categories
after	Particule
remoteness	Noun
remove	Verb
go away	Verb

Table 1: Different meanings of the word "بعد"

In table 1, there exist four different analyses for the word "بعد". This ambiguity can be resolved only in the phrase context.

Due to the Arabic is an agglutinative language, the morphological decomposition is required. So as mentioned above, both training and decoding use segmented Arabic. The final output of the decoder must therefore be recombined into a surface form. This proves to be a non-trivial challenge for a reason that Arabic uses diverse systems of prefixes, suffixes, and pronouns that are attached to the words (Soudi et al., 2007). For example, the Arabic sentence "قبل ت عرض ك" can be recombined as presented in table 2.

Recombined sentence	meanings
قبل تعرضك	Before exposure
قبلت عرضك	Accepted the offer

Table 2: Ambiguity in recombining sentence

6 Statistical Feature Language Model

One of the problems of statistical language models is to consider that the word is depending only on its previous history (words or classes). But in fact, in natural language the appearance of a word depends not only on its history but also on some others features. The word "كتب" (write) and "كتب" (books) are two different words, but we can't predict them if we don't know their features and their contexts.

In order to settle such problem we are trying to introduce knowledge about the word features by using a featured statistical language model: Statistical Feature Language Model (Smaïli et al., 2004).

Arabic is an inflected natural language, linguistic features are very useful to reduce translation errors due to homonyms. By employing SFLM, each word is considered as an array of m features:

$$w_i^{1..m} = \begin{pmatrix} f_1^i \\ f_2^i \\ . \\ . \\ f_m^i \end{pmatrix} \qquad (2)$$

Each f_j^i is a linguistic characteristic of w_i. These characteristics or features could be the surface word, its syntactic class, its gender, its number, its semantic class, ...

(Smaïli et al., 2004) substitute in the classical n-gram language model, the words by their feature arrays which contain surface words and their linguistic characteristics. Thus, a SFLM model is built up by analogy with the classical n-gram model given by:

$$P(w_1, w_2, \dots, w_L) = \prod_{i=1}^{L} P(w_i | w_{i-1} \dots w_{i-n+1}) \qquad (3)$$

To define SFLM model it is enough to replace each word w_i by its feature array $(f_1^i, f_2^i, \dots, f_m^i)^t$ as follows:

$$P\left(w_1^{1..m}, w_2^{1..m}, \dots, w_L^{1..m}\right) = \prod_{i=1}^{L} P\left(\begin{pmatrix} f_1^i \\ f_2^i \\ . \\ . \\ f_m^i \end{pmatrix} \middle| \begin{pmatrix} f_1^{i-1} \\ f_2^{i-1} \\ . \\ . \\ f_m^{i-1} \end{pmatrix} \dots \begin{pmatrix} f_1^{i-n+1} \\ f_2^{i-n+1} \\ . \\ . \\ f_m^{i-n+1} \end{pmatrix}\right) \qquad (4)$$

Where $(f_1^i, f_2^i, \dots, f_m^i)^t$ is the feature array corresponding to the ith word. This model is very simple to implement with classical language modeling toolkits like CMU (Clarkson and Rosenfeld, 1997) and SLRIM (Stolcke, 2002). In fact, we replace each word in the Arabic training and test corpora by its feature array. Thus the following notation is adopted:

$$w_i^{1...m} = f_1^i\_f_2^i, \dots, \_f_m^i \qquad (5)$$

The feature array $f_1^i\_f_2^i, \dots, \_f_m^i$ will be treated like only one string. In our experiments, we decided to employ a SFLM with two features. We choose to consider the word itself as first feature and its syntactic class (category) as second one. In this case, a word w_i is represented like the concatenation of the two strings w_i and $C(w_i)$ as follows:

$$w_i\_C(w_i) \qquad (6)$$

where $\mathbf{C(w_i)}$ represents the morpho-syntactic class of $\mathbf{w_i}$.

7 Arabic recombination

As mentioned in Section 1, Arabic is characterized by a rich morphology. In addition to being inflected for gender and number, words can be attached to various clitics for conjunction "و" (and), the definite article ال""the), prepositions) ب" .e.g)" (by/with), "ل" (for), "ك" (as)) and object pronouns (e.g. "هم" (their/them)).

We apply decomposition before aligning the training data, by splitting off each clitic and affix agglutinated to the word separately, such that any given word is split into at most five parts:

Proclitic + prefix+ stem +suffix + enclitic.

Then, the stem is associated with its morpho-syntactic feature. For example the word "أتعرفونهم" (in English: "do you know them" is replaced by:

أ ت عرف_ فعل ون هم

So in both training and decoding processes, segmented Arabic words are used. The final output of the decoder will be also a list of segmented words. Therefore this output must be recombined into a surface form to be able to evaluate the translation result by using the right surface words.

This proves to be a non-trivial challenge for a reason of order ambiguity: a segmented word can be recombined into two grammatically correct forms. Clitics can correspond to enclitic or proclitic. For example: in the segmented words: "سلم ت ك ذلك ال كتاب" the clitic "ك" can be recombined with the previous word ("ك": enclitic). So the segmented words "سلم ت ك ذلك ال كتاب" can b erecombined to "سلمتك ذلك الكتاب", in English: "I gave this book".

The clitic "ك" can be recombined also with the following word ("ك": proclitic), in this case, the segmented words "سلم ت ك ذلك" can be recombined to "سلمت كذلك الكتاب", in English: "I also gave the book".

Those two sentences have the same segmented form, but they have different meanings. By introducing morphological features (e.g. proclitic, prefix, stem, suffix and enclitic) for each segment, we may remove this ambiguity:

Therefore we apply reconstruction of the Arabic segmented words by agglutinating the morphological segments in the following order:

_هم suffix _فعل ون_ عرف prefix _ت proclitic _أ enclitic

8 Experiments

8.1 Used data

In this paper, we consider the translation task of texts from English into Arabic. We used IWSLT2010 data as a parallel corpus. For training the translation models, the train part of the IWSLT10 data was used which contains 19972 sentence pairs. For testing, we used a subset data made up of 469 sentences (there were 1 Arabic reference translation for each Arabic sentence). All BLEU scores presented in this paper are case-sensitive and include punctuations. For the Arabic language model we use trigrams to build up the baseline system and a 7-grams to build up our translation system. In fact, we use a 7-gram language model because in our system, each word in the training Arabic corpus is replaced by its list of morphological segments: proclitic, prefix, stem, suffix and enclitic.

8.2 Baseline system

The English-Arabic baseline system is built upon the open-source MT toolkit Moses (Koehn et al., 2007). Phrase pairs are extracted from word alignments generated by GIZA++ (Och and Ney. 2003). The phrase-based translation model provides direct and inverted frequency-based and lexical-based probabilities for each phrase pair. To train the trigram language models, SRILM (Stolcke, 2002) was used. The performances reported in this paper were measured using the BLEU score (Papineni et al., 2002).

8.3 Experimental results

- *Arabic word segmenter:*

In our method, each Arabic word, from the target training data, is replaced by its segmented form.

For example: the word "فعرفناهم" (in English: "and we have known them") is the result of the concatenation of the proclitic "ف" (then): coordinating conjunction, the suffix "نا" for the present masculine plural, enclitic "هم" (for the masculine plural posession pronoun), and the rest of the word "عرف" indicating the stem. So, the word "فعرفناهم" will be replaced by:

"ف عرف نا هم"

- *SFLM for introducing Morpho-syntactic features:*

For introducing morpho-syntactic features into the English-Arabic translation system, we use part of speech tagging provided by MORPH2. We believe that using these features can improve our language modeling when used with the SFLM model.

In our proposed method, each Arabic word, from the target Arabic training data, is replaced by the reduced word (obtained by removing its clitics and its affixes), combined with its syntactic class (category), where clitic and affix are featured with their morphological classes (e.g. proclitic, prefix, suffix and enclitic).

For example : the word "سيخبرهم" (in English: "he will notify them") is the result of the concatenation of the proclitic "س" indicating the future, the prefix "ي" for the present, enclitic "هم" (for the masculine plural posession pronoun), and the rest of the word "خبر" such as its syntactic class is verb: "فعل". So, the word "سيخبرهم" will be replaced by:

"enclitic_هم فعل_خبر prefix_ي proclitic_س "

In this notation, its morpho-syntactic feature (as verb "فعل", noun "اسم", particle "أداة" and proper noun "اسم علم"). The language model is then generated using the so obtained target Arabic training data, by the standard SRILM toolkit. The so obtained Arabic corpus in then used for training (without any change on the English side).

- Arabic post-processing

As mentioned above, both training and decoding phases use Arabic segmented words. The final output of the decoder will be also composed of segmented words. Therefore these words must be recombined into their surface forms. Therefore we apply reconstruction of the Arabic segmented words just by agglutinating the morphological segments in the following order:

Proclitic + prefix+ stem +suffix + enclitic.

The English-Arabic translation performance of this new system is reported in table3, and compared to the baseline system.

	Bleu
Baseline	12.58%
SMT hybrid	13.16%

Table 3: Comparison of the English-Arabic translation systems

Table 3 shows a significant improvement of the BLEU score when we use segmentation and introduce morpho-syntactic features into the English-Arabic translation system by using SFLM. The BLEU score increases from 12.58% to 13.16%.

These results attest that the use of morpho-syntactic features within SMT system can enhance translation performances, especially for agglutinative and inflectional languages, such as Arabic. Also, using the word category concatenated to the word, can avoid the problem of homographics and can improve language modeling efficacity.

9 Conclusion

English-to-Arabic machine translation has been a challenging research issue for many researchers in the field of Arabic Natural Language Processing. In this study, we have evaluated the effectiveness of morphological decomposition of the Arabic text and SFLM language modeling method to integrate morpho-syntactic features in English to Arabic machine translation. We also presented our method for recombining the segmented Arabic target. Our results suggest that morphological decomposition of the Arabic text is beneficial and that using morpho-syntactic features is a promising way to improve English to Arabic machine translation. The use of recombination of the target side technique is beneficial to overcome ambiguity in recombining Arabic text.

References

Badr I., Zbib R. and Glass J. 2008. Segmentation for English-to-Arabic statistical machine translation. Proceedings of the 46th Annual Meeting of the Association for Computational Linguistics on Human Language Technologies, Columbus, Ohio, 153-156.

Belguith L., Baccour L. and Mourad G. 2005. Segmentation des textes arabes basée sur l'analyse contextuelle des signes de ponctuations et de certaines particules". Actes de la 12éme Conférence annuelle sur le Traitement Automatique des Langues Naturelles, 451-456.

Besacier L., Ben-Youcef A. and Blanchon H. 2008. The LIG Arabic / English Speech Translation System. IWSLT08. Hawai. USA, 58-62.

Bilmes J. and Kirchhoff K. 2003. Factored language models and generalized parallel backoff". In Proceeding of Human Language Technology Conference, Edmonton, Canada. 4–6.

Brown P., Della Pietra V., Della Pietra S., and Mercer R. 1993. The mathematics of statistical machine translation: parameter estimation, Computational Linguistics, 19(1): 263–311.

Buckwalter T. 2002. Buckwalter Arabic morphological analyzer version 1.0. Linguistic Data Consortium, University of Pennsylvania.

Carpuat M, Marton Y, and Habash N. 2010. Improving arabic-to-english statistical machine translation by reordering post-verbal subjects for alignment. In Proceedings of the Association for Computational Linguistics (ACL 2010) Conference Short Papers, Uppsala, Sweden, 178–183.

Clarkson P. and Rosenfeld R. 1997, Statistical language modeling using the CMU-Cambridge toolkit. In Proceedings of the European Conference on Speech Communication and Technology, Rhodes, Greece, 2707-2710.

David Chiang, Yuval Marton, and Philip Resnik. 2008. Online large-margin training of syntactic and structural translation features. In Proceedings of the Conference on Empirical Methods in Natural Language Processing, EMNLP '08, 224–233, Stroudsburg, PA, USA.

Habash N. and Rambow O. 2005. Arabic Tokenization, Part-of-Speech Tagging and Morphological Disambiguation in One Fell Swoop. In Proc. of the 43rd Annual Meeting of the Association for Computational Linguistics (ACL), Ann Arbor, MI, 573–580.

Habash N. and Sadat F. 2006. Arabic Preprocessing Schemes for Statistical Machine Translation. In Proc. of the Human Language Technology Conference of the NAACL, Companion Volume: Short Papers, New York City, NY, 49–52.

Habash N., Dorr B., and Monz C. 2006. Challenges in Building an Arabic-English GHMT System with SMT Components. In Proceedings of the 11th annual conference of the European Association for Machine Translation (EAMT-2006), Norway, 56-65.

Kholy A. and Habash N. 2010. Techniques for arabic morphological detokenization and orthographic denormalization. In Proceedings of the seventh International Conference on Language Resources and Evaluation (LREC), Valletta, Malta.

Koehn P. and Hoang H. 2007. Factored translation models. In Proceedings of the 2007 Joint Conference on Empirical Methods in Natural Language Processing and Computational Natural Language Learning, Prague, 868–876.

Koehn P., Hoang H., Birch A., Callison-Burch C., Federico M., Bertoldi N., Cowa B., Shen W., Moran C., Zens R., Dyer C., Bojar O., Constantin A., and Herbst E., 2007. Moses: Open source toolkit for statistical machine translation, in Proceedings of the ACL-2007 Demoand Poster Sessions, Prague, Czeck Republic, 177–180.

Lee Y. S. 2004. Morphological Analysis for Statistical Machine Translation. In Proceedings of HLT-NAACL: Short Papers on XX, Boston, Massachusetts, 57-60.

Marcu D. and Wong W. 2002. A Phrase-Based, Joint Probability Model for Statistical Machine Translation. Proceedings of the Conference on Empirical Methods in Natural Language Processing (EMNLP-2002), Philadelphia, PA, 133-139.

Och F. J., and Ney H., 2003. A Systematic comparison of various statistical alignment models, Computational Linguistics, 29(1): 19-51.

Papineni K. A., Roukos S., Ward T., and Zhu W.J., 2002. Bleu: a method for automatic evaluation of machine translation. The Proc. of the 40th Annual Meeting of the Association for Computational Linguistics, Philadelphia, 311–318.

Sadat F. and Habash N. 2006. Combination of Arabic preprocessing schemes for statistical machine translation". In Proceedings of the 21st International Conference on Computational Linguistics and the 44th annual meeting of the ACL (Coling ACL'06), Sydney, Australia, 1–8.

Sarikaya R. and Deng Y. 2007. Joint Morphological-Lexical Language Modeling for Machine Translation. In Proc. of NAACL HLT, Rochester, NY, 145-148.

Sawaf H. 2010. Arabic Dialect Handling in Hybrid Machine Translation. In Proceedings of the Conference of the Association for Machine Translation in the Americas (AMTA 2010), Denver, Colorado.

Schwenk H., Déchelotte D. 2007. Bonneau-Maynard H. and Allauzen A., "Modèles statistiques enrichis par la syntaxe pour la traduction automatique". TALN 2007, Toulouse-France. 253-262.

Smaïli K., Jamoussi S., Langlois D. and Haton J. P. 2004. Statistical feature language model. INTERSPEECH, Korea, 1357-1360.

Soudi A., Bosch A. and Neumann G. 2007, Arabic Computational Morphology: Knowledge-based and Empirical Methods. In Arabic Computational Morphology, Springer, 3-14.

Stolcke A., 2002. SRILM an Extensible Language Modeling Toolkit. The Proc. of the Intl. Conf. on Spoken Language Processing, Denver, CO, USA, 901–904.

Experiments with POS-based restructuring and alignment-based re-ordering for statistical machine translation

Shuo Li, Derek F. Wong and Lidia S. Chao
Department of Computer and Information Science
University of Macau, Macau S.A.R., China.
leevis1987@gmail.com, {derekfw, lidiasc}@umac.mo

Abstract

This paper presents the methods which are based on the part-of-speech (POS) and auto alignment information to improve the quality of machine translation result and the word alignment. We utilize different types of POS tag to restructure source sentences and use an alignment-based reordering method to improve the alignment. After applying the reordering method, we use two phrase tables in the decoding part to keep the translation performance. Our experiments on Korean-Chinese show that our methods can improve the alignment and translation results. Since the proposed approach reduces the size of the phrase table, multi-tables are considered. The combination of all these methods together would get the best translation result.

1 Introduction

Translating between two morphological different languages is more difficult in the descriptions by Koehn (2005). In Statistical Machine Translation (SMT) system, the surface word in a morphologically poor language is difficult to be generated from a morphologically richer language. Take the example of Korean and Chinese, their morphologies are different from European languages. Korean is a kind of subject-object-verb (SOV) language while Chinese is subject-verb-object (SVO) language which is a little similar to English. This leads to a problem of word order: despite the automatic word alignment tool GIZA++ (Och and Ney, 2003) is widely applied, there are still many generated misaligned language pairs among these two languages.

In Korean, a functional word may have different morphologies under different conditions. The verb and adjective usually end with suffixes in a sentence to represent different meanings (Li et al., 2012). On the other hand, alignment mistakes are often generated when many Korean words with different morphologies are aligned with the same Chinese tokens in Korean-Chinese translation. We applied a simple but efficient approach by utilizing different part-of-speech (POS) information to restructure Korean, after restructuring, many Korean words share the same Chinese meaning with different morphologies can be restored to their original forms. In particular, we expect to reduce the problem of misalignment due to the verb and adjective variations. Besides word restructuring, an alignment–based word reordering method which would improve the alignment result indirectly was applied in our experiment. This method is simple but effective and language-independent by modifying some alignment files. The lack of the off-the-shelf Korean-Chinese corpus is also an important problem. Most of these corpora are not open source for users, so it is hard for people applying Korean-Chinese corpus in the experiments like Europarl (Koehn, 2005), we built a small size corpus by ourselves in a short time to do the experiments based on the proposed methods. A script is developed for crawling parallel corpus of some specific websites.

In this paper, section 2 will review previous related works. In section 3, the POS-based restructuring method and alignment-based reordering approaches to improve the quality of alignment will be introduced. Experimental results and the analysis will be given in the following section 4. Finally, section 5 is the conclusion.

2 Related work

Several studies have been proposed to use POS tags and morphological information to enrich languages to tackle some problems in SMT: Li et al. (2009) proposed an approach focused on using pre-processing and post-processing methods, such as reordering the source sentences in a Chinese-Korean phrase-based SMT using syntactic information. Lee et al. (2010) transformed the syntactic relations of Chinese SVO patterns and inserted the corresponding transferred relations as pseudo words to solve the problem of word order. In order to reduce the morpheme-level translation ambiguity in an English-Chinese SMT system, Wu et al. (2008) grouped the morphemes into morpheme phrase and used the domain information for translation candidate selection. A contraction separation for Spanish in a Spanish-English SMT system was proposed in (Gispert and Mariño, 2008). Habash et al. (2009) proposed methods to tackle the Arabic enclitics. The experiment in Stymne et al. (2008) described that using POS information to split the compounds in a morphologically rich language (German nouns and adjectives) gave an effect for translation output. Holmqvist et al. (2009) also reported that using POS-based and morphology-based sequence model would give an improvement to the translation quality between English and German in WMT09 shared task.

In accordance with adding richer information to the training model, reordering the source language text to make it more similar to the target side is confirmed to be another kind of method to improve the word alignment. Collins et al. (2005) employed the forms of syntactic analysis and hand–written rules on the corpus, Xia and McCord (2004) extracted the rules from a parallel text automatically. A statistical machine pre-reordering method which addressed the reordering problems as a translation from the source sentence to a monotonized source sentence was proposed by Costa-jussà and Fonollosa (2006). Visweswariah et al. (2011) proposed a method which learns a model that can directly reorder source side text from a small parallel corpus with high quality word alignment, but this is hard for people to get such a high-quality aligned parallel corpus. Ma et al. (2007) packed some words together with the help of the existing statistical word aligner, which simplify the task of automatic word alignment by packing consecutive words together.

These approaches are integrated with morphological information in the translation and decoding model. Our approach is inspired by the approach proposed by Lee et al (2006) which added POS information; reordered the word sequence in the source corpus; deleted case particle and final ending words in Korean; appended the external dictionary in the training step between Korean and English. In the experiment reported by Li et al. (2012), these pre-processing methods on the Korean to Chinese translation system took advantage of POS in their additional factored translation model. In these studies, POS information was reported that it would improve the translation quality, but their taxonomy of POS tag is sole and less. On the word alignment side, we try to implement the idea proposed by Holmqvist et al. (2012), which was reported as a simple, language-independent reordering method to improve the quality of word alignment. But their method did not consider the problem that the probability and the amount would be changed when updated with an improved word alignment. The accuracy of alignment would be improved but the size of phrase-table would be less than the original one because there are more sure alignments generated. The probabilities of word and phrase also have the same problem.

Our works are based on the integration of these two methods. We utilized POS information and applied a richer taxonomy of POS tags in the restructuring of Korean, applied reordering method on Korean-Chinese, and combined the POS-based restructuring and alignment-based reordering together in the experiment.

3 POS-based restructuring and alignment-based reordering

The POS information is helpful when dealing with morphologically rich languages. In the morphological analysis, the Korean POS tagger involves the analytical task to identify the stem and suffixes of Korean, followed by assigning corresponding POS tags to both the morphemes and extracted stems. As described in Li et al. (2012), Korean is considered as a highly agglutinative language: the verbs, adjectives and adverbs are able to attach with affixes and particles. We considered that different category of POS tag would lead to different results of the translation. The more complex of tag would get a better result of alignment and the quality of translation. The method of processing Chinese POS is similar to Korean, which applies a more complex POS tag category from a Chinese POS tagger. Another simple but effective and language-independent reordering method which

형식상의 번거롭고 불필요한 예절을 피하다.
9 tags:
형식상의/**N** 번거/**N+**롭/**X+**고/**E** 불필요한/**N** 예절/**N+**을/**J** 피하/**P+**다/**E** ./**S**
22 tags:
형식상의/**NC** 번거/**NC+**롭/**XS+**고/**EC** 불필요한/**NC** 예절/**NC+**을/**JC** 피하/**PV+**어다/**EC** ./**SF**
9 tags deleted:
형식상의 번거 롭 고 불필요한 예절 을 피하 **다** .
22 tags deleted:
형식상의 번거 롭 고 불필요한 예절 을 피하 **어다** .

Figure 1. Different types of POS tag of Korean

improves the quality of automatic word alignment is applied on Korean-Chinese. The method is implemented by modifying the alignment file in Moses (Koehn et al., 2007), which needs two runs of GIZA++. After this step, an improved word alignment is generated potentially. Then, we combine the restructuring and reordering together to compare the superposed quality of these two methods.

3.1 POS-based restructuring

Because Korean is a kind of morphologically rich language, most of Korean verbs, adjectives and adverbs can be taken as the compound words like Germany. For example, the negative verb "가지 않다 (do not go)" should be restored to its original form "가다 (go)" and the negative verb suffix "지 않다 (do not)". Another example is the future tense verb "가겠다 (will go)" is the combination of original stem "가 (go)" and suffix with future tense "겠다 (will)". With the help of POS tagger, we can restructure the Korean with the 22 tags category instead of 9 tags in (Li et al., 2012). Here is an example of Korean restructuring in Figure 1, POS tagger can be detected the compound word and analyze its combination (tagged with "+"). The taxonomy with 22 tags is more specific than 9 tags, when tagging a noun, 22 tags will use NC (normal noun) instead of N (noun, pronoun, numeral) in 9 tags. When dealing with the compound verb "피하다 (in order to avoid)", "피하 (avoid) +어다" is more reasonable than "피하+다", because "어다" represents "in order to" in corresponding Chinese grammar. Then the tags were removed and restructured to a new sentence. After restructuring, the length of original sentence increased from 5 to 9 (9 tags) and 10 (22 tags). Based on previous relative simple tags, more complex taxonomy gives a deeper analysis of the sentence which would influence the alignment and the lexical possibility between the source and target language.

3.2 Alignment-based reordering

The aim of utilizing the alignment information is to make the order in source text same as the target text. It is believed that statistical word alignment methods perform better on translation with similar word orders.

The method needs two runs of word alignment, in the first run of GIZA++: the alignment information is acquired based on the original order. Then the source text is reordered by the order of the target text based on the information in the first alignment. Next, the reordered source text and the original target text are applied on the second run of GIZA++, which means this new parallel corpus includes the word with more similar order than before. After this step, a new alignment file would be generated, which covers potential improved word alignment with the reordered source language. Finally, the order of source text in the new alignment file is restored in its original order but kept with its new alignment information.

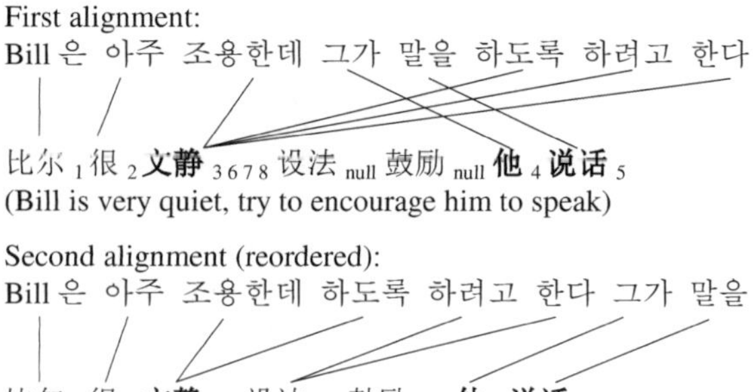

Figure 2. The alignment

The algorithm processes the corpus and the alignment results in a single direction: source side (Holmqvist et al., 2012). As an example, in the Korean-Chinese single direction in Figure 2, each Korean word aligns with the corresponding Chinese word, but Chinese is different. There are cross alignments between "그가", "말을", "하도록", "하려고", "한다" and "文静", "他",

"说话". Moreover, the alignment of these words is not totally correct.

Before the second run of GIZA++, the original Korean is reordered to the alignment of the Chinese side, so a new Korean sentence is generated by the Chinese order. After the second alignment, in Figure 2, there are no cross points and the additional correct alignment between "하려고", "한다" and "文静" is generated, the misalignment is decreased.

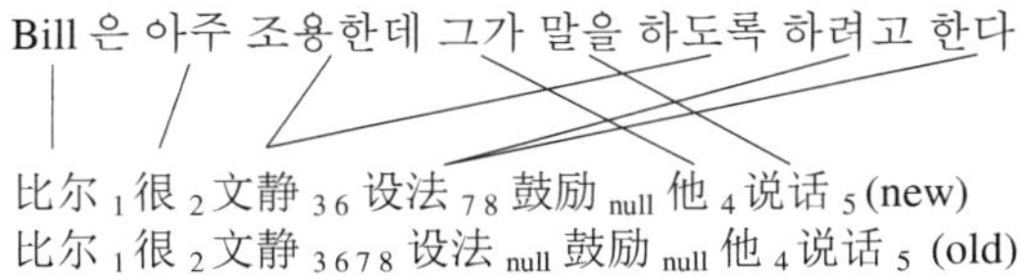

Figure 3. The improved alignment

In Figure 3, the new alignment information (new) is kept in the restored file. The crossing alignment still exists but it is more correct than the previous one (old). Based on this alignment, the establishment of word alignment, the estimation of lexical translation table and the extraction of phrase table are changed.

We assume that after applying our method, the size of the extracted words would increase because more alignments are generated at the end of the second run of GIZA++. Another assumption is that the size of the phrase table would decrease if two languages share such a different word order, because additional alignments would result in some cross alignments but the phrase extraction algorithm could not extract them. Based on two assumptions, we utilize multiple models in the decoding stage. This approach was proposed in (Koehn and Schroeder, 2007; Axelrod et al., 2011) which passes phrase and reordering tables in parallel. We used our modified tables (small size) as the main tables, and the baseline tables (big size) as the additional table when decoding. This can guarantee that if a phrase in testing sentence does not occur in the modified tables, the decoder would find the phrase in the original table. This method is effective in avoiding translation mistakes if our method harms the result.

4 Experimental results

We apply our methods on Korean-Chinese phrase-based statistical machine translation systems. The system is built based on Moses, and our reordering method is applied at the second step among the nine steps during the training in Moses. An additional combination of the POS-based restructuring and alignment-based reordering is considered in our experiment.

4.1 Corpus and system information

The Korean-Chinese (KOR-CHN) corpus is crawled from the Internet by our script[1] and we limited the length of sentence to be under 25 words. We use 990 sentences as the testing corpus. On the other hand, we use a monolingual corpus of 600k Chinese sentences to build a Chinese 3-gram language model. ICTCLAS[2] is an open source Chinese segmenter applied to delimiter the word boundaries and label with proper POS tags, while the Korean text is processed by the Korean POS tagger, HanNanum[3]. Table 1 shows the average information of each corpus. All the experiment was trained without tuning.

	Token	Avg. Length	Sentence
CHN	664,290	7.36	90,237
KOR	539,903	5.98	
KOR (9)	969,445	10.74	
KOR (22)	1,010,117	11.19	

Table 1. Summary of training corpora

4.2 Korean-Chinese machine translation

The Korean-Chinese translation system contains a reordering model in the translation model. The reordering model is trained as the default setting from the training corpus itself. The "grow-diag-final-and" symmetrization heuristic is applied in two directions word alignment. As described in the previous section, we restructured the Korean by POS tagger and applied our reordering approach to the translation system. Since the restructured Korean can be considered as a new corpus, it could be applied to our reordering method.

According to the study of Holmqvist et al. (2012), when dealing with the morphologically different language pair, reordering the morphologically richer side performs better. In the experiments, Korean was reordered and the experimental result is shown in Table 2.

From the results, applying more POS tags on the morphological analysis of Korean got a better performance and our reordering method im-

[1] http://nlp2ct.sftw.umac.mo/views/tools/WebpageCrawler
[2] http://ictclas.nlpir.org/
[3] http://semanticweb.kaist.ac.kr/home/index.php/HanNanum

proved the translation result from 14.98 to 15.50 in BLEU (Papineni et al., 2002). The combination of POS and reordering methods based on the multiple phrase tables and reordering tables got the best performance with BLEU score 17.35.

Corpus	KOR-CHN BLEU
Baseline	14.98
POS-based (9 tags)	16.61
POS-based (22 tags)	16.92
Alignment-based	15.50
POS (9 tags) + Alignment	16.71
POS (22 tags) + Alignment	17.03
POS (22 tags) + Alignment + two tables	17.35

Table 2. The translation results

4.3 Analysis and discussion

After the modification of the alignment file, the changes of size of the lexical file and the tables (phrase and reordering) file are shown in Table 3.

Tables	KOR-CHN baseline	KOR-CHN modified
Word	12.39 MB	12.52 MB
Phrase	19.41 MB	19.04 MB
Reordering	10.01 MB	9.83 MB

Table 3. The size changes of the word and phrase tables

From the table we found that the lexical extraction is bigger than the original system, but the size of phrase tables and the reordering tables decreased slightly. The result of these changes shows that our assumption is reasonable: our method can improve the quality of automatic alignment, but the phrase extracted from the corpus would decrease. The more word alignment points were generated by using our method, the more words would be extracted. But this will bring some cross alignments when dealing with two morphological different languages.

5 Conclusion

In this paper, we presented some preprocessing methods to deal with Korean, which is a morphological rich language. POS-based restructuring restores most of the Korean verbs, adjectives and adverbs to their original format. It is shown that the POS tag set with a richer taxonomy gives a higher translation result. Moreover, two runs of automatic alignment information got better results on the morphologically richer side. All of these methods can be combined together and improve the final translation. Finally, using two tables instead of one modified table in the decoding part will guarantee the translation quality if the reordering model harms the translation result.

Acknowledgments

This work is partially supported by the Research Committee of University of Macau, and Science and Technology Development Fund of Macau under the grants RG060/09-10S/CS/FST, and 057/2009/A2.

References

Amittai Axelrod, Xiaodong He, and Jianfeng Gao. 2011. Domain adaptation via pseudo in-domain data selection. In *Proceedings of the Conference on Empirical Methods in Natural Language Processing*. pages 355–362, Edinburgh, Scotland, UK.

Michael Collins, Philipp Koehn, and Ivona Kucerová. 2005. Clause restructuring for statistical machine translation. In *Proceedings of the 43rd Annual Meeting on Association for Computational Linguistics*. pages 531–540, Ann Arbor, Michigan.

Marta Ruiz Costa-jussà and José A. R. Fonollosa. 2006. Statistical machine reordering. In *Proceedings of the 2006 Conference on Empirical Methods in Natural Language Processing*, pages 70–76, Sydney, Australia.

Adriá de Gispert and José B. Mariño. 2008. On the impact of morphology in English to Spanish statistical MT. *Speech Communication*. Pages 50:1034–1046.

Maria Holmqvist, Sara Stymne, Jody Foo, and Lars Ahrenberg. 2009. Improving alignment for SMT by reordering and augmenting the training corpus. In *Proceedings of the Fourth Workshop on Statistical Machine Translation*, Athens, Greece.

Maria Holmqvist, Sara Stymne, Lars Ahrenberg, and Magnus Merkel. 2012. Alignment-based reordering for SMT. In *Proceedings of the Eight International Conference on Language Resources and Evaluation (LREC'12)*. pages 3436–3440, Istanbul, Turkey.

Nizar Habash, Owen Rambow, and Ryan Roth. 2009. MADA+TOKAN: A toolkit for arabic tokenization, diacritization, morphological disambiguation, pos tagging, stemming and lemmatization. In *Proceedings of the 2nd International Conference on Arabic Language Resources and Tools (MEDAR)*, pages 102–109, Cairo, Egypt.

Philipp Koehn. 2005. Europarl: A parallel corpus for statistical machine translation. In *Machine Translation Summit X*, pages 79-86, Phuket, Thailand.

Philipp Koehn, Hieu Hoang, Alexandra Birch, Chris Callison-Burch, Marcello Federico, Nicola Bertoldi, Brooke Cowan, Wade Shen, Christine Moran, Richard Zens, Chris Dyer, Ondrej Bojar, Alexandra Constantin, and Evan Herbst. 2007. Moses: Open source toolkit for statistical machine translation. In *Proceedings of the 45th Annual Meeting of the ACL, Demonstration session,* Prague, Czech Republic.

Philipp Koehn and Josh Schroeder. 2007. Experiments in domain adaptation for statistical machine translation. In *Proceedings of the Second Workshop on Statistical Machine Translation*, pages 224–227, Prague, Czech Republic.

Shuo Li, Derek F. Wong, and Lidia S. Chao. 2012. Korean-Chinese statistical translation model. In *Machine Learning and Cybernetics (ICMLC), 2012 International Conference*, 2:767-772, Xian, Shannxi, China.

Jin-Ji Li, Jungi Kim, Dong-Il Kim, and Jong-Hyeok Lee. 2009. Chinese syntactic reordering for adequate generation of Korean verbal phrases in Chinese-to-Korean SMT. In *Proceedings of the Fourth Workshop on Statistical Machine Translation*, pages 190–196, Athens, Greece.

Jae-Hee Lee, Seung-Wook Lee, Gumwon Hong, Young-Sook Hwang, Sang-Bum Kim, and Hae-Chang Rim. 2010. A post-processing approach to statistical word alignment reflecting alignment tendency between part-of-speeches. In *Proceedings of the 23rd International Conference on Computational Linguistics: Posters*, pages 623–629, Beijing, China.

Jonghoon Lee, Donghyeon Lee, and Gary Geunbae Lee. 2006. Improving phrase-based Korean-English statistical machine translation. In *Proceedings of the Ninth International Conference on Spoken Language Processing*, Pittsburgh, Pennsylvania.

Yanjun Ma, Nicolas Stroppa, and Andy Way. 2007. Bootstrapping word alignment via word packing. In *Proceedings of Annual Meeting-association for Computational Linguistic*, pages 304-311, Prague, Czech Republic.

Franz Josef Och and Hermann Ney. 2003. A systematic comparison of various statistical alignment models. *Computational Linguistics*, 29(1):19–51.

Kishore Papineni, Salim Roukos, Todd Ward, and Wei-Jing Zhu. 2002. BLEU: a method for automatic evaluation of machine translation. In *Proceedings of the 40th Annual Meeting on Association for Computational Linguistics*. pages 311–318, Philadelphia, USA.

Sara Stymne, Maria Holmqvist, and Lars Ahrenberg. 2008. Effects of morphological analysis in translation between German and English. In *Proceedings of the Third Workshop on Statistical Machine Translation*, pages 135–138, Columbus, Ohio, USA.

Karthik Visweswariah, Rajakrishnan Rajkumar, Ankur. Gandhe, Ananthakrishnan Ramanathan, and Jiri Navratil. 2011. A word reordering model for improved machine translation. In *Proceedings of the Conference on Empirical Methods in Natural Language Processing*, pages 486–496, Edinburgh, Scotland, UK.

Xianchao Wu, Naoaki Okazaki, Takashi Tsunakawa, and Jun'ichi Tsujii. 2008. Improving English-to-Chinese translation for technical terms using morphological information. In *Proceedings of the 8th AMTA Conference*, Hawaii, USA.

Fei Xia and Michael McCord. 2004. Improving a statistical MT system with automatically learned rewrite patterns. In *Proceedings of the 20th International Conference on Computational Linguistics*, pages 508, Geneva, Switzerland.

Building bilingual lexicon to create Dialect Tunisian corpora and adapt language model

Rahma Boujelbane
Miracl Laboratory, ANLP Research Group, University of Sfax, Tunisia
Rahma.boujelbane@gmail.com

Mariem Ellouze khemekhem
Miracl Laboratory, ANLP Research Group, University of Sfax, Tunisia
mariem.ellouze@planet.com

Siwar BenAyed
Faculty of Economics and Management of Sfax
siwar.ben.ayed@gmail.com

Lamia Hadrich Belguith
Miracl Laboratory, ANLP Research Group, University of Sfax, Tunisia
l.belguith@fsegs.rnu.tn

Abstract

Since the Tunisian revolution, Tunisian Dialect (TD) used in daily life, has became progressively used and represented in interviews, news and debate programs instead of Modern Standard Arabic (MSA). This situation has important negative consequences for natural language processing (NLP): since the spoken dialects are not officially written and do not have standard orthography, it is very costly to obtain adequate corpora to use for training NLP tools. Furthermore, there are almost no parallel corpora involving TD and MSA. In this paper, we describe the creation of Tunisian dialect text corpus as well as a method for building a bilingual dictionary, in order to create language model for speech recognition system for the Tunisian Broadcast News. So, we use explicit knowledge about the relation between TD and MSA.

1 Introduction

Recently, due to the political changes that have occurred in the Arab world, we noticed a new remarkable diversity in the media. Arabic dialects used in daily life have became progressively used and represented in interviews, news and debate programs instead of Modern Standard Arabic (MSA). In Tunisia for example, the revolution has affected not only the people but also the media. Since that, the media programs have been changed: television channels, political debates and broadcasts news have been multiplied. Therefore, this gave birth to a new kind of language. Indeed, the majority of speech is no longer on MSA but alternating between MSA and dialect. Thus, we can distinguish in the same speech, MSA words, TD words and MSA-TD words such as a word with an MSA component (stem) and dialectal affixes. This situation poses significant challenges to NLP, in fact applying NLP tools designed for MSA directly to TD yields significantly lower performance, making it imperative to direct the research to building resources and tools to process this kind of language. In our case we aim to convert this new language to text, but this process presents a series of linguistic and computational challenges some of these relate to language modeling: studying large amounts of text to learn about patterns of words in a language. This task is complicated because of the total lack of TD-MSA resources, whether parallel text or paper dictionaries. In this paper, we describe a method to create Tunisian Dialect (TD) text corpora and the associated lexical resources as well as building bilingual dictionary MSA-TD.

2 Related work

Spoken languages which have no written form can be classified as limited-resources languages. Therefore, several studies has attempted to overcome the problems of computerization of these languages. (Scherrer, 2008) in order to computerize the existing dialect in Switzerland, developed a translation system: standard German to any variety of the dialect continuum of German-speaking Switzerland. Moreover, (Shaalan et al, 2007) proposed a system of translation MSA-Egyptian dialect. For this, they tried to build a parallel corpus between Egyptian dialect and MSA-based on mapping rules EGY-MSA. Besides dialects, there are several languages from the group of limited-resources languages that do not have a relation with a well-resourced language. Indeed, (Nimaan et al., 2006) presented several scenarios to collect corpora in order to

process the Somali language: Collecting corpus from the web, automatic synthesis of texts and machine translation French-Somali. (SENG, 2010) selected news sites in Khmer to collect data in order to solicit the lack of resources in Khmer.
The literature shows that there is little work that dealt with the Tunisian Arabic, the target language of this work. (Graja et al, 2011), for example, treated the Tunisian Dialect for understanding speech. To train their system, researchers relied on manual transcripts of conversations between agents at the train station and travelers. However, a limited vocabulary is a problem if we want to model a language model for a system of recognition of television's programs with a wide and varied vocabulary.

3 Method to create Tunisian Dialect Corpora

In Arabic there are almost no parallel corpora involving TD and MSA. Therefore, Machine Translation (MT) is not easy, especially when there are no MT resources available such as naturally occurring parallel text or transfer lexicon. So, to deal with this problem, we proposed to leverage the large available annotated MSA resources by exploiting MSA/dialect similarities and addressing known differences. Our approach consists first on studying the morphological, syntactic and lexical difference by exploiting the Penn Arabic Treebank. Second, presenting these differences by developing rules and building dialectal concepts. Finally, storing these transformations into dictionaries.

3.1 Penn Arabic TreeBank corpora to create bilingual lexicon MSA-TD

Treebanks, are an important resources that allows for important research in general NLP applications. In the case of Arabic, two important treebanking efforts exist: the Penn Arabic Treebank (PATB) (Maamouri et al., 2004; Maamouri et al., 2009) and the Prague Arabic Dependency Treebank (PADT) (Smrž and Haji, 2007; Smrž et al., 2008). The PATB not only provides tokenization, complex POS tags, and syntactic structure; it also provides empty categories, diacritizations, lemma choices. The PATB consists of 23,611 parse-annotated sentences (Bies and Maamouri, 2003; Maamouri and Bies, 2004) from Arabic newswire text in MSA. The PATB annotation scheme involves 497 different POS-tags with morphological information. In this work we attempted to mitigate the genre differences by transforming the MSA-ATB to look like TD-ATB. This will allow us to create in tandem a bilingual lexicon with different dialectal concept (Figure1). For this, we adopted a transformation method based on the parts of speech of ATB's word.

Figure1- Methodology for creating TD resources

3.2 Modeling verbal lexical entries for the bilingual dictionary

As we aim to adapt MSA tools to TD, we tried to build for TD verbs the same concepts as those in MSA. Therefore, we focused in this work on the study of correspondence that may exist among the concepts of MSA verbs and dialect verbs. In Arabic there are three principal verbal concepts:
1-Root: It is the basic source of all forms of Arabic verb. The root is not a real word rather it is a sequence of three consonants that can be found in all words that are related to it. Most roots are composed of three letters, very few are of four or five consonants.
2-Pattern: In MSA, patterns are models with different structures that are applied to the root to create a lemma. For example, for the root خ ر ج: *xrj*, we can apply different patterns, which give different lemmas with different meanings
Root1*: xrj/*خ رج*/ C1C2C3+ verbal pattern1: AistaC1oC2a3 =lemma1* اِسْتَخْرَجَ*/ to extract*
Root1*: xrj/*خرج*/C1C2C3+ verbal pattern2 FoEaL(FaEal)=lemma2* خَرَجَ*/ to go out .*
Root1: *xrj (*خ رج*)/C1C2C3+ verbal pattern3 >aC1oC2aC3=lemma3* أَخْرَجَ*/ to eject*
2-Lemma: The lemma is a fundamental concept in the processing of texts in at least some languages. Arabic words can be analyzed as consisting of a root inserted into a pattern.
TD-lemma building: Verbs in the PATB corpus are presented in their inflected forms. So, we extracted lemmas and their roots using the morphological analyzer developed by Elexir FM (Smrz, 2007). As we are native speakers of TD, we associate to each MSA-Lemma a TUN-Lemma. As a result, we found that 60% of verbs change totally by passing from MSA to TD. As we have 1500 TD-Lemmas, and starting from the fact that

MSA verbs have patterns describing their morphological behavior during conjugation, we tried to assign, if possible, to each TD-Lemma a TD-Pattern.

TD-pattern building: The challenge on building TD-pattern was to find patterns similar to those in MSA. Thus, by studying the morphology of TD-lemmas, we remarked that it's possible to assign to TD-lemmas the same pattern as those on MSA but with defining other patterns that will be sub-patterns to these patterns. In fact, this process has allowed distinguishing 32 patterns for dialect verbs while there were 15 in MSA. This was due to the morphological richness and the frequent change of vowel within TD-lemmas. For example:

In MSA *$Arak/yu$Arik/to participate* and *dAfaE/yudAFiE/to defend* belongs to the *patternII: CACaC(perfectiveform)/yiCACiC* (imperfectiveform). In TD the model of these tow verbs remains *CACVC/yVCACVC* but the vowel of the second consonant of the pattern (vowel letter ع / E) change. The mark of this vowel is a fundamental criterion for classifying a verb in MSA (Ouerhani, 2009), that's why we proposed to define tow sub-pattern for the pattern II, by dividing the pattern-II to *II-i: CACiC/yVCACiC* and *II-a:CACaC/yVCACaC*. As consequence, *$Arak/yu$Arik/* becomes in TD *$Arik/yi$Arik/* belongs to *CACiC/yVCACiC* and *dAfaE/yudAFiE* becomes in TD *dAfaE/yidAFaE* belongs to *CACaC/yiVCACaC*.

Therefore, by adopting this reasoning, we succeeded with the ATB's verbs to define pattern for the TD verb. Thus, knowing these new patterns, we will be able to assign a pattern for all TD verbs.

TD-root building: In Tunisian dialect, there is no standard definition for the root. For this, construction of root dialect was not obvious, especially when the root verb changes completely through the MSA to the dialect. In fact, to define a root for TD verbs, we have adopted a deductive method. Indeed, in MSA, the rule says: root + pattern= Lemma (1). In our case, we have already defined the TD-lemma and the TD-pattern. Following rule (1), the extraction of the root is then made easy. For example, we classified the lemma إستنى */Aistan ~ aY/Wait* in the pattern *AistaCCaC then root(?) + AistaCCaC=* إستنى */ ~ YAistana~*

Following (1), the root for the verb إستنى */Aistan ~ aY/Wait* is *"نني" [NNY]*. In fact, we can say that the definition of roots is a problematic issue which could allow more discussion. According to (1), it was like we have forced the roots to be *[NNY]*. However, if we classified *Aistann ~ aY* under the pattern *AiCCaCal*, the root in this case must be *snn*. The root can also be quadrilateral سنني / snnY if we classified *Aistann~ aY* under the pattern *AiCCaCaC*. But as there's no standard, we have done in our best to be the most logical possible to define dialectal root.

3.3 Structure of verbal lexicon entries

Different verbal transformations described above are modeled and stored at a dictionary of verb as follows: to each MSA verbal block containing MSA-lemma, MSA-pattern and MSA-root will correspond TD- block which containing TD-lemma, TD-root and TD-pattern. So, knowing the pattern and the root we will able to generate automatically various inflected forms of the TUN verbs. That's why we stored in our dictionary the active and the passive form of the TD-lemma in perfective and imperfective tense. We also store the inflected forms in the imperative (CV). Figure 2 shows the structure that we have defined for the dictionary to present the TD-verbal concepts (in section 4 we will explain how we will automate the enrichment of this dictionary).

```
<DIC_TUN_VERBS_FORM>
 <LEXICAL-ENTRY POS="VERB">
<VERB ID-VERB="48">
   <MSA-LEMMA>
    <Headword-sa>عَايَنَ</Headword-MSA
    <Pattern>فاعل</Pattern>
    <Root-Msa>عين</Root-Msa>
    <Gloss lang= "fr" > Observer</Gloss>
   </MSA-LEMMA>
<TUN-VERB Sense= "1" >
<Cat-Tun-Verb Category= "TUN--VERB--I--au--yi" />
<Root-Tun-Verb>شوف</Root-Tun-Verb>
<Conjug-Tun-Verb>
<TENSE>
<FORM Type= "IV" >
<VOICE Label="Active">
<Features Val_Number_Gender="1S">
<Verb_Conj>نشُوفْ</Verb_Conj>
<Struct-Deriv>Ø+شوف+ن</Struct-Deriv>
</Features>
</VOICE>
:::
</DIC_TUN_VERBS_FORM>
```

Figure2- Verbal structure in dictionary

3.4 Modeling lexical entries for tools words in the bilingual dictionary

Tools words or syntactic tools are an area that reflects the specific syntax of the dialect. It has a large amount in the Treebank and all MSA-texts. However, their transformation was not trivial and required, for each tool a study of its different context. In our approach, we defined two kinds of transformations. The first requires the study of different context of a tool word. In fact, the same word may have different translations depending on its context. Thus, to deal with the variation of context, we developed mapping rules. Note that among these contexts, there are those that cause a change in the syntactic order of words by passing to the dialect. The second transformation is direct, the word remains unchanged whatever the context.

3.5 Context dependent transformation

We mean by transformation-based context, the passage MSA-DT which is based on transformation rules. Indeed given a word W, we say that the transformation of W is based on context if it gives a new translation whenever it changes on context. RT : X + W + Y = TDk

$$\mathbf{X} = \sum_{j=1}^{m} Wj : POSj \text{ ; } \mathbf{Y} = \sum_{i=1}^{n} Wi : POSi \text{ ; } \mathbf{k} \textbf{ varies from 1 to z ;}$$

RTk: transformation rules n°k ; POS : Part of speech ; W :word tool, TDk: Translation n°k

The transformation of a tool word may depend to the words that it precedes (X), or the following word (Y), or both. If none of the contexts is presented, then a default translation will be assigned to the word tool. For example, For the tool word *"حتى" [hatY]/So that* which have the POS: Preposition, we developed three different mapping rules depending to the context in the ATB corpora.

1- حَتَّى / HatY + verb = باش(TUN-particle) + TUN_verb
2- حَتَّى/ HatY + NEG_PART = باش(TUN-particle)+ TUN_NEG_PART
otherwise
3- حَتَّى/HatY = حَتَّى /HatY

In total, we developed 316 rules for the ATB's tools words. Figure 3 shows how we present a transformation rule in the dictionary. For each tool word we have defined a set of contexts, each context contains one or more configurations. The configuration describes the position and the part of speech of the words of context. Each context corresponds to a new translation of the tool word.

```
<PREP-MSA ID="9">
   <MSA-LEMMA>حَتَّى</MSA-LEMMA>
   <GLOSS lang="ANG ">until </GLOSS>
   <CONTEXT ID="1">
     <CONFIG ID= "1" Position="Après" PRC="DET" />
               <CONFIG ID="2" Position="Après"
                POS="NOUN">ساعة</CONFIG>
<CONFIG ID="3" Position="Après" POS="NOUN_NUM" />
       <TOKEN>
        <TUN ID="1">حَتَّى-ل</TUN>
        <TUN ID="2" POS="NOUN_NUM" />
      </TOKEN>
     </CONTEXT>
     ......
     <CONTEXT ID="6">
       .....
</Prep-MSA>
```

Figure3- Context dependent rule structure in dictionary

Syntactic transformation:
The order of the elements in the dialect sentence seems to be relatively less important than in other languages . However, the canonical word order in Tunisian verbal sentences is SVO (Subject-Verb-Object) (Baccouche , 2004). In contrast, MSA word order can have the following three forms: SVO / VSO / VOS (2).
(1) TD: الطْفُل كْتِبْ الدَرْسْ/AlTfol ktib aldars/the child wrote the lesson: SVO
(2) MSA: كتب الطفل الدرس/ktib Altfol Ald~ars/wrote the boy the lesson: VSO.
This opposition bestween the MSA and the dialect is clearer in the case of proper names. In fact, MSA order is VSO (3) while the order in TD is SVO. (Mahfoudhi, 2002)
(3) MSA: أكل القط الفئران/>akal Alqit Alfi>rAn / Cats rats
(4) TD: القط أكل الفئران/ Alqit >akal Alfi>rAn /Cats eat rats
There are other types of simple dialect sentences named nominal sentences which do not contain a verb. They have the same order in both Tunisian and MSA. For example:
MSA: حار الطقس/TaKs HAr/ weather is hot
TD: سْخُونْ الطَقْسْ/ TaKs sxuwn/ weather is hot
In our work, we discussed the syntactic level at some nominal groups. The word order is generally reversed by passing to TD. For example:
(1)MSA: ADV + ADJ:
أيضا />ayDaA/Also+ مُثَقَّف /muvaK~af/also educated
(2) TD: ADJ +ADV:
TD: ADJ/ مُثَقَّف +ADV/ زاده
(2)MSA: Noun + ADJ:
كُتُب كَثِيرة /kutubun kavira/many books

TD: ADJ + Noun:
برشا كتُب /bar$A ktub

In the dictionary, we present this kind of rule as shown in the figure 4.

```
<ADV-MSA ID="5">
<MSA-LEMMA> أَيْضً ا </MSA- LEMMA>
<GLOSS ang="ang">Also</GLOSS>
<CONTEXT ID="1">
<CONFIG ID="1" Position="Before" POS="ADJ" />
<TOKEN>
<TUN ID="1" DIC="ADJECTIVES" POS="ADJ" />
<TUN ID="2" />
<TUN ID=" زَادا<" 3 </TUN>
</TOKEN>
</CONTEXT>
```

Figure 4- Syntactic rule representation in the dictionary

3.6 Context independent transformation

In addition to the context-dependent transformations, the translation of some tools words in the corpus was direct "word to word", eg; the word remains the same regardless of the context. Figure 5 shows an example of how we represented this kind of translation in the dictionary

```
<SUB_CONJ-MSA ID="7">
<MSA-LEMMA>كَيْ</MSA-LEMMA>
<GLOSS lang="ANG">In order to
</GLOSS>
<TOKEN>
<TUN ID="1">بَاشْ</TUN>
</TOKEN>
</SUB_CONJ-MSA>
```

Figure 5- Direct translation structure in the dictionary

4 Automatic generation of Tunisian Dialect corpora

To test and improve the developed bilingual models, we tried by exploiting our dictionaries to automate the task of converting MSA corpora to a corpora with a dialect appearance.

For this, we developed a tool called Tunisian Dialect Translator (TDT) which enables to produce TD texts and to enrich the MSA-TD dictionary (Figure 6). This tool works according to the following steps:

1-Morphosyntactic annotation of MSA texts: TDT annotate each MSA text morphosyntactically by using MADA analyzer (Morphological Analyser and disambiguisator of Arabic) (Habash, 2010). MADA is a toolkit that, given a raw MSA text, adds as much lexical and morphological information as possible by disambiguating in one operation part-of-speech tags, lexemes, diacritizations and full morphological analyses.

2-Exploiting MSA-TD Dictionaries: Based on each part of speech of the MSA-word, TDT propose for each MSA structure the corresponding TD translation by exploiting the MSA-TD dictionaries.

3-Enriching lexicon: As the lexical database does not cover all Arabic words, texts resulting from the previous step are not totally translated. Therefore, in order to improve the quality of translation and to enrich our dictionaries to be well used even in other NLP application, we added to TDT a semi-automatic enrichment module. This module filters first all MSA words for which a translation has not been provided. Then, TDT assigned for them their corresponding MSA-lemmas and POS, the user proposes, if the POS is verb or noun, a TD-root and a TD-pattern (described in subsection 3.2) and the TDT proposes automatically the appropriate Tunisian lemma and it's inflected forms.

5 Evaluation

To evaluate different translations of the verbs dictionary, we asked 47 judges (native speakers) to translate a sample containing 10% of verbs in the dictionary. The evaluation consists in comparing what we have proposed as a translation of lexical items taken from the ATB with the proposals of judges who are native speakers of Tunisian dialect. The percentages calculated reflect the percentage of agreement for each verb translations between judges and the translation proposed in our lexicon. Table 1 shows the obtained results.

Verbs	Unchanged	Changed	Total
Number of verbs in the sample	52	98	150
Agreement	97,17%	63,21%	74,97%

Table 1- Evaluation of verb translation

For the same context, an MSA-Verb may have many translations. The agreement decreases for changed verbs because the judges may propose a valid translation different from what we have proposed in the dictionary. Moreover, as the translation of the majority of tool words depends on context, we asked 5 judges to translate 89 sentences containing 133 words tools. In this sample, we made some tools words repeated in the same sentence but in different context. Table

(2) gives the percentages of agreement between the translations of the judges and those of our dictionaries of tools words. The variation in percentage is due to the fact that for some words, judges do not agree among themselves. The table also shows the percentage of disagreement between judges and dictionaries.

	2 juges	3 juges	4 juges	5 juges
Agreement	72,69 %	74,53 %	71,34 %	71,23 %
Disgreement	18,79 %	15,03 %	14,28 %.	12,03 %

Table 2- Evaluation of tool word translation

In fact, the disagreement arises when no judge gives translation similar to the translation proposed in the dictionaries. But, by increasing the number of judges, the disagreement decreases which proves that our dictionaries are able to give acceptable translations by several judges

6 Conclusion

This paper presented an effort to create resources and translation tool for Tunisian dialect.

To deal with the total lack of written resource in Tunisian dialect, we described first a methodology that allowed the creation of bilingual dictionaries with in tandem TD-ATB. In fact, TD-ATB will serve as a source of insight on the phenomena that need to be addressed and as corpora to train TD-NLP tools. We focused second on describing TDT a tool to generate automatically TD corpora and to enrich semi-automatically the dictionaries we have built.

We plan to continue working on improving the TD-resources by studying the transformation of nouns. We also plan to validate our approach by measuring the ability of a language model, built on a corpus translated by our TDT tool, to model transcriptions of Tunisian broadcast news.

Experiments in progress showed that the integration of translated data improves significantly lexical coverage and perplexity of language models.

References

Bies Ann. 2002. Developing an Arabic Treebank: Methods , Guidelines , Procedures , and Tools.

Sopheap Seng, Sethserey Sam, Viet-Bac Le, Brigitte Bigi, Laurent Besacier , 2010. Reconnaissance automatique de la parole en langue khmère : quelles unités pour la modélisation du langage et la modélisation acoustique.

Diki-kidiri Marcel. 2007. Comment assurer la présence d 'une langue dans le cyberespace

Habash Nizar., Rambow Owen and Roth Ryan. MADA + TOKAN: A Toolkit for Arabic Tokenization , Diacritization , Morphological Disambiguation , POS Tagging , Stemming and Lemmatization.2009. In Proceedings of the 2nd International Conference on Arabic Language Resources and Tools (MEDAR), Cairo, Egypt.

Graja Marwa, Jaoua Maher, Belguith Lamia. 2011. Building ontologies to understand spoken, CoRR.

Maamouri Mahmoud and Bies Ann. 2004. Developing an Arabic Treebank: Methods, Guidelines, Procedures, and Tools, *Workshop on Computational Approaches to Arabic Script-based Languages, COLING.*

Mohamed Maamouri , Ann Bies , Seth Kulick , Wajdi Zaghouani , David Graff , Michael Ciul. 2010. From Speech to Trees: Applying Treebank Annotation to Arabic Broadcast News, (Lrec).

Emad Mohamed, Behrang Mohit and Kemal Oflazer 2012. Transforming Standard Arabic to Colloquial Arabic, (July), 176–180.

Abdillahi Nimaan, Pascal Nocera, Juan-Manuel orres-Moreno. 2006. Boîte à outils TAL pour des langues peu informatisées: le cas du Somali, JADT.

Ouerhani Bechir, Interférence entre le dialectal et le littéral en Tunisie: Le cas de la morphologie verbale, 75–84.

Scherrer Yyves. 2008. Transducteurs à fenêtre glissante pour l'induction lexicale, Genève

Smrž Otakar. 2007. Computational Approaches to Semitic Languages, ACL, Prague

Otakar Smrž, Viktor Bielický, Iveta Kourilová, Jakub Kráčmar, Jan Hajic, Petr Zemánek. 2008. Prague Arabic Dependency Treebank: A Word on the Million Words

A Hybrid Word Alignment Model for Phrase-Based Statistical Machine Translation

Santanu Pal*, **Sudip Kumar Naskar†** and **Sivaji Bandyopadhyay***
*Department of Computer Science & Engineering
Jadavpur University, Kolkata, India
santanu.pal.ju@gmail.com, sivaji_cse_ju@yahoo.com
† Department of Computer & System Sciences
Visva-Bharati University, Santiniketan, India
sudip.naskar@gmail.com

Abstract

This paper proposes a hybrid word alignment model for Phrase-Based Statistical Machine translation (PB-SMT). The proposed hybrid alignment model provides most informative alignment links which are offered by both unsupervised and semi-supervised word alignment models. Two unsupervised word alignment models (GIZA++ and Berkeley aligner) and a rule based aligner are combined together. The rule based aligner only aligns named entities (NEs) and chunks. The NEs are aligned through transliteration using a joint source-channel model. Chunks are aligned employing a bootstrapping approach by translating the source chunks into the target language using a baseline PB-SMT system and subsequently validating the target chunks using a fuzzy matching technique against the target corpus. All the experiments are carried out after single-tokenizing the multi-word NEs. Our best system provided significant improvements over the baseline as measured by BLEU.

1 Introduction

Word alignment is the backbone of PB-SMT system or any data driven approaches to Machine Translation (MT) and it has received a lot of attention in the area of statistical machine translation (SMT) (Brown et al., 1993; Och and Ney, 2003; Koehn et al., 2003). Word alignment is not an end task in itself and is usually used as an intermediate step in SMT. Word alignment is defined as the detection of corresponding alignment of words from parallel sentences that are translation of each other. Statistical machine translation usually suffers from many-to-many word links which existing statistical word alignment algorithms can not handle well.

The unsupervised word alignment models are based on IBM models 1–5 (Brown et al., 1993) and the HMM model (Ney and Vogel, 1996; Och and Ney, 2003). Models 3, 4 and 5 are based on fertility based models which are asymmetric. To improve alignment quality, the Berkeley Aligner is based on the symmetric property by intersecting alignments induced in each translation direction.

In the present work, we propose improvement of word alignment quality by combining three word alignment tables (i) GIZA++ alignment (ii) Berkeley Alignment and (iii) rule based alignment. Our objective is to perceive the effectiveness of the Hybrid model in word alignment by improving the quality of translation in the SMT system. In the present work, we have implemented a rule based alignment model by considering several types of chunks which are automatically extracted on the source side. Each individual source chunk is translated using a baseline PB-SMT system and validated with the target chunks on the target side. The validated source-target chunks are added in the rule based alignment table. Work has been carried out into three directions: (i) three alignment tables are combined together by taking their union; (ii) extra alignment pairs are added into the alignment table. This is a well-known practice in domain adaptation in SMT (Eck et al., 2004; Wu et al., 2008); (iii) the alignment table is updated through semi-supervised alignment technique.

The remainder of the paper is organized as follows. Section 2 discusses related work. The proposed hybrid word alignment model is described in Section 3. Section 4 presents the tools and resources used for the various experiments. Section 5 includes the results obtained, together with some analysis. Section 6 concludes and provides avenues for further work.

2 Related Works

Zhou et al. (2004) proposed a multi lingual filtering algorithm that generates bilingual chunk alignment from Chinese-English parallel corpus. The algorithm has three steps, first, from the parallel corpus; the most frequent bilingual chunks are extracted. Secondly, the participating chunks for alignments are combined into a cluster and finally one English chunk is generated corresponding to a Chinese chunk by analyzing the highest co-occurrences of English chunks. Bilingual knowledge can be extracted using chunk alignment (Zhou et. al., 2004). Pal et, al. (2012) proposed a bootstrapping method for chunk alignment; they used an SMT based model for chunk translation and then aligned the source-target chunk pairs after validating the translated chunk. Ma et. al. (2007) simplified the task of automatic word alignment as several consecutive words together correspond to a single word in the opposite language by using the word aligner itself, i.e., by bootstrapping on its output. A Maximum Entropy model based approach for English—Chinese NE alignment which significantly outperforms IBM Model4 and HMM has been proposed by Feng et al. (2004). They considered 4 features: translation score, transliteration score, source NE and target NE's co-occurrence score and the distortion score for distinguishing identical NEs in the same sentence. Moore (2003) presented an approach where capitalization cues have been used for identifying NEs on the English side. Statistical techniques are applied to decide which portion of the target language corresponds to the specified English NE, for simultaneous NE identification and translation.

To improve the learning process of unlabeled data using labeled data (Chapelle et al., 2006), the semi-supervised learning method is the most useful learning technique. Semi-supervised learning is a broader area of Machine Learning. Researchers have begun to explore semi-supervised word alignment models that use both labeled and unlabeled data. Fraser and Marcu (2006) proposed a semi-supervised training algorithm. The weighting parameters are learned from discriminative error training on labeled data, and the parameters are estimated by maximum-likelihood EM training on unlabeled data. They have also used a log-linear model which is trained on the available labeled data to improve performance. Interpolating human alignments with automatic alignments has been proposed by Callison-Burch et al. (2004), where the alignments of higher quality have gained much higher weight than the lower-quality alignments. Wu et al. (2006) have developed two separate models of standard EM algorithm which learn separately from both labeled and unlabeled data. Two models are then interpolated as a learner in the semi-supervised Ada-Boost algorithm to improve word alignment. Ambati et al. (2010) proposed active learning query strategies to identify highly uncertain or most informative alignment links under an unsupervised word alignment model.

Intuitively, multiword NEs on the source and the target sides should be both aligned in the parallel corpus and translated as a whole. However, in the state-of-the-art PB-SMT systems, the constituents of multiword NE are marked and aligned as parts of consecutive phrases, since PB-SMT (or any other approaches to SMT) does not generally treat multiword NEs as special tokens. This is the motivations behind considering NEs for special treatment in this work by converting into single tokens that makes sure that PB-SMT also treats them as a whole

Another problem with SMT systems is the erroneous word alignment. Sometimes some words are not translated in the SMT output sentence because of the mapping to NULL token or erroneous mapping during word alignment. Verb phrase translation also creates major problems. The words inside verb phrases are generally not aligned one-to-one; the alignments of the words inside source and target verb phrases are mostly many-to-many particularly so for the English—Bengali language pair.

The first objective of the present work is to see how single tokenization and alignment of NEs on both the sides affects the overall MT quality. The second objective is to see whether Hybrid word alignment model of both unsupervised and semi-supervised techniques enhance the quality of translation in the SMT system rather than the single tokenized NE level parallel corpus applied to the hybrid model.

We carried out the experiments on English—Bengali translation task. Bengali shows high morphological richness at lexical level. Language resources in Bengali are not widely available.

3 Hybrid Word Alignment Model

The hybrid word alignment model is described as the combination of three word alignment models as follows:

3.1 Word Alignment Using GIZA++

GIZA++ (Och and Ney, 2003) is a statistical word alignment tool which incorporates all the IBM 1-5 models. GIZA++ facilitates fast development of statistical machine translation (SMT) systems. In case of low-resource language pairs the quality of word alignments is typically quite low and it also deviates from the independence assumptions made by the generative models. Although huge amount of parallel data enables the model parameters to acquire better estimation, a large number of language pairs still lacks from the unavailability of sizeable amount of parallel data. GIZA++ has some draw-backs. It allows at most one source word to be aligned with each foreign word. To resolve this issue, some techniques have already been applied such as: the parallel corpus is aligned bidirectionally; then the two alignment tables are reconciled using different heuristics e.g., intersection, union, and most recently grow-diagonal-final and grow-diagonal-final-and heuristics have been applied. In spite of these heuristics, the word alignment quality for low-resource language pairs is still low and calls for further improvement. We describe our approach of improving word alignment quality in the following three subsections.

3.2 Word Alignment Using Berkley Aligner

The recent advancements in word alignment is implemented in Berkeley Aligner (Liang et al., 2006) which allows both unsupervised and supervised approach to align word from parallel corpus. We initially train the parallel corpus using unsupervised technique. We make a few manual corrections to the alignment table produced by the unsupervised aligner. Then we apply this corrected alignment table as gold standard training data for the supervised aligner. The Berkeley aligner is an extension of the Cross Expectation Maximization word aligner. Berkeley aligner is a very useful word aligner because it allows for supervised training, enabling us to derive knowledge from already aligned parallel corpus or we can use the same corpus by updating the alignments using some rule based methods. Our approach deals with the latter case. The supervised technique of Berkeley aligner helps us to align those words which could not be aligned by rule based word aligner.

3.3 Rule Based Word Alignment

The proposed Rule based aligner aligns Named Entities (NEs) and chunks. For NE alignment, we first identify NEs from the source side (i.e. English) using Stanford NER. The NEs on the target side (i.e. Bengali) are identified using a method described in (Ekbal and Bandyopadhyay, 2009). The accuracy of the Bengali Named Entity recognizers (NER) is much poorer compared to that of English NER due to several reasons: (i) there is no capitalization cue for NEs in Bengali; (ii) most of the common nouns in Bengali are frequently used as proper nouns; (iii) suffixes (case markers, plural markers, emphasizers, specifiers) get attached to proper names as well in Bengali. Bengali shallow parser[1] has been used to improve the performance of NE identification by considering proper names as NE. Therefore, NER and shallow parser are jointly employed to detect NEs from the Bengali sentences. The source NEs are then transliterated using a modified joint source-channel model (Ekbal et al., 2006) and aligned to their target side equivalents following the approach of Pal et al. (2010). The target side equivalents NEs are transformed into canonical form after omitting their '*matras*'. Similarly Bengali NEs are also transformed into canonical forms as Bengali NEs may differ in their choice of *matras* (vowel modifiers). The transliterated NEs are then matched with the corresponding parallel target NEs and finally we align the NEs if match is found.

After identification of multiword NEs on both sides, we pre-processed the corpus by replacing space with the underscore character ('_'). We have used underscore ('_') instead of hyphen ('-') since there already exists some hyphenated words in the corpus. The use of the underscore ('_') character also facilitates to de-tokenize the single-tokenized NEs after decoding.

For chunk alignment, the source sentences of the parallel corpus are parsed using Stanford POS tagger. The chunks of the sentences are extracted using CRF chunker[2]. The chunker detects the boundaries of noun, verb, adjective, adverb

[1] http://ltrc.iiit.ac.in/showfile.php?filename=downloads/shallow_parser.php

[2] http://crfchunker.sourceforge.net/

and prepositional chunks from the sentences. In case of prepositional phrase chunks, we have taken a special attention: we have expanded the prepositional phrase chunk by examining a single noun chunk followed by a preposition or a series of noun chunks separated by conjunctions such as *'comma', 'and'* etc. For each individual chunk, the head word is identified. Similarly target side sentences are parsed using a shallow parser. The individual target side Bengali chunks are extracted from the parsed sentences. The head words for all individual chunks on the target side are also marked. If the translated head word of a source chunk matches with the headword of a target chunk then we hypothesize that these two chunks are translations of each other.

The extracted source chunks are translated using a baseline SMT model trained on the same corpus. The translated chunks are validated against the target chunks found in the corresponding target sentence. During the validation process, if any match is found between the translated chunk and a target chunk then the source chunk is directly aligned with the original target chunk. Otherwise, the source chunk is ignored in the current iteration for any possible alignment and is considered in the next iterations.

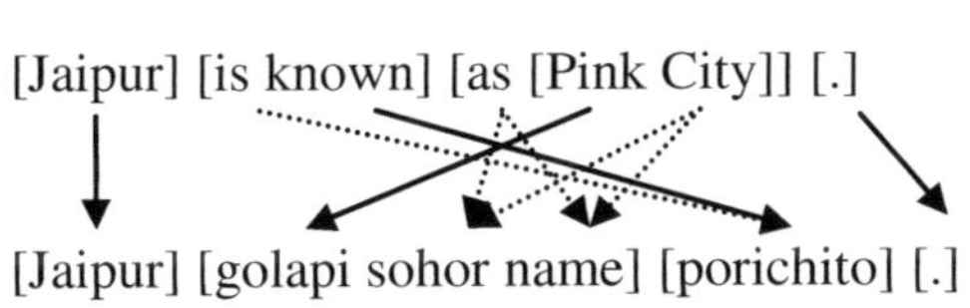

Figure 1.a: Rule based alignments

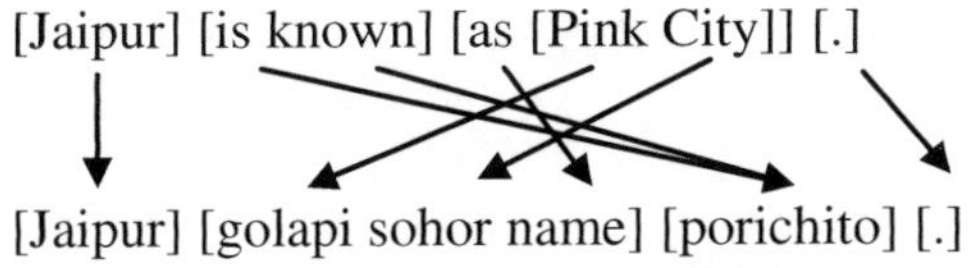

Figure 1.b: Gold standard alignments

Figure 1: Establishing alignments through Rule based methods.

The extracted chunks on the source side may not have a one to one correspondence with the target side chunks. The alignment validation process is focused on the proper identification of the head words and not between the translated source chunk and target chunk. The matching process has been carried out using a fuzzy matching technique. If both sides contain only one chunk after aligning the remaining chunks then the alignment is trivial. After aligning the individual chunks, we also establish word alignments between the matching words in those aligned chunks. Thus we get a sentence level source-target word alignment table.

Figure 1 shows how word alignments are established between a source-target sentence pair using the rule based method. Figure 1.a shows the alignments obtained through rule based method. The solid links are established through transliteration (for NEs) and translation. The dotted arrows are also probable candidates for intra-chunk word alignments; however they are not considered in the present work. Figure 1.b shows the gold standard alignments for this sentence pair.

3.4 Hybrid Word alignment Model

The hybrid word alignment method combines three different kinds of word alignments – Giza++ word alignment with grow-diag-final-and (GDFA) heuristic, Berkeley aligner and rule based aligner. We have followed two different strategies to combine the three different word alignment tables.

Union

In the union method all the alignment tables are united together and duplicate entries are removed.

ADD additional Alignments

In this method we consider either of the alignments generated by GIZA++ GDFA (A1) or Berkeley aligner (A2) as the standard alignment as the rule based aligner fails to align all words in the parallel sentences. From the three set of alignments A1, A2 and A3, we propose an alignment combination method as described in algorithm 1.

ALGORITHM: 1

Step 1: Choose either A1 or A2 as the standard alignment (SA).
Step 2: Correct the alignments in SA using the alignment table of A3.
Step 3: if A2 is considered as SA then find additional alignment from A1 and A3 using intersection method ($A1 \cap A3$) otherwise find additional alignment from A2 and A3 (using $A2 \cap A3$).
Step 4: Add additional entries with SA.

3.5 Berkeley Semi-supervised Alignment

The correctness of the alignments is verified by manually checking the performance of the various alignment system. We start with the combined alignment table which is produced by Algorithm 1. Iinitially, we take a subset of the alignments by manually inspecting from the combined alignment table. Then we train the Barkley supervised aligner with this labeled data. A subset of the unlabeled data from the combined alignment table is tested with the supervised model. The output is then added as additional labeled training data for the supervised training method for the next iteration. Using this bootstrapping approach, the amount of labeled training data for the supervised aligner is gradually increased. The process is continued until there are no more unlabelled training data. In this way we tune the whole alignment table for the entire parallel corpus. The process is carried out in a semi-supervised manner.

4 Tools and resources Used

A sentence-aligned English-Bengali parallel corpus containing 23,492 parallel sentences from the travel and tourism domain has been used in the present work. The corpus has been collected from the consortium-mode project "Development of English to Indian Languages Machine Translation (EILMT) System - Phase II"[3]. The Stanford Parser[4] and CRF chunker[5] have been used for identifying chunks and Stanford NER has been used to identify named entities in the source side of the parallel corpus.

The target side (Bengali) sentences are parsed by using the tools obtained from the consortium mode project "Development of Indian Language to Indian Language Machine Translation (IL-ILMT) System - Phase II[6]".

The effectiveness of the present work has been tested by using the standard log-linear PB-SMT model as our baseline system: phrase-extraction heuristics described in (Koehn et al., 2003), , MERT (minimum-error-rate training) (Och, 2003) on a held-out development set, target language model trained using SRILM toolkit (Stolcke, 2002) with Kneser-Ney smoothing (Kneser and Ney, 1995) and the Moses decoder (Koehn et al., 2007) have been used in the present study.

5 Experiments and Results

We have randomly selected 500 sentences each for the development set and the test set from the initial parallel corpus. The rest are considered as the training corpus. The training corpus was filtered with the maximum allowable sentence length of 100 words and sentence length ratio of 1:2 (either way). Finally the training corpus contained 22,492 sentences. In addition to the target side of the parallel corpus, a monolingual Bengali corpus containing 488,026 words from the tourism domain was used for building the target language model. We experimented with different n-gram settings for the language model and the maximum phrase length and found that a 4-gram language model and a maximum phrase length of 7 produced the optimum baseline result. We carried out the rest of the experiments using these settings.

We experimented with the system over various combinations of word alignment models. Our hypothesis focuses mainly on the theme that proper alignment of words will result in improvement of the system performance in terms of translation quality.

141,821 chunks were identified from the source corpus, of which 96,438 (68%) chunks were aligned by the system. 39,931 and 28,107 NEs were identified from the source and target sides of the parallel corpus respectively, of which 22,273 NEs are unique in English and 22,010 NEs in Bengali. A total of 14,023 NEs have been aligned through transliteration.

The experiments have been carried out with various experimental settings: (i) single tokenization of NEs on both sides of the parallel corpus, (ii) using Berkeley Aligner with unsupervised training, (iii) union of the three alignment models: rule based, GIZA++ with GDFA and Berkeley Alignment, (iv) hybridization of the three alignment models and (v) supervised Berkeley Aligner. Eextrinsic evaluation was carried out on the MT quality using BLEU (Papineni et al., 2002) and NIST (Doddington, 2002).

[3] The EILMT project is funded by the Department of Electronics and Information Technology (DEITY), Ministry of Communications and Information Technology (MCIT), Government of India.

[4] http://nlp.stanford.edu/software/lex-parser.shtml

[5] http://crfchunker.sourceforge.net/

[6] The IL-ILMT project is funded by the Department of Electronics and Information Technology (DEITY), Ministry of Communications and Information Technology (MCIT), Government of India.

Experiment	Exp no.	BLEU	NIST
Baseline system using GIZA++ with GDFA	1	10.92	4.13
PB-SMT system using Berkeley Aligner	2	11.42	4.16
Union of all Alignments	3	11.12	4.14
PB-SMT System with Hybrid Alignment by considering (a) GIZA++ as the standard alignment) (b) Berkeley alignment as the standard alignment)	4a†	15.38	4.30
	4b†	15.92	4.36
Single tokenized NE + Exp 1	5	11.68	4.17
Single tokenized NE + Exp 2	6	11.82	4.19
Single tokenized NE + (a) Exp 4a (b) Exp 4b	7a†	16.58	4.45
	7b†	17.12	4.49
PB-SMT System with semi-supervised Berkeley Aligner + Single tokenized NE	8†	**20.87**	**4.71**

Table: 1 Evaluation results for different experimental setups. (The '†' marked systems produce statistically significant improvements on BLEU over the baseline system)

The baseline system (Exp 1) is the state-of-art PB-SMT system where GIZA++ with grow-diag-final-and has been used as the word alignment model. Experiment 2 provides better results than experiment 1 which signifies that Berkeley Aligner performs better than GIZA++ for the English-Bengali translation task. The union of all thee alignments (Exp 3) provides better scores than the baseline; however it cannot beat the results obtained with the Berkeley Aligner alone.

Hybrid alignment model with GIZA++ as the standard alignment (Exp 4a) produces statistically significant improvements over the baseline. Similarly the use of Berkeley Aligner as the standard alignment for hybrid alignment model (Exp 4b) also results in statistically significant improvements over Exp 2. These two experiments (Exp 4a and 4b) demonstrate the effectiveness of the hybrid alignment model. It is to be noticed that hybrid alignment model works better with the Berkeley Aligner than with GIZA++.

Single-tokenization of the NEs (Exp 5, 6, 7a and 7b) improves the system performance to some extent over the corresponding experiments without single-tokenization (Exp 1, 2, 4a and 4b); however, these improvements are not statistically significant. The Berkeley semi-supervised alignment method using a bootstrapping approach together with single-tokenization of NEs provided the overall best performance in terms of both BLEU and NIST and the corresponding improvement is statistically significant on BLEU over rest of the experiments.

6 Conclusion and Future Work

The paper proposes a hybrid word alignment model for PB-SMT. The paper also shows how effective pre-processing of NEs in the parallel corpus and direct incorporation of their alignment in the word alignment model can improve SMT system performance. In data driven approaches to MT, specifically for scarce resource data, this approach can help to upgrade the state-of-art machine translation quality as well as the word alignment quality. . The hybrid model with the use of the semi-supervised technique of the Berkeley word aligner in a bootstrapping manner, together with single tokenization of NEs, provides substantial improvements (9.95 BLEU points absolute, 91.1% relative) over the baseline. On manual inspection of the output we found that our best system provides more accurate lexical choice as well as better word ordering than the baseline system.

As future work we would like to explore how to get the best out of multiple word alignments. Furthermore, integrating the knowledge about multi-word expressions into the word alignment models is another future direction for this work.

Acknowledgement

The work has been carried out with support from the project "Development of English to Indian Languages Machine Translation (EILMT) System - Phase II" funded by Department of Information Technology, Government of India.

References

Alexander Fraser and Daniel Marcu. 2006. Semi-supervised training for statistical word alignment. In ACL-44: Proceedings of the 21st International Conference on Computational Linguistics and the 44th annual meeting of the Association for Computational Linguistics (ACL-2006), Morristown, NJ, USA. pages 769–776.

Brown, Peter F., Stephen A. Della Pietra, Vincent J. Della Pietra, and Robert L. Mercer. 1993. The mathematics of statistical machine translation: parameter estimation. Computational Linguistics, 19(2):263-311.

Chris Callison-Burch, David Talbot, and Miles Osborne. 2004. Statistical machine translation with word- and sentence-aligned parallel corpora. In ACL 2004, page 175, Morristown, NJ, USA. Association for Computational Linguistics.

Dempster, A.P., N.M. Laird, and D.B. Rubin. 1977). Maximum Likelihood from Incomplete Data via the EM Algorithm. Journal of the Royal Statistical Society, Series B (Methodological) 39 (1): 1–38.

Doddington, George. 2002. Automatic evaluation of machine translation quality using n-gram cooccurrence statistics. In Proceedings of the Second International Conference on Human Language Technology Research (HLT-2002), San Diego, CA, pp. 128-132.

Eck, Matthias, Stephan Vogel, and Alex Waibel. 2004. Improving statistical machine translation in the medical domain using the Unified Medical Language System. In Proc. of the 20th International Conference on Computational Linguistics (COLING 2004), Geneva, Switzerland, pp. 792-798.

Ekbal, Asif, and Sivaji Bandyopadhyay. 2008. Maximum Entropy Approach for Named Entity Recognition in Indian Languages. International Journal for Computer Processing of Languages (IJCPOL), Vol. 21 (3), 205-237.

Ekbal, Asif, and Sivaji Bandyopadhyay. 2009. Voted NER system using appropriate unlabeled data. In proceedings of the ACL-IJCNLP-2009 Named Entities Workshop (NEWS 2009), Suntec, Singapore, pp.202-210.

Feng, Donghui, Yajuan Lv, and Ming Zhou. 2004. A new approach for English-Chinese named entity alignment. In Proceedings of the 2004 Conference on Empirical Methods in Natural Language Processing (EMNLP-2004), Barcelona, Spain, pp. 372-379.

Feng, Donghui, Yajuan Lv, and Ming Zhou. 2004. A new approach for English-Chinese named entity alignment. In Proceedings of the 2004 Conference on Empirical Methods in Natural Language Processing (EMNLP-2004), Barcelona, Spain, pp. 372-379.

Franz Josef Och and Hermann Ney. 2003. A systematic comparison of various statistical alignment models. Computational Linguistics, pages 19–51.

Huang, Fei, Stephan Vogel, and Alex Waibel. 2003. Automatic extraction of named entity translingual equivalence based on multi-feature cost minimization. In Proceedings of the ACL-2003 Workshop on Multilingual and Mixed-language Named Entity Recognition, 2003, Sapporo, Japan, pp. 9-16.

HuaWu, HaifengWang, and Zhanyi Liu. 2006. Boosting statistical word alignment using labeled and unlabeled data. In Proceedings of the COLING/ACL on Main conference poster sessions, pages 913–920, Morristown, NJ, USA. Association for Computational Linguistics.

Kneser, Reinhard, and Hermann Ney. 1995. Improved backing-off for m-gram language modeling. In Proceedings of the IEEE Internation Conference on Acoustics, Speech, and Signal Processing (ICASSP), vol. 1, pp. 181–184. Detroit, MI.

Koehn, Philipp, Franz Josef Och, and Daniel Marcu. 2003. Statistical phrase-based translation. In Proceedings of HLT-NAACL 2003: conference combining Human Language Technology conference series and the North American Chapter of the Association for Computational Linguistics conference series, Edmonton, Canada, pp. 48-54.

Koehn, Philipp, Hieu Hoang, Alexandra Birch, Chris Callison-Burch, Marcello Federico, Nicola Bertoldi, Brooke Cowan, Wade Shen, Christine Moran, Richard Zens, Chris Dyer, Ondřej Bojar, Alexandra Constantin, and Evan Herbst. 2007. Moses: open source toolkit for statistical machine translation. In Proceedings of the 45th Annual meeting of the Association for Computational Linguistics (ACL 2007): Proceedings of demo and poster sessions, Prague, Czech Republic, pp. 177-180.

Koehn, Philipp. 2004. Statistical significance tests for machine translation evaluation. In EMNLP-2004:

Proceedings of the 2004 Conference on Empirical Methods in Natural Language Processing, 25-26 July 2004, Barcelona, Spain, pp 388-395.

O. Chapelle, B. Sch¨olkopf, and A. Zien, editors. 2006. Semi-Supervised Learning. MIT Press, Cambridge, MA.

Och, Franz J. 2003. Minimum error rate training in statistical machine translation. In Proceedings of the 41st Annual Meeting of the Association for Computational Linguistics (ACL-2003), Sapporo, Japan, pp. 160-167.

Pal, Santanu, Sivaji Bandyopadhyay. 2012, "Bootstrapping Chunk Alignment in Phrase-Based Statistical Machine Translation", Joint Workshop on Exploiting Synergies between Information Retrieval and Machine Translation (ESIRMT) and Hybrid Approaches to Machine Translation (HyTra), EACL-2012, Avignon, France, pp. 93-100 .

Pal, Santanu., Sudip Kumar Naskar, Pavel Pecina, Sivaji Bandyopadhyay and Andy Way. 2010, Handling Named Entities and Compound Verbs in Phrase-Based Statistical Machine Translation, In proc. of the workshop on Multiword expression: from theory to application (MWE-2010), The 23rd International conference of computational linguistics (Coling 2010),Beijing, Chaina, pp. 46-54.

Papineni, Kishore, Salim Roukos, Todd Ward, and Wei-Jing Zhu. 2002. BLEU: a method for automatic evaluation of machine translation. In Proceedings of the 40th Annual Meeting of the Association for Computational Linguistics (ACL-2002), Philadelphia, PA, pp. 311-318.

Percy Liang, Ben Taskar, Dan Klein. 2006. 6th Proceedings of the main conference on Human Language Technology Conference of the North American Chapter of the Association of Computational Linguistics, HLT-NAACL-2006, Pages 104-111

Stolcke, A. SRILM—An Extensible Language Modeling Toolkit. Proc. Intl. Conf. on Spoken Language Processing, vol. 2, pp. 901–904, Denver (2002).

Vamshi Ambati, Stephan Vogel, Jaime Carbonell. 2010, 10th Proceedings of the NAACL HLT 2010 Workshop on Active Learning for Natural Language Processing (ALNLP-2010), Pages 10-17.

Vogel, Stephan, Hermann Ney, and Christoph Tillmann. 1996. HMM-based word alignment in statistical translation. In Proc. of the 16th International Conference on Computational Linguistics (COLING 1996), Copenhagen, pp. 836-841.

Wu, Hua Haifeng Wang, and Chengqing Zong. 2008. Domain adaptation for statistical machine translation with domain dictionary and monolingual corpora. In Proc. of the 22nd International Conference on Computational Linguistics (COLING 2008), Manchester, UK, pp. 993-1000.

X. Zhu. 2005. Semi-Supervised Learning Literature Survey. Technical Report 1530, Computer Sciences, University of Wisconsin-Madison. http://www.cs.wisc.edu/_jerryzhu/pub/ssl_survey.pdf.

Lexical Selection for Hybrid MT with Sequence Labeling

Alex Rudnick and Michael Gasser
Indiana University, School of Informatics and Computing
{alexr,gasser}@indiana.edu

Abstract

We present initial work on an inexpensive approach for building large-vocabulary lexical selection modules for hybrid RBMT systems by framing lexical selection as a sequence labeling problem. We submit that Maximum Entropy Markov Models (MEMMs) are a sensible formalism for this problem, due to their ability to take into account many features of the source text, and show how we can build a combination MEMM/HMM system that allows MT system implementors flexibility regarding which words have their lexical choices modeled with classifiers. We present initial results showing successful use of this system both in translating English to Spanish and Spanish to Guarani.

1 Introduction

Lexical ambiguity presents a serious challenge for rule-based machine translation (RBMT) systems, since many words have several possible translations in a given target language, and more than one of them may be syntactically valid in context. A translation system must choose a translation for each word or phrase in the input sentence, and simply taking the most common translation will often fail, as a word in the source language may have translations in the target language with significantly different meanings. Even when choosing among near-synonyms, we would like to respect selectional preferences and common collocations to produce natural-sounding output text.

Writing lexical selection rules by hand is tedious and error-prone; even if informants familiar with both languages are available, they may not be able to enumerate the contexts under which they would choose one translation alternative over another. Thus we would like to learn from corpora where possible.

Framing the resolution of lexical ambiguities in machine translation as an explicit classification task has a long history, dating back at least to early SMT work at IBM (Brown et al., 1991). More recently, Carpuat and Wu have shown how to use word-sense disambiguation techniques to improve modern phrase-based SMT systems (Carpuat and Wu, 2007), even though the language model and phrase tables of these systems can mitigate the problem of lexical ambiguities somewhat. Treating lexical selection as a word-sense disambiguation problem, in which the sense inventory for each source-language word is its set of possible translations, is often called cross-lingual WSD (CL-WSD). This framing has received enough attention to warrant shared tasks at recent SemEval workshops; the most recent running of the task is described in (Lefever and Hoste, 2013).

Intuitively, machine translation implies an "all-words" WSD task: we need to choose a translation for every word or phrase in the source sentence, and the sequence of translations should make sense taken together. Here we begin to explore CL-WSD not just as a classification task, but as one of sequence labeling. We describe our approach and implementation, and present two experiments. In the first experiment, we apply the system to the SemEval 2013 shared task on CL-WSD (Lefever and Hoste, 2013), translating from English to Spanish, and in the second, we perform an all-words labeling task, translating text from the Bible from Spanish to Guarani. This is work in progress and our code is currently "research-quality", but we are developing the software in the open[1], with the intention of using it with free RBMT systems and producing an easily reusable package as the system matures.

[1] http://github.com/alexrudnick/clwsd

2 Related Work

To our knowledge, there has not been work specifically on sequence labeling applied to lexical selection for RBMT systems. However, there has been work recently on using WSD techniques for translation into lower-resourced languages, such as the English-Slovene language pair, as in (Vintar et al., 2012).

The Apertium team has a particular practical interest in improving lexical selection in RBMT; they recently have been developing a new system, described in (Tyers et al., 2012), that learns finite-state transducers for lexical selection from the available parallel corpora. It is intended to be both very fast, for use in practical translation systems, and to produce lexical selection rules that are understandable and modifiable by humans.

Outside of the CL-WSD setting, there has been work on framing all-words WSD as a sequence labeling problem. Particularly, Molina *et al.* (2002) have made use of HMMs for all-words WSD in a monolingual setting.

3 Sequence Labeling with HMMs

In building a sequence-based CL-WSD system, we first tried using the familiar HMM formalism. An HMM is a generative model, giving us a formula for $P(S,T) = P(T) * P(S|T)$. Here by S we mean a sequence of source-language words, and by T we mean a sequence words or phrases in the target language. In practice, the input sequence S is a given, and we want to find the sequence T that maximizes the joint probability, which means predicting an appropriate label for each word in the input sequence.

Using the (first-order) Markov assumption, we approximate $P(T)$ as $P(T) = \prod_i P(t_i|t_{i-1})$, where i denotes each index in the input sentence. Then we imagine that each source-language word s_i is generated by the corresponding unobserved label t_i, through the emission probabilities $P(s|t)$. This generative model is admittedly less intuitive for CL-WSD than for POS-tagging (where it is more traditionally applied), in that it requires the target-language words to be generated in the source order.

Training the transition model – roughly an n-gram language model – for target-language words or phrases in the source order is straightforward with sentence-aligned bitext. We use one-to-many alignments in which each source word corresponds with zero or more target-language words, and we take the sequence of target-language words aligned with a given source word to be its label. NULL labels are common; if a source word is not aligned to a target word, it gets a NULL label. Similarly , we can learn the emission probabilities, $P(s|t)$, simply by counting which source words are paired with which target words and smoothing.

For decoding with this model, we can use the Viterbi algorithm, especially for a first-order Markov model – although we must be careful in the inner loops only to consider the possible target-language words and not the entire target-language vocabulary. The Viterbi algorithm may still be used with second- or higher-order models, although it slows down considerably. In the interest of speed, in this work we performed decoding for second-order HMMs with a beam search.

4 Sequence Labeling With MEMMs and HMMs

Contrastingly, an MEMM is a discriminative sequence model, with which we can calculate the conditional probability $P(T|S)$ using individual discriminative classifiers that model $P(t_i|F)$ (for some features F). Like an HMM, an MEMM models transitions over labels, although the input sequence is considered given. This frees us to include any features we like from the source-language sentence. The "Markov" aspect of the MEMM is that, unlike a standard maximum entropy classifier, we can include information from the previous k labels as features, for a k-th order MEMM. So at every step in the sequence labeling, we want a classifier that models $P(t_i|S, t_{i-1} ... t_{i-k})$, and the probability of a sequence T is just the product of each of the individual transition probabilities.

To avoid the intractable task of building a single classifier that might return thousands of different labels, we could in principle build a classifier for each individual word in the source-language vocabulary, each of which will produce perhaps tens of possible target-language labels. However, there will be tens or hundreds of thousands of words in the source-language vocabulary, and most word-types will only occur very rarely; it may be prohibitively expensive to train and store classifiers for each of them.

We would like a way to focus our efforts on some words, but not all, and to back off to a simpler model when a classifier is not available for a given word. Here, in order to approximate $P(t_i|S, t_{i-1}...t_{i-k})$, we use an HMM, as described in the previous section, with which we can estimate $P(s_i, t_i|t_{i-1}...t_{i-k})$ as $P(t_i|t_{i-1}...t_{i-k}) * P(s_i|t_i)$. This gives us the joint probability, which we divide by $P(s_i)$ – prior probabilities of each source-language word must be stored ahead of time – and thus we can approximate the conditional probability that we need to continue the sequence labeling.

In the implementation, we can specify criteria under which a source-language word will have its translations explicitly modeled with a maximum entropy classifier. When training a system, one might choose, for example, the 100 most common ambiguous words, all words that are observed a certain number of times in the training corpus, or words that are particularly of interest for some other reason.

At training time, we find all of the instances of the words that we want to model with classifiers, along with their contexts, so that we can extract appropriate features for training the classifiers. Then we train classifiers for those words, and store the classifiers in a database for retrieval at inference time.

For inference with this model, we use a beam search rather than the Viterbi algorithm, for convenience and speed while using a second-order Markov model. A sketch of the beam search implementation is presented in Figure 1.

5 Experiments

So far, we have evaluated our sequence-labeling system in two different settings, the English-Spanish subset of a recent SemEval shared task (Lefever and Hoste, 2013), and an all-words prediction task in which we want to translate, from Spanish to Guarani, each word in a test set sampled from the Bible.

5.1 SemEval CL-WSD task

In the SemEval CL-WSD task, systems must provide translations for twenty ambiguous English nouns given a small amount of context, typically a single sentence. The test set for this task consists of fifty short passages for each ambiguous word, for a thousand test instances in total. Each passage contains one or a few uses of the ambiguous word. For each test passage, the system must produce a translation of the noun of interest into the target language. These translations may be a single word or a short phrase in the target language, and they should be lemmatized. The task allows systems to produce several output labels, although the scoring metric encourages producing one best guess, which is matched against several reference translations provided by human annotators. The details of the scoring are provided in the task description paper, and the scores reported were calculated with a script provided by the task organizers.

As a concrete example, consider the following sentences from the test set:

(1) But a quick look at today's *letters* to the editor in the Times suggest that here at least is one department of the paper that could use a little more fact-checking.

(2) All over the ice were little Cohens, little Levys, their names sewed in block *letters* on the backs of their jerseys.

A system should produce *carta* (a message or document) for Sentence (1) and *letra* or *carácter* (a symbol or handwriting) for (2). During sequence labeling, our system chooses a translation for each word in the sentence, but the scoring only takes into account the translations for the words marked in italics.

For simplicity and comparability with previous work, we trained our system on the Europarl Intersection corpus, which was provided for developing CL-WSD systems in the shared task. The Europarl Intersection is a subset of the sentences from Europarl (Koehn, 2005) that are available in English and all five of the target languages for the task, although for these initial experiments, we only worked with Spanish. There were 884603 sentences in our training corpus.

We preprocess the Europarl training data by tokenizing with the default NLTK tokenizer (Bird et al., 2009), getting part-of-speech tags for the English text with the Stanford Tagger (Toutanova et al., 2003), and lemmatizing both sides with TreeTagger (Schmid, 1995). We aligned the untagged English text with the Spanish text using the Berkeley Aligner (DeNero and Klein, 2007) to get one-to-many alignments from English to Spanish, since the target-language labels in this setting may be multi-word phrases. We used nearly the default settings for Berkeley Aligner, except that we

```
def beam_search(sequence, HMM, source_word_priors, classifiers):
    """Search over possible label sequences, return the best one we find."""
    candidates = [Candidate([], 0)] # empty label sequence with 0 penalty
    for t in range(len(sequence)):
        sourceword = sequence[t]
        for candidate in candidates:
            context = candidate.get_context(t) # labels at positions (t-2, t-1)
            if sourceword in classifiers:
                features = extract_features(sequence, t, context)
                label_distribution = classifiers[sourceword].prob_classify(features)
            else:
                label_distribution = Distribution()
                for label in get_vocabulary(sourceword):
                    label_distribution[label] = (HMM.transition(context, label) +
                                                 HMM.emission(sourceword, label) -
                                                 source_word_priors[sourceword])
            # extend candidates for next time step to include labels for next word
            add_new_candidates(candidate, label_distribution, new_candidates)
        candidates = filter_top_k(new_candidates, BEAMWIDTH)
    return get_best(candidates)
```

Figure 1: Python-style code sketch for MEMM/HMM beam search. Here we are using negative log-probabilities, which we interpret as penalties to be minimized.

ran 20 iterations each of IBM Model 1 and HMM alignment.

We trained classifiers for all of the test words, and also for any words that appear more than 500 times in the corpus. The classifiers used the previous two labels and all of the tagged, lemmatized words within three tokens on either side of the target word as features. Training was done with the MEGA Model optimization package [2] and its corresponding NLTK interface.

At testing time, for each test instance, we labeled the test sentences with four different sequence labeling methods: first-order HMMs, second-order HMMs, MaxEnt classifiers with no sequence features, and the MEMMs with HMM backoff. We then compared the system output against the reference translations for the target words using the script provided by the task organizers.

5.2 All-words Lexical Selection for Spanish-Guarani

Since we are primarily interested in lexical selection for RBMT systems in lower-resource settings, we also experimented with translating from Spanish to Guarani, using the Bible as bitext. In this experiment, we labeled all of the text in the test set using each of the different sequence labeling models, and we report the classification accuracy over the test set.

For example, for the following sentences – from Isaiah and Psalms, respectively – the system should predict the corresponding Guarani roots for each Spanish word. Here we show the inflected Spanish and Guarani text with English translation for the sake of readability, although the system was given the roots of the Spanish words as produced by the morphological analyzer.

(3) a. Plantaréis viñas y *comeréis* su fruto.
    b. Peñotỹ parral ha *pe'u* hi'a.
    c. You will plant vineyards and *eat* their fruit.

(4) a. *Comieron* y se saciaron.
    b. *Okaru* hikuái hyguãtã meve.
    c. They *ate* and were well filled.

In this example, the correct translation of *comer* depends on transitivity: if transitive, it should be an inflected form of *'u* as in (3), if intransitive it should be *karu*, as in (4).

In preparing the corpus, since different translations of the Bible do not necessarily have direct correspondences between verse numbers (they are not unique identifiers across language!), we selected only the chapters that contain the same number of verses in our Spanish and Guarani translations. This only leaves 879 chapters out of 1189, for a total of 22828 bitext verses of roughly one sentence each. We randomly sampled 100 verses from the corpus and set these aside as the test set.

[2] http://www.umiacs.umd.edu/~hal/megam/

Here we trained the HMM and MEMM as before, but with lemmatized Spanish as the source language, and the roots of Guarani words as the target. As Guarani is a much more morphologically rich language than either English or Spanish, this requires the use of a sophisticated morphological analyzer, described in section 6. Due to the much smaller data set, in this setting we stored classifiers for any Spanish word that occurs more than 20 times in the training data and backed off to the HMM during decoding otherwise.

6 Morphological Analysis for Guarani

We analyze the Spanish and Guarani Bible using our in-house morphological analyzer, originally developed for Ethiopian Semitic languages (Gasser, 2009). As in other, more familiar, modern morphological analyzers such as (Beesley and Karttunen, 2003), analysis in our system is modeled by cascades of finite-state transducers (FSTs). To solve the problem of long-distance dependencies, we extend the basic FST framework using an idea introduced by Amtrup (2003). Amtrup starts with the well-understood framework of weighted FSTs, familiar from speech recognition. For speech recognition, FST arcs are weighted with probabilities, and a successful traversal of a path through a transducer results in a probability that is the product of the probabilities on the arcs that are traversed, as well as an output string as in conventional transducers. Amtrup showed that probabilities could be replaced by feature structures and multiplication by unification. In an FST weighted with feature structures, the result of a successful traversal is the unification of the feature structure "weights" on the traversed arcs, as well as an output string. Because a feature structure is accumulated during the process of transduction, the transducer retains a sort of memory of where it has been, permitting the incorporation of long-distance constraints such as those relating the negative prefix and suffix of Guarani verbs.

In our system, the output of the morphological analysis of a word is a root and a feature structure representing the grammatical features of the word. We implemented separate FSTs for Spanish verbs, for Guarani nouns, and for the two main categories of Guarani verbs and adjectives. Since Spanish nouns and adjectives have very few forms, we simply list the alternatives in the lexicon for these categories. For this paper, we are only concerned with the roots of words in our corpora, so we ignore the grammatical features that are output with each word.

7 Results

The scores for the first experiment are presented in Figure 2. Here we use the precision metric calculated by the scripts for the SemEval shared task (Lefever and Hoste, 2013), which compare the answers produced by the system against several reference answers given by human annotators. There are two "most frequent sense" baselines reported. The first one ("with tag"), is the baseline in which we always take the most frequent label for a given source word, conditioned on its POS tag. The other MFS baseline is not conditioned on POS tag; this was the baseline for the SemEval task. Perhaps unsurprisingly, we see part-of-speech tagging doing some of the lexical disambiguation work.

Neither of the HMM systems beat the most-frequent-sense baselines, but both the non-sequence MaxEnt classifier and the MEMM system did, which suggests that the window features are useful in selecting target-language words. Furthermore, the MEMM system outperforms the MaxEnt classifiers.

The scores for the second experiment are presented in Figure 3. Here we did not have human-annotated reference translations for each word, so we take the labels extracted from the alignments as ground truth and can only report per-word classification accuracy, rather than the more sophisticated precision metric used in the shared task.

Here we see similar results. Neither of the HMM systems beat the MFS baseline, and the trigram model was noticeably worse. The training set here is probably too sparse to train a good trigram model. The MEMM system, however, did beat the baseline, posting the highest results: just over two-thirds of the time, we were able to predict the correct label for each Spanish word, whereas the most frequent label was correct about 60% of the time.

8 Conclusions and Future Work

We have described a work-in-progress lexical selection system that takes a sequence labeling approach, and shown some initial successes in using it for cross-language word sense disambiguation tasks for English to Spanish and Spanish to Guarani. We have demonstrated a hybrid se-

system	features	score (precision)
MFS (with tag)		24.97
MFS (without tag)		23.23
HMM1	current word, previous label	21.17
HMM2	current word, previous two labels	21.23
MaxEnt	three-word window	25.64
MEMM	three-word window, previous two labels	**26.49**

Figure 2: Results for the first experiment; SemEval 2013 CL-WSD task.

system	features	score (accuracy %)
MFS		60.39
HMM1	current word, previous label	57.40
HMM2	current word, previous two labels	43.04
MEMM	three-word window, previous two labels	**66.82**

Figure 3: Results for the second experiment; all-words lexical selection on the Guarani Bible

quence labeling strategy that combines MEMMs and HMMs, which will allow users to set parameters sensibly for their computational resources and available training data.

In future work, we will continue to refine the approach, exploring different parameter settings, such as beam widths, numbers of classifiers for the MEMM component, and the effects of different features as input to the classifiers. We are also interested in making use of multilingual information sources, as in the work of Lefever and Hoste (2011). We may also consider more sophisticated sequence tagging models, such as CRFs (Lafferty et al., 2001), although we may not have enough training data to make use of richer models.

Our goal for this work is practical; we are trying to produce a hybrid Spanish-Guarani MT system that can be used in Paraguay. We have a small amount of Guarani training data available, and plan to collect more. At the time of writing, our lexical selection system is a prototype and not yet integrated with our RBMT engine, but this integration is among our near-term goals.

A limitation of the current design is that we do not yet have a good way to make use of monolingual training data. In SMT, it is common practice to train a language model for the target language from a monolingual corpus that is much larger than the available bitext. There is a substantial amount of available Guarani text on the Web, but our current model can only be trained on aligned bitext. Given Guarani text that had been rearranged into a Spanish-like word order, we could build a better model for the transition probabilities in the HMM component of the system. It might be feasible to use a Guarani-language parser and some linguistic knowledge for this purpose. We will also investigate ways to translate multiword expressions as a unit rather than word-by-word.

References

Jan Amtrup. 2003. Morphology in machine translation systems: Efficient integration of finite state transducers and feature structure descriptions. *Machine Translation*, 18.

Kenneth R. Beesley and Lauri Karttunen. 2003. *Finite State Morphology*. CSLI Publications.

Steven Bird, Ewan Klein, and Edward Loper. 2009. *Natural Language Processing with Python*. O'Reilly Media.

Peter F. Brown, Stephen A. Della Pietra, Vincent J. Della Pietra, and Robert L. Mercer. 1991. Word-Sense Disambiguation Using Statistical Methods. In *Proceedings of the 29th Annual Meeting of the Association for Computational Linguistics*.

Marine Carpuat and Dekai Wu. 2007. How Phrase Sense Disambiguation Outperforms Word Sense Disambiguation for Statistical Machine Translation. In *11th Conference on Theoretical and Methodological Issues in Machine Translation*.

John DeNero and Dan Klein. 2007. Tailoring Word Alignments to Syntactic Machine Translation. In *Proceedings of the 45th Annual Meeting of the Association of Computational Linguistics*. Association for Computational Linguistics, June.

Michael Gasser. 2009. Semitic morphological analysis and generation using finite state transducers with feature structures. In *Proceedings of the 12th Conference of the European Chapter of the ACL.*

Philipp Koehn. 2005. Europarl: A Parallel Corpus for Statistical Machine Translation. In *Proceedings of The Tenth Machine Translation Summit.*

John D. Lafferty, Andrew McCallum, and Fernando C. N. Pereira. 2001. Conditional Random Fields: Probabilistic Models for Segmenting and Labeling Sequence Data. In *ICML.*

Els Lefever and Véronique Hoste. 2013. SemEval-2013 Task 10: Cross-Lingual Word Sense Disambiguation. In *Proceedings of the 7th International Workshop on Semantic Evaluation (SemEval 2013).*

Els Lefever, Véronique Hoste, and Martine De Cock. 2011. ParaSense or How to Use Parallel Corpora for Word Sense Disambiguation. In *Proceedings of the 49th Annual Meeting of the Association for Computational Linguistics: Human Language Technologies.*

Antonio Molina, Ferran Pla, and Encarna Segarra. 2002. A Hidden Markov Model Approach to Word Sense Disambiguation. In *IBERAMIA.*

Helmut Schmid. 1995. Improvements In Part-of-Speech Tagging With an Application To German. In *Proceedings of the ACL SIGDAT-Workshop.*

Kristina Toutanova, Dan Klein, Christopher D. Manning, and Yoram Singer. 2003. Feature-Rich Part-of-Speech Tagging with a Cyclic Dependency Network. In *PROCEEDINGS OF HLT-NAACL.*

F. M. Tyers, F. Sánchez-Martínez, and M. L. Forcada. 2012. Flexible finite-state lexical selection for rule-based machine translation. In *Proceedings of the 17th Annual Conference of the European Association of Machine Translation, EAMT12.*

Špela Vintar, Darja Fišer, and Aljoša Vrščaj. 2012. Were the clocks striking or surprising? Using WSD to improve MT performance. In *Proceedings of the Joint Workshop on Exploiting Synergies between Information Retrieval and Machine Translation (ESIRMT) and Hybrid Approaches to Machine Translation (HyTra).*

Two Approaches to Correcting Homophone Confusions in a Hybrid Machine Translation System

Pierrette Bouillon[1], **Johanna Gerlach**[1], **Ulrich Germann**[2], **Barry Haddow**[2], **Manny Rayner**[1]
(1) FTI/TIM, University of Geneva, Switzerland
{Pierrette.Bouillon,Johanna.Gerlach,Emmanuel.Rayner}@unige.ch
(2) School of Informatics, University of Edinburgh, Scotland
{ugermann,bhaddow}@inf.ed.ac.uk

Abstract

In the context of a hybrid French-to-English SMT system for translating online forum posts, we present two methods for addressing the common problem of homophone confusions in colloquial written language. The first is based on hand-coded rules; the second on weighted graphs derived from a large-scale pronunciation resource, with weights trained from a small bicorpus of domain language. With automatic evaluation, the weighted graph method yields an improvement of about $+0.63$ BLEU points, while the rule-based method scores about the same as the baseline. On contrastive manual evaluation, both methods give highly significant improvements ($p < 0.0001$) and score about equally when compared against each other.

1 Introduction and motivation

The data used to train Statistical Machine Translation (SMT) systems is most often taken from the proceedings of large multilingual organisations, the generic example being the Europarl corpus (Koehn, 2005); for academic evaluation exercises, the test data may well also be taken from the same source. Texts of this kind are carefully cleaned-up formal language. However, real MT systems often need to handle text from very different genres, which as usual causes problems.

This paper addresses a problem common in domains containing informally written text: spelling errors based on homophone confusions. Concretely, the work reported was carried out in the context of the ACCEPT project, which deals with the increasingly important topic of translating online forum posts; the experiments we describe were performed using French data taken from the Symantec forum, the concrete task being to translate it into English. The language in these posts is very far from that which appears in Hansard. People write quickly and carelessly, and no attempt is made to clean up the results. In particular, spelling is often uncertain.

One of the particular challenges in the task considered here is that French has a high frequency of homophones, which often cause confusion in written language. Everyone who speaks English is familiar with the fact that careless writers may confuse *its* ("of or belonging to it") and *it's* (contraction of "it is" or "it has"). French has the same problem, but to a much greater degree. Even when someone is working in an environment where an online spell-checker is available, it is easy to write *ou* ("or") instead of *où* ("where"), *la* ("the-feminine") instead of *là* ("there") or *ce* ("this") instead of *se* ("him/herself"). Even worse, there is systematic homophony in verb-form endings: for example, *utiliser* ("to use") *utilisez* ("you use") and *utilisé* ("used") are all homophones.

In French posts from the Symantec forum, we find that between 10% and 15% of all sentences contain at least one homophone error, depending on exactly how the term is defined[1]. Substituting a word with an incorrect homophone will often result in a translation error. Figure 1 shows typical examples of homophone errors and their effect on translation.

The core translation engine in our application is a normal SMT system, bracketed between pre- and post-editing phases. In what follows, we contrast two different approaches to handling homophone errors, which involve pre-editing in different ways. The first approach is based on knowledge-intensive construction of regular expression rules, which use the surrounding context to correct the most frequent types of homophone

[1]Unclear cases include hyphenation, elison and some examples of missing or incorrect accents.

	source	automatic translation
original	**La sa** ne pose pas de problème ...	**The its** is not the issue ...
corrected	**Là ça** ne pose pas de problème ...	**Here it** is not a problem
original	... (du moins on ne **recoit** pas l'alerte).	... (at least **we do not recoit** alert).
corrected	... (du moins on ne **reçoit** pas l'alerte).	.. (at least **it does not receive** the alert).

Figure 1: Examples of homophone errors in French forum data, contrasting English translations produced by the SMT engine from plain and corrected versions.

confusions.

The second is an engineering method: we use a commercial pronunciation-generation tool to generate a homophone dictionary, then use this dictionary to turn the input into a weighted graph where each word is replaced by a weighted disjunction of homophones. Related, though less elaborate, work has been reported by Bertoldi et al. (2010), who address spelling errors using a character-level confusion network based on common character confusions in typed English and test them on artificially created noisy data. Formiga and Fonollosa (2012) also used character-based models to correct spelling on informally written English data.

The two approaches in the present paper exploit fundamentally different knowledge sources in trying to identify and correct homophone errors. The rule-based method relies exclusively on source-side information, encoding patterns indicative of common French homophone confusions. The weighted graph method shifts the balance to the target side; the choice between potential homophone alternatives is made primarily by the target language model, though the source language weights and the translation model are also involved.

The rest of the paper is organised as follows. Section 2 describes the basic framework in more detail, and Section 3 the experiments. Section 4 summarises and concludes.

2 Basic framework

The goal of the ACCEPT project is to provide easy cross-lingual access to posts in online forums. Given the large variety of possible technical topics and the limited supply of online gurus, it frequently happens that users, searching forum posts online, find that the answer they need is in a language they do not know.

Currently available tools, for example Google Translate, are of course a great deal better than nothing, but still leave much to be desired. When one considers that advice given in an online forum may not be easy to follow even for native language speakers, it is unsurprising that a Google-translated version often fails to be useful. There is consequently strong motivation to develop an infrastructure explicitly designed to produce high-quality translations. ACCEPT intends to achieve this by a combination of three technologies: pre-editing of the source; domain-tuned SMT; and post-editing of the target. The pre- and post-editing stages are performed partly using automatic tools, and partly by manual intervention on the part of the user communities which typically grow up around online forums. We now briefly describe the automatic parts of the system.

2.1 SMT engine and corpus data

The SMT engine used is a phrase-based system trained with the standard *Moses* pipeline (Koehn et al., 2007), using GIZA++ (Och and Ney, 2000) for word alignment and SRILM (Stolcke, 2002) for the estimation of 5-gram Kneser-Ney smoothed (Kneser and Ney, 1995) language models.

For training the translation and lexicalised reordering models we used the releases of europarl and news-commentary provided for the WMT12 shared task (Callison-Burch et al., 2012), together with a dataset from the ACCEPT project consisting mainly of technical product manuals and marketing materials.

For language modelling we used the target sides of all the parallel data, together with approximately 900 000 words of monolingual English data extracted from web forums of the type that we wish to translate. Separate language models were trained on each of the data sets, then these were linearly interpolated using SRILM to minimise perplexity on a heldout portion of the forum data.

For tuning and testing, we extracted 1022 sentences randomly from a collection of monolingual French Symantec forum data (distinct from the monolingual English forum data), translated these using Google Translate, then post-edited to create references. The post-editing was performed by a native English speaker, who is also fluent in French. This 1022-sentence parallel text was then split into two equal halves (`devtest_a` and `devtest_b`) for minimum error rate tuning (MERT) and testing, respectively.

2.2 Rule-based pre-editing engine

Rule-based processing is carried out using the Acrolinx engine (Bredenkamp et al., 2000), which supports spelling, grammar, style and terminology checking. These methods of pre-editing were originally designed to be applied by authors during the technical documentation authoring process. The author gets error markings and improvement suggestions, and decides about reformulations. It is also possible to apply the provided suggestions automatically as direct reformulations. Rules are written in a regular-expression-based formalism which can access tagger-generated part-of-speech information. The rule-writer can specify both positive evidence (patterns that will trigger application of the rule) and negative evidence (patterns that will block application).

3 Experiments

We compared the rule-based and weighted graph approaches, evaluating each of them on the 511 sentence `devtest_b` corpus. The baseline SMT system, with no pre-editing, achieves an average BLEU score of 42.47 on this set.

3.1 The rule-based approach

Under the ACCEPT project, a set of lightweight pre-editing rules have been developed specifically for the Symantec Forum translation task. Some of the rules are automatic (direct reformulations); others present the user with a set of suggestions. The evaluations described in Gerlach et al. (2013) demonstrate that pre-editing with the rules has a significant positive effect on the quality of SMT-based translation.

The implemented rules address four main phenomena: differences between informal and formal language (Rayner et al., 2012), differences between local French and English word-order, elision/punctuation, and word confusions. Rules for resolving homophone confusions belong to the fourth group. They are shown in Table 1, together with approximate frequencies of occurrence in the development corpus.

Table 1: Hand-coded rules for homophone confusions and per-sentence frequency of applicability in the development corpus. Some of the rules also cover non-homophone errors, so the frequency figures are slight overestimates as far as homophones are concerned.

Rule	Freq.
a/as/à	4.17%
noun phrase agreement	3.20%
incorrect verb ending (er/é/ez)	2.90%
missing hyphenation	2.08%
subject verb agreement	1.90%
missing elision	1.26%
du/dû	0.35%
la/là	0.32%
ou/où	0.28%
ce/se	0.27%
Verb/noun	0.23%
tous/tout	0.22%
indicative/imperative	0.19%
future/conditional tense	0.14%
sur/sûr	0.10%
quel que/quelque	0.08%
ma/m'a	0.06%
quelle/qu'elle/quel/quels	0.05%
ça/sa	0.04%
des/dès	0.04%
et/est	0.02%
ci/si	0.01%
m'y/mi/mis	0.01%
other	0.17%
Total	18.09%

The set of Acrolinx pre-editing rules potentially relevant to resolution of homophone errors was applied to the `devtest_b` set test corpus (Section 2.1). In order to be able to make a fair comparison with the weighted-graph method, we only used rules with a unique suggestion, which could be run automatically. Applying these rules produced 430 changed words in the test corpus, but did not change the average BLEU score significantly (42.38).

Corrections made with a human in the loop, used as "oracle" input for the SMT system, by the way, achieve an average BLEU score[2] of 43.11 — roughly on par with the weighted-graph approach described below.

3.2 The weighted graph approach

In our second approach, the basic idea is to transform the input sentence into a *confusion network* (Bertoldi et al., 2008) which presents the translation system with a weighted list of homophone alternatives for each input word. The system is free to choose a path through a network of words that optimizes the internal hypothesis score; the weighting scheme for the alternatives can be used to guide the decoder. The conjecture is that the combination of the confusion network weights, the translation model and the target language model can resolve homophone confusions.

3.2.1 Defining sets of confusable words

To compile lists of homophones, we used the commercial Nuance Toolkit `pronounce` utility as our source of French pronunciation information.

We began by extracting a list of all the lexical items which occurred in the training portion of the French Symantec forum data, giving us 30 565 words. We then ran `pronounce` over this list. The Nuance utility does not simply perform table lookups, but is capable of creating pronunciations on the fly; it could in particular assign plausible pronunciations to most of the misspellings that occurred in the corpus. In general, a word is given more than one possible pronunciation. This can be for several reasons; in particular, some sounds in French can systematically be pronounced in more than one way, and pronunciation is often also dependent on whether the word is followed by a consonant or vowel. Table 2 shows examples.

Using the data taken from `pronounce`, we grouped words together into clusters which have a common pronunciation; since words typically have more than one pronunciation, they will typically also belong to more than one cluster. We then contructed sets of possible alternatives for words by including, for each word W, all the words W' such that W and W' occurred in the same cluster; since careless French writing is also characterised by mistakes in placing accents, we added all words W' such that W and W' are identical up to dropping accents. Table 3 shows typical results.

[2]With parameter sets from tuning the system on raw input and input preprocessed with the fully automatic rules; cf. Sec. 3.3.

Word	Pronunciation
ans	A~
	A~z
prévu	p r E v y
	p r e v y
québec	k e b E k
roule	r u l
	r u l *

Table 2: Examples of French pronunciations generated by `pronounce`. The format used is the Nuance version of ARPABET.

Intuitively, it is in general unlikely that, on seeing a word which occurs frequently in the corpus, we will want to hypothesize that it may be a misspelling of one which occurs very infrequently. We consequently filtered the sets of alternatives to remove all words on the right whose frequency was less than 0.05 times that of the word on the left.

Table 3: Examples of sets of possible alternatives for words, generated by considering both homophone and accent confusions.

Word	Alternatives
aux	au aux haut
créer	créer créez créé créée créées créés
côte	cote coté côte côté quot quote
hôte	haut haute hôte hôtes
il	e elle elles il ils l le y
mène	main mené mène
nom	nom noms non
ou	ou où
saine	sain saine saines scène seine
traits	trait traits tray tre tres très

3.2.2 Setting confusion network weights

In a small series of preliminary experiments we first tested three naïve weighting schemes for the confusion networks.

- using a **uniform** distribution that assigns equal weight to all spelling alternatives;
- setting weights proportional to the **unigram probability** of the word in question;
- computing the weights as state probabilities in a trellis with the **forward-backward** algorithm (Rabiner, 1989), an algorithm widely

Table 4: Decoder performance with different confusion network weighting schemes.

weighting scheme	av. BLEU[a]	std.
none (baseline system)	42.47	± .22
uniform	41.50	± .37
unigram	41.58	± .26
fwd-bwd (bigram)	41.81	± .16
bigram context (interpolated)	43.10	± .32

[a]Based on muliple tuning runs with random parameter initializations.

used in speech recognition. Suppose that each word $\hat{w}_i$ in the observed translation input sentence is produced while the writer has a particular "true" word $w_i \in C_i$ in mind, where C_i is the set of words confusable with $\hat{w}_i$. For the sake of simplicity, we assume that within a confusion set, all "true word" options are equally likely, i.e., $p(\hat{w}_i \mid w_i = x) = \frac{1}{|C_i|}$ for $x \in C_i$. The writer chooses the next word w_{i+1} according to the conditional word bigram probability $p(w_{i+1} \mid w_i)$.

The *forward* probability $fwd_i(x)$ is the probability of arriving in state $w_i = x$ at time i, regardless of the sequence of states visited en-route; the backward probability $bwd_i(x)$ is the probability of arriving at the end of the sentence coming from state $w_i = x$, regardless of the path taken. These probabilities can be computed efficiently with dynamic programming.

The weight assigned to a particular homophone alternative x at position i in the confusion network is the joint forward and backward probability:

$$weight_i(x) = fwd_i(x) \cdot bwd_i(x).$$

In practice, it turns out that these three naïve weighting schemes do more harm than good, as the results in Table 4 show. Clearly, they rely too much on overall language statistics (unigram and bigram probabilities) and pay too little attention to the actual input.

We therefore designed a fourth weighting scheme ("**bigram context interpolated**") that gives more weight to the observed input and computes the weights as the average of two score components. The first is a binary feature function that assigns 1 to each word actually observed in the input, and 0 to its homophone alternatives. The second component is the bigram-based in-context probability of each candidate. Unlike the forward-backward weighting scheme, which considers all possible context words for each candidate (as specified in the respective confusion sets), the new scheme only considers the words in the actual input as context words.

It would have be desirable to keep the two score components separate and tune their weights together with all the other parameters of the SMT system. Unfortunately, the current implementation of confusion network-based decoding in the *Moses* decoder allows only one single weight in the specification of confusion networks, so that we had to combine the two components into one score before feeding the confusion network into the decoder.

With the improved weighting scheme, the confusion network approach does outperform the baseline system, giving an average BLEU of 43.10 ($+0.63$).

3.3 Automatic evaluation (BLEU)

Due to the relatively small size of the evaluation set and instability inherent in minimum error rate training (Foster and Kuhn, 2009; Clark et al., 2011), results of *individual* tuning and evaluation runs can be unreliable. We therefore preformed multiple tuning and evaluation runs for each system (baseline, rule-based and weighted graph). To illustrate the precision of the BLEU score on our data sets, we plot in Fig. 2 for each individual tuning run the BLEU score achieved on the tuning set (x-axis) against the performance on the evaluation set (y-axis). The variance along the x-axis for each system is due to search errors in parameter optimization. Since the search space is not convex, the tuning process can get stuck in local maxima. The apparent poor local correlation between performance on the tuning set and performance on the evaluation set for each system shows the effect of the sampling error.

With larger tuning and evaluation sets, we would expect the correlation between the two to improve. The scatter plot suggests that the weighted-graph system does on average produce significantly better translations (with respect to BLEU) than both the baseline and the rule-based system, whereas the difference between the baseline and the rule-based system is within the range

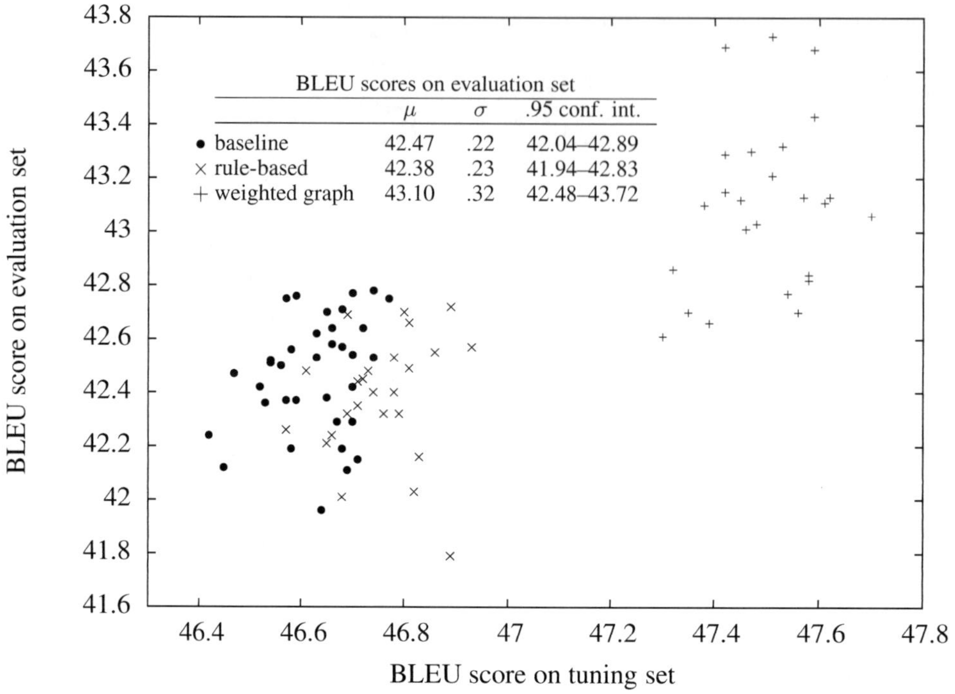

Figure 2: BLEU scores (in points) for the baseline, rule-based and weighted graph-based systems.

of statistical error.

To study the effect of tuning condition (tuning on raw vs. input pre-processed by rules), we also translated both the raw and the pre-processed evaluation corpus with all parameter setting that we had obtained during the various experiments. Figure 3 plots (with solid markers) performance on raw input (x-axis) against translation of pre-processed input (y-axis). We observe that while preprocessing harms performance for certain parameter settings, most of the time proprocessing does lead to improvements in BLEU score. The slight deterioration we observed when comparing system tuned on exactly the type of input that they were to translate later (i.e., raw or preprocessed) seems to be a imprecision in the measurement caused by training instability and sampling error rather than the result of systematic input deterioration due to preprocessing. Overall, the improvements are small and not statistically significant, but there appears to be a positive trend.

To gauge the benefits of more extensive preprocessing and input error correction we produced and translated 'oracle' input by also applying rules from the Acrolinx engine that currently require a human in the loop who decides whether or not the rule in question should be applied. The boost in performance is shown by the hollow markers in Fig. 3. Here, translation of pre-processed input consistently fares better than translation of the raw input.

3.4 Human evaluation

Although BLEU suggests that the weighted-graph method significantly outscores both the baseline and the rule-based method ($p < 0.05$ over 25 tuning runs), the absolute differences are small, and we decided that it would be prudent to carry out a human evaluation as well. Following the methodology of Rayner et al. (2012), we performed contrastive judging on the Amazon Mechanical Turk (AMT) to compare different versions of the system. Subjects were recruited from Canada, a bilingual French/English country, requesting English native speakers with good written French; we also limited the call to AMT workers who had already completed at least 50 assignments, at least 80% of which had been accepted. Judging assignments were split into groups of 20 triplets, where each triplet consisted of a source sentence and two different target sentences; the judge was asked to say which translation was better, using a five-point scale {better, slightly-better, about-equal, slightly-worse, worse}. The order of the two targets was

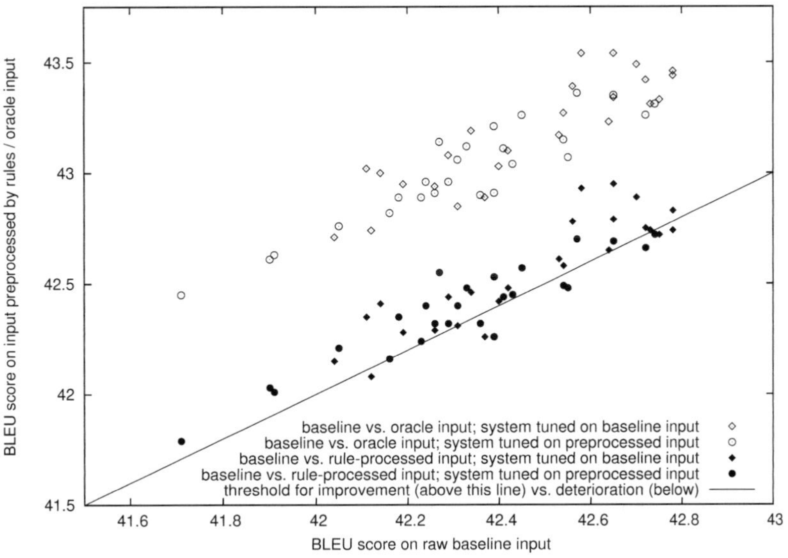

Figure 3: BLEU scores (in points) the two input conditions "baseline" and "rule-based" (solid markers). The hollow markers show the BLEU score on human-corrected 'oracle' input using a more extensive set of rules / suggestions from the Acrolinx engine that require a human in the loop.

randomised. Judges were paid $1 for each group of 20 triplets. Each triplet was judged three times.

Using the above method, we posted AMT tasks to compare a) the baseline system against the rule-based system, b) the baseline system against the best weighted-graph system (**interpolated-bigram**) from Section 3.2.2 and c) the rule-based system and the weighted-graph system against each other. The results are shown in Table 5; in the second and third columns, disagreements are resolved by majority voting, and in the fourth and fifth we only count cases where the judges are unanimous, the others being scored as unclear. In both cases, we reduce the original five-point scale to a three-point scale {better, equal/unclear, worse}[3]. Irrespective of the method used to resolve disagreements, the differences "rule-based system/baseline" and "weighted-graph system/baseline" are highly significant ($p < 0.0001$) according to the McNemar sign test, while the difference "rule-based system/weighted-graph system" is not significant.

Table 5: Comparison between baseline, rule-based and weighted-graph versions, evaluated on the 511-utterance `devtest_b` corpus and judged by three AMT-recruited judges. Figures are presented both for majority voting and for unanimous decisions only.

	Majority		Unanimous	
baseline vs rule-based				
baseline better	83	16.2%	48	9.4%
r-based better	204	40.0%	161	31.5%
Unclear	36	7.0%	93	18.1%
Equal	188	36.8%	209	40.9%
baseline vs weighted-graph				
baseline better	115	22.5%	52	10.1%
w-graph better	193	37.8%	119	23.3%
Unclear	46	9.0%	99	19.4%
Equal	157	30.7%	241	47.2%
rule-based vs weighted-graph				
r-based better	141	27.6%	68	13.3%
w-graph better	123	24.1%	70	13.7%
Unclear	25	4.9%	142	27.8%
Equal	222	43.4%	231	45.2%

We were somewhat puzzled that BLEU makes the weighted-graph system clearly better than the rule-based one, while manual evaluation rates them as approximately equal. The explanation seems to be to do with the fact that manual evaluation operates at the sentence level, giving equal importance to all sentences, while BLEU oper-

[3]For reasons we do not fully understand, we get better inter-judge agreement this way than we do when we originally ask for judgements on a three-point scale.

ates at the word level and consequently counts longer sentences as more important. If we calculate BLEU on a per-sentence basis and then average the scores, we find that the results for the two systems are nearly the same; per-sentence BLEU differences also correlate reasonably well with majority judgements (Pearson correlation coefficient of 0.39). It is unclear to us, however, whether the difference between per-sentence and per-word BLEU evaluation points to anything particularly interesting.

4 Conclusions

We have presented two methods for addressing the common problem of homophone confusions in colloquial written language in the context of an SMT system. The weighted-graph method produced a small but significant increase in BLEU, while the rule-based one was about the same as the baseline. Both methods, however, gave clearly significant improvements on contrastive manual evaluation carried out through AMT, with no significant difference in performance when the two were compared directly.

The small but consistent improvements in BLEU score that we observed with the human-in-the-loop oracle input over the fully automatic rule-based setup invite further investigation. How many of the decisions currently left to the human can be automated? Is there a fair way of comparing and evaluating fully automatic against semi-automatic setups? Work on these topics is in preparation and will be reported elsewhere.

Acknowledgements

The work described in this paper was performed as part of the Seventh Framework Programme ACCEPT project, under grant agreement 288769.

References

Bertoldi, Nicola, Mauro Cettolo, and Marcello Federico. 2010. "Statistical machine translation of texts with misspelled words." *NAACL*. Los Angeles, CA, USA.

Bertoldi, Nicola, Richard Zens, Marcello Federico, and Wade Shen. 2008. "Efficient speech translation through confusion network decoding." *IEEE Transactions on Audio, Speech & Language Processing*, 16(8):1696–1705.

Bredenkamp, Andrew, Berthold Crysmann, and Mirela Petrea. 2000. "Looking for errors : A declarative formalism for resource-adaptive language checking." *LREC*. Athens, Greece.

Callison-Burch, Chris, Philipp Koehn, Christof Monz, et al. (eds.). 2012. *Seventh Workshop on Statistical Machine Translation (WMT)*. Montréal, Canada.

Clark, Jonathan H., Chris Dyer, Alon Lavie, and Noah A. Smith. 2011. "Better hypothesis testing for statistical machine translation: Controlling for optimizer instability." *ACL-HLT*. Portland, OR, USA.

Formiga, Lluis and José A. R. Fonollosa. 2012. "Dealing with input noise in statistical machine translation." *COLING*. Mumbai, India.

Foster, George and Roland Kuhn. 2009. "Stabilizing minimum error rate training." *WMT*. Athens, Greece.

Gerlach, Johanna, Victoria Porro, Pierrette Bouillon, and Sabine Lehmann. 2013. "La préédition avec des règles peu coûteuses, utile pour la TA statistique?" *TALN-RECITAL*. Sables d'Olonne, France.

Kneser, Reinhard and Hermann Ney. 1995. "Improved backing-off for m-gram language modeling." *ICASSP*. Detroit, MI, USA.

Koehn, Philipp. 2005. "Europarl: A parallel corpus for statistical machine translation." *MT Summit X*. Phuket, Thailand.

Koehn, Philipp, Hieu Hoang, Alexandra Birch, et al. 2007. "Moses: Open source toolkit for statistical machine translation." *ACL Demonstration Session*. Prague, Czech Republic.

Och, Franz Josef and Hermann Ney. 2000. "Improved statistical alignment models." *ACL*. Hong Kong.

Rabiner, Lawrence R. 1989. "A tutorial on hidden markov models and selected applications in speech recognition." *Proceedings of the IEEE*, 257–286.

Rayner, Manny, Pierrette Bouillon, and Barry Haddow. 2012. "Using source-language transformations to address register mismatches in SMT." *AMTA*. San Diego, CA, USA.

Stolcke, Andreas. 2002. "SRILM - an extensible language modeling toolkit." *ICSLP*. Denver, CO, USA.

Uses of Monolingual In-Domain Corpora for Cross-Domain Adaptation with Hybrid MT Approaches

An-Chang Hsieh, Hen-Hsen Huang and Hsin-Hsi Chen
Department of Computer Science and Information Engineering
National Taiwan University
No. 1, Sec. 4, Roosevelt Road, Taipei, 10617 Taiwan
{achsieh,hhhuang}@nlg.csie.ntu.edu.tw;hhchen@ntu.edu.tw

Abstract

Resource limitation is challenging for cross-domain adaption. This paper employs patterns identified from a monolingual in-domain corpus and patterns learned from the post-edited translation results, and translation model as well as language model learned from pseudo bilingual corpora produced by a baseline MT system. The adaptation from a government document domain to a medical record domain shows the rules mined from the monolingual in-domain corpus are useful, and the effect of using the selected pseudo bilingual corpus is significant.

1 Introduction

Bilingual dictionary and corpus are important resources for MT applications. They are used for lexical choice and model construction. However, not all resources are available in bilingual forms in each domain. For example, medical records are in English only in some countries. In such a case, only bilingual dictionary and monolingual corpus is available. Lack of bilingual corpus makes domain adaptation more challenging.

A number of adaptation approaches (Civera and Juan, 2007; Foster and Kuhn 2007; Foster et al., 2010, Matsoukas et al., 2009; Zhao et al., 2004) have been proposed. They address the reliability of a model in a new domain and count the domain similarities between a model and the in-domain development data. The domain relevance in different granularities including words, phrases, sentences, documents and corpora are considered. Ueffing et al. (2007) propose semi-supervised methods which use monolingual data in source language to improve translation performance. Schwenk (2008) present lightly-supervised training to generate additional training data from the translation results of monolingual data. To deal with the resource-poor issue, Bertoldi and Federico (2009) generate a pseudo bilingual corpus from the monolingual in-domain corpus, and then train a translation model from the pseudo bilingual corpus.

Besides counting similarities and generating pseudo bilingual in-domain corpus, text simplification (Zhu et al., 2010; Woodsend and Lapata, 2011; Wubben et al., 2012) is another direction. Simplifying a source language text makes the translation easier in a background MT system. Chen et al. (2012a) propose a method to simplify a sentence before MT and to restore the translation of the simplified part after MT. They focus on the treatments of input text only, but do not consider how to adapt the background MT to the specific domain. The translation performance depends on the coverage of the simplification rules and the quality of the background system.

This paper adopts the simplification-translation-restoration methodology (Chen et al., 2012a), but emphasizes on how to update bilingual translation rules, translation model and language model, which are two kernels of rule-based and statistics-based MT systems, respectively. This paper is organized as follows. Section 2 specifies the proposed hybrid MT approaches to resource-limited domains. The characteristics of available resources including their types, their linguality, their belonging domains, and their belonging languages are analyzed and their uses in translation rule mining and model construction are presented. Section 3 discusses how to adapt an MT system from a government document domain to a medical record domain. The experimental setups reflect various settings. Section 4 concludes the remarks.

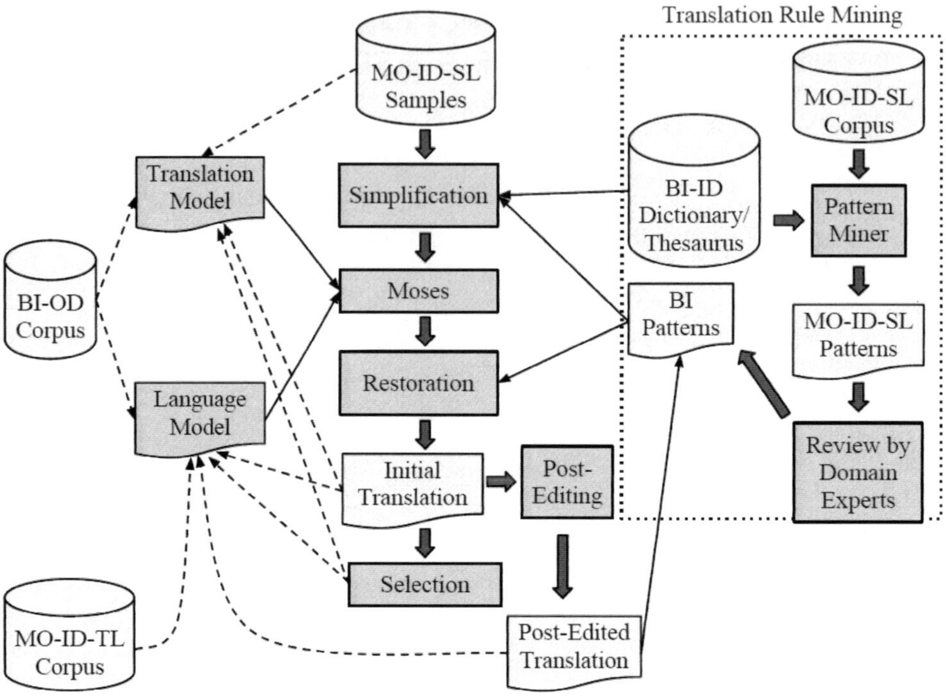

Figure 1: Hybrid MT Approaches

2 Hybrid MT Approaches

Figure 1 sketches the overall picture of our proposed hybrid MT approaches. A resource is represented in terms of its *linguality*, *domain*, *language*, and *type*, where MO/BI denotes monolingual/bilingual, ID/OD denotes in-domain/out-domain, and SL/TL denotes source language/target language. For example, an MO-ID-SL corpus and an MO-ID-TL corpus mean monolingual in-domain corpora in source and in target languages, respectively. Similarly, a BI-OD corpus and a BI-ID dictionary denote a bilingual out-domain corpus, and a bilingual in-domain dictionary, respectively.

Resources may be provided by some organizations such as LDC, or collected from heterogeneous resources. The MO-ID-SL/TL corpus, the BI-OD corpus, and the BI-ID dictionary belong to this type. Besides, some outputs generated by the baseline MT systems are regarded as other kinds of resources for enhancing the proposed methods incrementally. Initial translation results, selected translation results, and post-edited translation results, which form pseudo bilingual in-domain corpora, belong to this type.

The following subsections first describe the baseline systems with the original resources and then specify the advanced systems with the generated resources.

2.1 A baseline translation system

In an extreme case, only a bilingual out-domain corpus, a monolingual in-domain corpus in source/target language, a bilingual in-domain dictionary and a monolingual in-domain thesaurus in source language are available. The bilingual out-domain corpus is used to train translation and language models by Moses. They form a background out-domain translation system.

A pattern miner is used to capture the written styles in the monolingual in-domain corpus in source language. A monolingual in-domain thesaurus in source language is looked up to extract the class (sense) information of words. Monolingual patterns are mined by counting frequent word/class n-grams. Then, the bilingual in-domain dictionary is introduced to formulate translation rules based on the mined monolingual patterns. Here in-domain experts may be involved in reviewing the bilingual rules. The human cost will affect the number of translation rules formulated and thus its coverage.

The baseline translation system is composed of four major steps shown as follows. (1) and (2) are pre-processing steps before kernel MT, and (4) is a post-processing step after kernel MT.

(1) Identifying and translating in-domain segments from an input sentence by using translation rules.

(2) Simplifying the input sentence by replacing the in-domain segments as follows.
   (a) If an in-domain segment is a term in the bilingual in-domain dictionary, we find a related term (i.e., hypernym or synonym) in the in-domain thesaurus which has relatively more occurrences in the background SMT system to replace the term.
   (b) If an in-domain segment is a noun phrase, we keep its head only, and find a related term of the head as (a).
   (c) If an in-domain segment is a verb phrase composed of a verb and a noun phrase, we keep the verb and simplify the noun phrase as (b).
   (d) If an in-domain segment is a verb phrase composed of a verb and a prepositional phrase, we keep the verb and remove the prepositional phrase if it is optional. If the prepositional phrase is mandatory, it is kept and simplified as (e).
   (e) If an in-domain segment is a prepositional phrase, we keep the preposition and simplify the noun phrase as (b).
   (f) If an in-domain segment is a clause, we simplify its children recursively as (a)-(e).
(3) Translating the simplified source sentence by using the out-domain background MT system.
(4) Restoring the results of the bilingual in-domain segments translated in (1) back to the translation results generated in (3). The restoration is based on the internal alignment between the source and the target sentences.

2.2 Incremental learning

There are several alternatives to update the baseline translation system incrementally. The first consideration is the in-domain translation rules. They are formed semi-automatically by domain experts. The cost of domain experts results that only small portion of n-gram patterns along with the corresponding translation are generated. The post-editing results suggests more translation rules and they are fed back to revise the baseline translation system.

The second consideration is translation model and language model in the Moses. In an ideal case, the complete monolingual in-domain corpus in source language is translated by the baseline translation system, then the results are post-edited by domain experts, and finally the complete post-edited bilingual corpus is fed back to revise both translation model and language model. However, the post-editing cost by domain experts is high. Only some samples of the initial translation are edited by domain experts. On the one hand, the sampled post-edited in-domain corpus in target language is used to revise the language model. On the other hand, the in-domain bilingual translation result before post-editing is used to revise the translation model and the language model. Size and translation quality are two factors to be considered. We will explore the effect of different size of imperfect in-domain translation results on refining the baseline MT system. Moreover, a selection strategy, e.g., only those translation results completely in target language are considered, is introduced to sample "relatively more accurate" bilingual translation results.

In the above incremental learning, translation rules, translation model and language model are revised individually. The third consideration is to merge some refinements together and examine their effects on the translation performance.

3 Cross-Domain Adaptation

To evaluate the feasibility of the proposed hybrid MT approaches, we adapt an English-Chinese machine translation system from a government document domain to a medical record domain. The linguistic resources are described first and then the experimental results.

3.1 Resource description

Hong Kong parallel text (LDC2004T08), which contains official records, law codes, and press releases of the Legislative Council, the Department of Justice, and the Information Services Department of the HKSAR, respectively, and UN Chinese-English Parallel Text collection (LDC2004E12) is used to train the translation model. These two corpora contain total 6.8M sentences. The Chinese counterpart of the above parallel corpus and the Central News Agency part of the Tagged Chinese Gigaword (LDC2007T03) are used to train trigram language model. These two corpora contain total 18.8M sentences. The trained models are used in Step (3) of the baseline translation system.

Besides the out-domain corpora for the development of translation model and language model, we select 60,448 English medical records (1.8M sentences) from National Taiwan University

Hospital (NTUH) to learn the n-gram patterns. Metathesaurus of the Unified Medical Language System (UMLS) provides medical classes of in-domain words. A bilingual medical domain dictionary composed of 71,687 pairs is collected. Total 7.2M word/class 2-grams~5-grams are identified. After parsing, there remain 57.2K linguistic patterns. A higher order pattern may be composed of two lower order patterns. Keeping the covering patterns and ruling out the covered ones further reduce the size of the extracted patterns. The remaining 40.1K patterns are translated by dictionary look-up. Because of the high cost of medical record domain experts (i.e., physicians), only a small portion is verified. Finally, 981 translation rules are formulated. They are used in Step (1) of the baseline MT system. The detail rule mining and human correction process please refer to Chen et al. (2012b).

We further sample 2.1M and 1.1M sentences from NTUH medical record datasets, translate them by the baseline MT system, and get 2.1M- and 1.1M-pseudo bilingual in-domain corpora. We will experiment the effects of the corpus size. On the other hand, we apply the selection strategy to select 0.95M "good" translation from 2.1M-pseudo bilingual in-domain corpus. Furthermore, some other 1,004 sentences are post-edited by the domain experts. They are used to learn the advanced MT systems.

To evaluate the baseline and the advanced MT systems, we sample 1,000 sentences different from the above corpora as the test data, and translate them manually as the ground truth.

3.2 Results and discussion

Table 1 lists the methods along with the resources they used. B is the baseline MT system. Most patterns appearing in the 57.2K learned n-grams mentioned in Section 3.1 are not reviewed by physicians due to their cost. Part of these unreviewed patterns may occur in the post-edited data. They will be further introduced into M1. In the experiments, patterns appearing at least two times in the post-edited result are integrated into M1. Total 422 new patterns are identified. Translation model and language model in M1 is the same as those in baseline system.

In M2-M6, the translation rules are the same as those in baseline MT system, only translation model and/or language model are re-trained. In

	Translation Rules	Translation Model	Language Model	Tuning Data
B	981 bilingual translation rules	6.8M government domain bilingual sentences	18.8M government/news domain Chinese sentences	1000 government domain bilingual sentences
M1	981 bilingual translation rules + 422 mined rules from post-editing	6.8M government domain bilingual sentences	18.8M government/news domain Chinese sentences	200 post-edited medical domain sentences
M2	981 bilingual translation rules	6.8M government domain bilingual sentences	804 post-edited Chinese sentences	200 post-edited medical domain sentences
M3	981 bilingual translation rules	6.8M government domain bilingual sentences	30,000 Chinese sentences selected from medical literature	200 post-edited medical domain sentences
M4	981 bilingual translation rules	1.1M pseudo medical domain bilingual sentences generated by M1	1.1M pseudo medical domain Chinese sentences generated by M1	200 post-edited medical domain sentences
M5	981 bilingual translation rules	2.1M pseudo medical domain bilingual sentences generated by M1	2.1M pseudo medical domain Chinese sentences generated by M1	200 post-edited medical domain sentences
M6	981 bilingual translation rules	0.95M selected pseudo medical domain bilingual sentences generated by M1	0.95M selected pseudo medical domain Chinese sentences generated by M1	200 post-edited medical domain sentences
M12	981 bilingual translation rules + 422 mined rules from post-editing	6.8M government domain bilingual sentences	804 post-edited Chinese sentences	200 post-edited medical domain sentences
M13	981 bilingual translation rules + 422 mined rules from post-editing	6.8M government domain bilingual sentences	30,000 medical domain Chinese sentences	200 post-edited medical domain sentences
M14	981 bilingual translation rules + 422 mined rules from post-editing	1.1M pseudo medical domain bilingual sentences generated by M1	1.1M pseudo medical domain Chinese sentences generated by M1	200 post-edited medical domain sentences
M15	981 bilingual translation rules + 422 mined rules from post-editing	2.1M pseudo medical domain bilingual sentences generated by M1	2.1M pseudo medical domain Chinese sentences generated by M1	200 post-edited medical domain sentences
M16	981 bilingual translation rules + 422 mined rules from post-editing	0.95M selected pseudo medical domain bilingual sentences generated by M1	0.95M selected pseudo medical domain Chinese sentences generated by M1	200 post-edited medical domain sentences

Table 1: Resources used in each hybrid MT method

Method	Bleu	Method	Bleu	Method	Bleu	Method	Bleu	Method	Bleu	Method	Bleu
B	28.04	M2	39.45	M3	32.03	M4	34.86	M5	35.09	M6	40.48
M1	39.72	M12	39.72	M13	32.85	M14	35.11	M15	35.52	M16	40.71

Table 2: BLEU of each hybrid MT method

M2, 804 post-edited sentences are used to train a new language model, without changing the translation model. In M3, paper abstracts in medical domain are used to derive a new language model. M4, M5 and M6 are similar except that different sizes of corpora are used. M4 and M5 use 1.1M and 2.1M sentences, respectively, while M6 uses 0.95M sentences chosen by using the selection strategy. M12-M16 are combinations of M1 and M2-M6, respectively. Translation rules, translation model and language model are refined by using different resources. Total 200 of the 1,004 post-edited sentences are selected to tune the parameters of Moses in the advanced methods.

Table 2 shows the BLEU of various MT methods. The BLEU of the MT system without employing simplification-translation-restoration methodology (Chen et al., 2012a) is 15.24. Apparently, the method B, which employs the methodology, achieves the BLEU 28.04 and is much better than the original system. All the enhanced systems are significantly better than the baseline system B by t-test (p<0.05). Comparing M1 and M12-M16 with the corresponding systems, we can find that introducing the mined patterns has positive effects. M1 is even much better than B. Although the number of the post-edited sentences is small, M2 and M12 show such a resource has the strongest effects. The results of M3 and M13 depict that 30,000 sentences selected from medical literature are not quite useful for medical record translation. Comparing M4 and M5, we can find larger pseudo corpus is useful. M6 shows using the selected pseudo subset performs much better. Comparing the top 4 methods, the best method, M16, is significantly better than M12 and M1 (p<0.05), but is not different from M6 significantly (p=0.1662).

We further analyze the translation results of the best methods M6 and M16 from two perspectives. On the one hand, we show how the mined rules improve the translation. The following list some examples for reference. The underlined parts are translated correctly by new mined patterns in M16.

(1) Example: Stenting was done from distal IVC through left common iliac vein to external iliac vein.
M6: 支架置入術 是 從 遠端 下腔靜脈 通過 從 左髂總靜脈 到 髂外靜脈 。
M16: 完成 支架置入術 從 遠端 下腔靜脈 通過 從 左髂總靜脈 到 髂外靜脈 。

(2) Example: We shifted the antibiotic to cefazolin.
M6: 我們 把 抗生素 頭孢唑啉 。
M16: 我們 把 抗生素 更換 為 頭孢唑啉 。

(3) Example: Enhancement of right side pleural, and mild pericardial effusion was noted .
M6: 增強 方面 的 權利 胸腔 、 和 發現 有 輕微 的 心包積液 。
M16: 增強 的 右 胸腔 、 輕微 心包積液 被 注意到 。

On the other hand, we touch on which factors affect the translation performance of M16. Three factors including word ordering errors, word sense disambiguation errors and OOV (out-of-vocabulary) errors are addressed as follows. The erroneous parts are underlined.

(1) Ordering errors
Example: Antibiotics were discontinued after 8 days of treatment.
M16: 抗生素 中斷 後 8 天 的 治療 。
Analysis: The correct translation result is "8 天 的 治療 後 抗生素 中斷。" The current patterns are 2-5 grams, so that the longer patterns cannot be captured.

(2) Word sense disambiguation errors
Example: After tracheostomy, he was transferred to our ward for post operation care.
M16: 氣管切開術 後， 他 被 轉送到 我們 病房 為 員額 關懷 行動 。
Analysis: The correct translation of "post operation care" should be "術後照護". However, the 1,004 post-edited sentences are still not large enough to cover the possible patterns. Incremental update will introduce more patterns and may decrease the number of translation errors.

(3) OOV errors
Example: Transcatheter intravenous urokinase therapy was started on 1/11 for 24 hours infusion.
M16: transcatheter 靜脈 尿激酶 在 1/11 開始 進行 治療 24 小時 輸液 。
Analysis: The word "transcatheter" is an OOV. Its translation should be "導管".

4 Conclusion

This paper considers different types of resources in cross-domain MT adaptation. Several methods are proposed to integrate the mined translation rules, translation model and language model. The adaptation experiments show that the rules mined from the monolingual in-domain corpus are useful, and the effect of using the selected pseudo bilingual corpus is significant.

Several issues such as word ordering errors, word sense disambiguation errors, and OOV errors still remain for further investigation in the future.

Acknowledgments

This work was partially supported by National Science Council (Taiwan) and Excellent Research Projects of National Taiwan University under contracts NSC101-2221-E-002-195-MY3 and 102R890858. We are very thankful to National Taiwan University Hospital for providing NTUH the medical record dataset.

References

N. Bertoldi and M. Federico. 2009. Domain adaptation for statistical machine translation with monolingual resources. In *Proceedings of the Fourth Workshop on Statistical Machine Translation*, pages 182–189.

H.B. Chen, H.H. Huang, H.H. Chen and C.T. Tan. 2012a. A simplification-translation-restoration framework for cross-domain SMT applications. In *Proceedings of COLING 2012*, pages 545–560.

H.B. Chen, H.H. Huang, J. Tjiu, C.Ti. Tan and H.H. Chen. 2012b. A statistical medical summary translation system. In *Proceedings of 2012 ACM SIGHIT International Health Informatics Symposium*, pages. 101-110.

J. Civera and A. Juan. 2007. Domain adaptation in statistical machine translation with mixture modeling. In *Proceedings of the Second Workshop on Statistical Machine Translation*, pages 177–180.

G. Foster and R. Kuhn. 2007. Mixture-model adaptation for SMT. In *Proceedings of the Second Workshop on Statistical Machine Translation*, pages 128–135.

G. Foster, C. Goutte, and R. Kuhn. 2010. Discriminative instance weighting for domain adaptation in statistical machine translation. In *Proceedings of EMNLP 2010*, pages 451–459.

S. Matsoukas, A.I. Rosti, and B. Zhang. 2009. Discriminative corpus weight estimation for machine translation. In *Proceedings of EMNLP 2009*, pages 708–717.

H. Schwenk. 2008. Investigations on large-scale lightly-supervised training. In *Proceedings of IWSLT 2008*, pages 182–189.

N. Ueffing, G. Haffari and A. Sarkar. 2007. Transductive learning for statistical machine translation. In *Proceedings of the 45th Annual Meeting of the Association of Computational Linguistics*, pages 25–32,

K. Woodsend and M. Lapata. 2011. Learning to simplify sentences with quasi-synchronous grammar and integer programming. In *Proceedings of EMNLP 2011*, pages 409–420.

S. Wubben and A. van den Bosch, and E. Krahmer. 2012. Sentence simplification by monolingual machine translation. In *Proceedings of ACL 2012*, pages 1015–1024.

B. Zhao, M. Eck, M. and S. Vogel. 2004. Language model adaptation for statistical machine translation via structured query models. In *Proceedings of COLING 2004*, pages 411–417.

Z. Zhu, D. Bernhard, and I. Gurevych. 2010. A monolingual tree-based translation model for sentence simplification. In *Proceedings of COLING 2010*, pages 1353–1361.

Language-independent hybrid MT with PRESEMT

George Tambouratzis
ILSP, Athena R.C
giorg_t@ilsp.gr

Sokratis Sofianopoulos
ILSP, Athena R.C
s_sofian@ilsp.gr

Marina Vassiliou
ILSP, Athena R.C
mvas@ilsp.gr

Abstract

The present article provides a comprehensive review of the work carried out on developing PRESEMT, a hybrid language-independent machine translation (MT) methodology. This methodology has been designed to facilitate rapid creation of MT systems for unconstrained language pairs, setting the lowest possible requirements on specialised resources and tools. Given the limited availability of resources for many languages, only a very small bilingual corpus is required, while language modelling is performed by sampling a large target language (TL) monolingual corpus. The article summarises implementation decisions, using the Greek-English language pair as a test case. Evaluation results are reported, for both objective and subjective metrics. Finally, main error sources are identified and directions are described to improve this hybrid MT methodology.

1 Introduction and background

Currently a large proportion of language-independent MT approaches are based on the statistical machine translation (SMT) paradigm (Koehn, 2010). A main benefit of SMT is that it is directly amenable to new language pairs, provided appropriate training data are available for extracting translation and language models. The main obstacle to the creation of an SMT system is the requirement for SL-TL parallel corpora of a sufficient size to allow the extraction of meaningful translation models. Such corpora (of the order of million sentences) are hard to obtain, particularly for less resourced languages. On the other hand, the translation accuracy of such systems largely depends on the quality and size of the bilingual corpora, as well as their relevance to the domain of text being translated. Even if such parallel corpora exist for a language pair, they are frequently restricted to a specific domain (or a narrow range of domains). As a consequence, these corpora are not suitable for creating MT systems that focus on other domains. For this reason, in SMT, researchers are investigating the extraction of information from monolingual corpora, including lexical translation probabilities (Klementiev et al., 2012) and topic-specific information (Su et al., 2011).

Alternative techniques for creating MT systems using less informative but readily available resources have been proposed. Even if these methods do not provide a translation quality as high as SMT, their ability to develop hybrid MT systems with very limited specialised resources represents an important advantage. Such methods include automatic inference of templates for structural transfer from SL to TL (Caseli et al., 2008 and Sanchez-Martinez et al., 2009). Similarly, Carbonell et al. (2006) propose an MT method that needs no parallel text, but relies on a lightweight translation model utilising a full-form bilingual dictionary and a decoder for long-range context. Other systems using low-cost resources include METIS (Dologlou et al., 2003) and METIS-II (Markantonatou et al., 2009; Carl et al., 2008), which utilise a bilingual lexicon and monolingual corpora to translate SL texts. METIS/METIS II, which have studied translation only towards English, employ pattern recognition algorithms to retrieve the most appropriate translation from a monolingual corpus.

2 The MT methodology in brief

The MT methodology has been developed within the PRESEMT (Pattern REcognition-based Statistically Enhanced MT) project, funded by the European Commission (cf. www.presemt.eu). It comprises three stages:

(i) pre-processing, where the input sentence is tagged and lemmatised

(ii) main translation, where the actual translation output is generated and

(iii) post-processing, where the corresponding tokens are generated from lemmas.

The main translation process is split in two phases, namely (a) the establishment of the translation structure in terms of phrase order and (b) the definition of word order and resolution of lexical ambiguities at an intra-phrase level.

In terms of resources, PRESEMT utilises a bilingual lemma dictionary providing SL – TL lexical correspondences. It also employs an extensive TL monolingual corpus, compiled automatically via web crawling (Pomikalek et al., 2008) to generate a comprehensive phrase-based language model. The provision of the monolingual corpus allows PRESEMT to use only a very small bilingual corpus for mapping the transfer from SL to TL sentence structures. This bilingual corpus only numbers a few hundred sentences, reducing reliance on costly linguistic resources. The corpus is assembled from available parallel corpora, only replacing free translations with more literal ones, to allow the accurate extraction of structural modifications. The parallel corpus coverage is not studied prior to integration in PRESEMT, which would have allowed an optimisation of translation performance.

3 Extracting information from corpora

3.1 Parallel corpus

Initially, both the bilingual and the monolingual corpora are annotated [1] so as to incorporate lemma and Part-of-Speech (PoS) information and other salient language-specific morphological features (e.g. case, number, tense etc.). Furthermore, for the TL side, a shallow parser or chunker (hereafter referred to as parser) is used to split the sentences into syntactic phrases. As the proposed methodology has been developed to maximise the use of publicly-available software, the user is free to select any desired parser for the TL language.

To avoid either an additional SL side parser or potential incompatibilities between the two parsers, the Phrase Aligner module (**PAM**, Tambouratzis et al., 2011) is implemented. PAM transfers the TL side parsing scheme, which encompasses lemma, tag and parsing information, to the SL side, based on lexical information coupled with statistical data on PoS tag correspondences extracted from the lexicon. The parsing scheme includes phrase boundaries and phrase labels. PAM follows a 3-step process, involving (a) lexicon-based alignment, (b) alignment based on similarity of grammatical features and PoS tag correspondence and (c) alignment on the evidence of already aligned neighbouring words.

The SL side of the aligned corpus is subsequently processed by the Phrasing model generator (**PMG**), to create an SL phrasing model which will then parse sentences input for translation. The original PMG implementation (Tambouratzis et al., 2011) has utilised Conditional Random Fields (CRF), due to the considerable representation capabilities of this model (Lafferty et al., 2001). CRF is a statistical modelling method that takes context into account to predict labels for sequences of input samples.

The implementation of an alternative PMG methodology (termed PMG-simple) based on template-matching principles has also been pursued. PMG-simple locates phrases that match

[1] For the annotation task readily available tools are employed. For the experiments reported here, TreeTagger (Schmid, 1994) has been used for the TL text processing and the FBT PoS tagger (Prokopidis et al., 2011) has been employed for the processing of the SL text..

exactly what it has seen before, based on a simple template-matching algorithm (Duda et al., 2001). The templates used are the phrases to which the SL side sentences of the bilingual corpus have been segmented. In contrast to CRF, PMG-simple implements a greedy search (Black, 2005) without backtracking. Initially all phrases are positioned in an ordered list according to their likelihood of being accurately detected. Starting from the phrase with the highest likelihood, PMG-simple examines if each phrase occurs in the input sentence. If it does and the constituent words are not part of an already established phrase, the constituent words are marked as parts of this phrase and are no longer considered in the phrase-matching process. If the phrase pattern does not occur, the next in-line phrase is considered, until the table is exhausted. Comparative results between CRF and PMG-simple are reported in the results section.

3.2 Monolingual corpus

The TL monolingual corpus is processed to extract two complementary types of information. The first type supports disambiguation between multiple possible translations, while the second determines the order of words in the final translation and the addition or removal of functional words, using a TL phrase model derived from an indexing based on (i) phrase type, (ii) phrase head lemma and (iii) phrase head PoS tag.

The TL phrases are then organised in a hash map that allows the storage of multiple values for each key, using as a key the three aforementioned criteria. For each phrase the number of occurrences within the corpus is retained. Each hash map is stored in a separate file to minimise access time during translation.

4 Translation phase 1: Structure selection

The Structure selection phase determines the type and relative position of TL phrases to which the SL ones are translated. To achieve this, PRESEMT consults the SL-to-TL structural modifications as contained in the PAM-processed parallel corpus. In that respect, it resembles EBMT (Hutchins, 2005).

Translation phase 1 receives as input an SL sentence, annotated with tag & lemma information and segmented into phrases by the PMG. A dynamic programming algorithm then determines for each SL side the most similar (in terms of phrase structure) SL sentence from the bilingual corpus. Similarity is calculated by taking into account structural information such as the phrase type, the PoS tag and case (if applicable) of the phrase head and phrase functional head info. The phrases of the input sentence are then reordered to generate the translation structure by combining the phrase alignments established by the algorithm and the SL-TL phrase alignment information stored in the pair of parallel sentences.

The dynamic programming algorithm compares structures from the same language. The most similar SL structure from the bilingual corpus, that will determine the TL translation structure, is thus selected purely on SL properties. The similarity of two sentences is calculated as a weighted internal product between the two sentences, traversing both sentences in parallel from their start towards their end. The implemented method utilises the Smith-Waterman variant (Smith and Waterman, 1981).

The last step of this phase is the translation of words using the bilingual lexicon.[2] All translation alternatives are disambiguated during the subsequent translation phase.

5 Translation Phase 2: Translation equivalent selection

Issues resolved in the second phase are phrase-internal and include (i) word order within each phrase, (ii) introduction or deletion of functional words and (iii) selection of the best candidate in the case of translation ambiguities. These are resolved using the phrase-based indexing of the TL monolingual corpus.

For each phrase of the sentence being translated, the algorithm searches the TL phrase model for similar phrases. If the search is successful, all retrieved TL phrases are compared to the phrase to be translated. The comparison is based on the words included, their tags and lemmas and the morphological features.

[2] If an SL word is not included in the lexicon, it is retained in the translation in its original SL form.

1. Retrieve the relevant phrases from the TL corpus based on the head word
2. Compare the phrase with all the TL relevant phrases and store the one that scores the highest similarity score
3. For any words that the TL model cannot disambiguate, use the lemma frequency model for selecting the best translation
4. Return the new translated Phrase instance.

Figure 1. Pseudocode for Translation equivalent selection

For the purposes of the proposed methodology, the stable-marriage algorithm (Gale & Shapley, 1962) is applied for calculating the similarity and aligning the words of a phrase pair. In comparison to other relevant algorithms, the Gale-Shapley algorithm, results in potentially non-optimal solutions, but possesses the advantage of a substantially lower complexity and thus a reduced processing time.

Using the most similar TL phrase and the word alignments generated by the stable-marriage algorithm, word reordering, translation disambiguation and addition or removal of functional words is performed for each phrase of the input sentence. The final translation is produced by combining all of its translated phrases.

6 Developing new Language Pairs

The porting of the proposed methodology to new language pairs is straightforward. The summary presented herewith is based on the creation of a new Greek-to-Italian language pair, and is typical of porting to new TLs. Initially, the NLP tools need to be selected for the new language (tagger & lemmatiser, shallow parser). In addition, a TL monolingual corpus and a bilingual lexicon need to be provided. The following steps are then taken:

A. Create a java wrapper class for the Italian annotation tools, and provide rules for identifying heads of phrases.

B. Tag/lemmatise and chunk the TL corpus, which takes less than a day.

C. Process the chunked Italian corpus to generate the phrase model. This operation is fully automated and performed off-line (e.g. for a corpus of 100 million words, approx. 1.5 days are needed).

D. For the parallel corpus, train the PAM/PMG suite for the relevant language pair (less than 2 hours needed).

7 Objective Evaluation Experiments

The evaluation results reported in this article focus on the Greek – English language pair. Two datasets have been used (a development set and a test set), each of which comprises 200 sentences, with a length of between 7 and 40 words. For every sentence, exactly one reference translation has been created, by SL-language native speakers and then the translation correctness was cross-checked by TL-language native speakers.

Number of sentences	200	**Source**		web
Reference translations	1	**Language pair**		EL–EN
MT system	**Metrics**			
	BLEU	**NIST**	**Meteor**	**TER**
PRESEMT	0.3254	6.9793	0.3880	51.5330
METIS-2	0.1222	3.1655	0.2698	82.878
Systran	0.2930	6.4664	0.3830	49.721
Bing	0.4600	7.9409	0.4281	37.631
Google	0.5544	8.8051	0.4665	29.791
WorldLingo	0.2659	5.9978	0.3666	50.627

Table 1. Objective metrics results for PRESEMT & other MT systems (development set)

To objectively evaluate the translation accuracy, four automatic evaluation metrics have been chosen, namely BLEU (Papineni et al., 2002), NIST (NIST 2002), Meteor (Denkowski and Lavie, 2011) and TER (Snover et al., 2006). When developing the MT methodology, extensive evaluation was carried out at regular intervals (Sofianopoulos et al., 2012). The evolution of translation accuracy is depicted within Figure 2. The falling trend for TER, signifies a continuously improving translation performance. The current results for a number of MT systems for the development set are reported in Table 1. These results show that at the current stage of development the proposed approach has a quality exceeding that of WorldLingo and Systran, but is still inferior to Google and Bing. The results are particularly promising, taking into account that the proposed methodology has been developed for a substantially shorter period than the other systems, and has no language-specific information injected into it. According to an error analysis carried out, most of the errors are due to the lack of syntactic information (e.g. the inability to distinguish between object/subject). Also a point which can be improved concerns the mapping of sentence structures from SL to TL. To address this, additional experiments are currently under way involving larger monolingual corpora.

Even without this type of knowledge, the proposed methodology has shown substantial scope for improvement, as evidenced by the evolution of the objective translation metrics (cf. Figure 2). It is expected that this trend will be continued in future versions of the MT system.

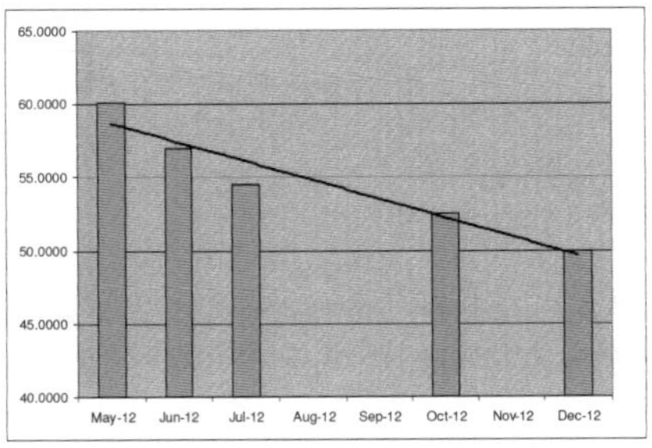

Figure 2. Evolution of translation accuracy reflected by TER scores for the PRESEMT system together with the associated trend line

Number of sentences	200	**Source**		web
Reference translations	1	**Language pair**		EL–EN
PMG type	**Metrics**			
	BLEU	**NIST**	**Meteor**	**TER**
CRF-based	0.3167	6.9127	0.3817	52.509
PMG-simple	0.3254	6.9793	0.3880	51.533

Table 2. Effect on PRESEMT translation accuracy of using the two distinct PMG variants

Recent activity towards improving translation accuracy has focussed on the effect of using different PMG approaches, as summarised in section 3. According to Table 2, an improvement in all four metrics is achieved using PMG-simple instead of CRF. For the limited training set defined by the parallel corpus, PMG-simple extracts more effectively the phrasing model. An improvement of approx. 3% in the BLEU score is achieved over the CRF-based system. The reduction in TER is almost 2% indicating a sizable improvement in translation quality, while NIST and METEOR scores are improved by 1% and 1.9% respectively.

8 Subjective Evaluation Results

To fully evaluate translation quality, both objective and subjective evaluation have been implemented. The latter type is carried out by humans who assess translation quality.

Human evaluation is considered to be more representative of the actual MT quality (Callison-Burch, et al., 2008 & 2011), though on the other hand it is time-consuming and laborious. Furthermore, it lacks objectivity (single evaluators may not be consistent in assessing a given translation through time while two evaluators may yield completely different judgements on the same text) and must be repeated for every new test result.

For the human evaluation, for each language pair, a total of 15 language professionals were recruited, who were either language professionals, closely associated with MT tasks, or postgraduate university students in the area of linguistics. Two types of subjective evaluation were carried out. The first one involves the experts grading translations generated by the PRESEMT system regarding their adequacy and fluency. Adequacy refers to the amount of information from the SL text that is retained in the translation, based on a 1-5 scale of scores (with a score of 1 corresponding to the worst translation). Fluency measures whether the translation is well-formed, also on a 1-5 scale, with emphasis being placed on grammaticality.

The second type of subjective evaluation involves direct comparison between the translations generated by PRESEMT and by other established MT systems over the same dataset. In this case, each evaluator ranks the translations of the different systems, these systems being presented in randomised order to ensure the dependability of the feedback received.

Subjective evaluation activities were carried out during two distinct periods (namely October and December 2012), separated by two months. The purpose of implementing two sessions has been to judge the improvement in the system within the intervening period. Thus, two distinct versions of the EL-EN MT system corresponding to these two time points were used. For reference, the objective evaluation results obtained for the test sentences are listed in Table 3. In both cases, the CRF-based PMG was used since it was more mature at the time of evaluation.

A specifically-designed platform has been developed to support subjective evaluation activities[3]. This platform has been used to (a) collect the human evaluators' feedback for the different language pairs and (b) support the subsequent assessment of the results via statistical methods.

Number of sentences	200	Source	web	
Reference translations	1	Language pair	EL–EN	
MT system	Metrics			
	BLEU	NIST	Meteor	TER
PRESEMT (phase 1)	0.2627	6.2001	0.3329	60.0420
PRESEMT (phase 2)	0.2666	6.2061	0.3335	59.3360
Bing	0.4793	8.1357	0.4486	35.7220
Google	0.5116	8.4549	0.4580	32.6860
WorldLingo	0.3019	6.3799	0.3814	46.7350

Table 3. Objective metrics results for PRESEMT & other MT systems (test set)

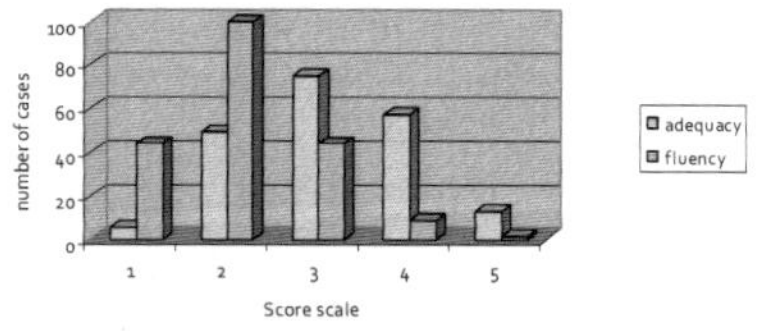

Figure 3. Histogram of adequacy and fluency over all sentences (1st human evaluation phase)

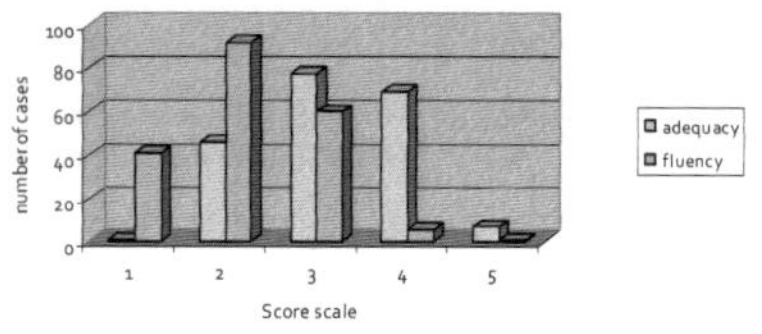

Figure 4. Histogram of adequacy and fluency over all sentences (2nd human evaluation phase)

For the proposed methodology, in phase 1 relatively low values of both adequacy and fluency measurements were recorded. By comparing the scores in the first and second evaluation phases (Figures 3 and 4, respectively), it can be seen that both adequacy and fluency histograms move towards higher values (notably fluency ratings with a score of 3 and adequacy ratings with scores of 3 and 4 have substantially higher frequencies). This reflects improved translation quality in the later version of the proposed MT system in comparison to the earlier one.

Number of sentences	200	Source	web	
Reference translations	1	Language pair	EL–EN	
MT system	Adequacy		Fluency	
	average	stdev.	average	stdev.
PRESEMT (phase 1)	3.08	0.27	2.17	0.27
PRESEMT (phase 2)	3.14	0.24	2.16	0.25
Google	4.17	0.39	3.51	0.50
Bing	3.75	0.77	3.02	0.61
WorldLingo	3.77	0.45	3.11	0.51

Table 4. Summary of measurements (in terms of average and standard deviation) for fluency and adequacy for various MT systems (test set)

In addition, in phase 2 of subjective evaluation, adequacy and fluency measurements were collected for the three operational systems used as reference systems (namely Google Translate, Bing and WorldLingo). These operational systems have higher adequacy and fluency values than PRESEMT, as indicated in Table 4. Furthermore, paired t-tests have confirmed that at a 0.99 level of significance, these three systems have statistically superior subjective measurements to the proposed methodology. To provide a reference, for the same set of 200 sentences, objective metrics are shown in Table 3 for each system. As can be seen the relative order of the systems in the subjective evaluations (in terms of adequacy and fluency) is confirmed by the objective measurements.

A second subjective evaluation focused on ranking comparatively the translations of the four studied MT systems. Evaluators were presented with the outputs of the four systems in randomized order, to conceal the identity of each system. The evaluators were requested to order the four translations from higher to lower quality (with 1 denoting the more accurate translation.

[3] www.presemt.eu/presemt_eval/

To transform this ranking into a single score, the individual rankings per evaluator have been accumulated and normalized over the number of evaluators. Then the representative scoring has been defined as a weighted sum of frequency of a system being ranked as first, second, third and fourth best over all evaluators, by multiplying with weights of 40, 30, 20 and 10 respectively. The average scores of the proposed methodology were the lowest, followed by the ranking results for WorldLingo. The results of Bing and Google are comparable with the Google results giving the best results. A statistical analysis was carried out using paired t-tests for all six pairings of the four systems being studied. This has confirmed that the differences in subjective scores are statistically significant at a level of 0.95.

To summarise, subjective evaluation has shown that the PRESEMT methodology has an inferior translation performance in terms of subjective measurements to the three operational systems. This can be justified as the proposed methodology refrains from utilising language-specific information as a priori grammatical knowledge. Inferior translations also reflect the much shorter development time available as well as the very limited amount of expensive resources provided. The effect on translation quality of using pre-existing tools (to ease portability to new language pairs) needs to be stressed, as no modification of these tools was performed to remedy systematic shortcomings identified. For the newer MT versions now available, a new round of subjective evaluations is planned. It has been observed that improvements in objective metrics are followed by improved subjective evaluation performance. Thus, for these new versions, an improved accuracy is expected.

9 Discussion

In the present article the principles and implementation of a novel language-independent MT methodology have been presented. This methodology draws on information from a large TL monolingual corpus and a very small bilingual one. The overwhelming majority of linguistic information is extracted in an automated manner using pattern recognition techniques.

Two types of evaluation have been reported, these concerning objective and subjective evaluations. Experimental results using objective metrics through a period of time have indicated a rising trend in terms of translation quality. Also, it has been shown that by introducing a new phrasing model for the sentences to be translated a substantial improvement is achieved. Subjective evaluation activities have indicated a higher translation accuracy achieved by other MT systems. A limiting factor for the PRESEMT methodology is admittedly the requirement for portability to new language pairs. This leads to the extraction of knowledge from texts via algorithmic means and the adoption of already existing linguistic tools, without modifications.

On the other hand, subsequent versions of the proposed MT system have shown a trend of improving translation accuracy. In this respect, objective evaluation results are promising, especially taking into account the fact that for several aspects, scope for improvement has been identified. This includes the revision of the structure selection phase, where smaller sub-sentential structures need to be combined to improve generalisation. In addition, improvements in the bilingual corpus compilation procedure need to be studied. The results of these ongoing experiments will be reported in the future.

References

Paul E. Black. 2005. *Dictionary of Algorithms and Data Structures*. U.S. National Institute of Standards and Technology (NIST).

Chris Callison-Burch, Cameron Fordyce, Philipp Koehn, Christof Monz and Josh Schroeder. 2009. *Further Meta-Evaluation of Machine Translation*. Proceedings of the WMT-08 Workshop, Colombus, Ohio.

Chris Callison-Burch, Philip Koehn, Christof Monz, Omar F. Zaidan. 2011. *Findings of the 2011Workshop on Statistical Machine Translation*. Proceedings of the 6th Workshop on Statistical Machine Translation, Edinburgh, UK, pp. 22–64.

Jaime Carbonell, Steve Klein, David Miller, Michael Steinbaum, Tomer Grassiany and Jochen Frey. 2006. *Context-Based Machine Translation*. Proceedings of the 7th AMTA Conference, Cambridge, MA, USA, pp. 19-28.

Michael Carl, Maite Melero, Toni Badia, Vincent Vandeghinste, Peter Dirix, Ineke Schuurman, Stella Markantonatou, Sokratis Sofianopoulos,

Marina Vassiliou and Olga Yannoutsou. 2008. METIS-II: Low Resources Machine Translation: Background, Implementation, Results and Potentials. *Machine Translation*, 22 (1-2):pp. 67-99.

Helena M. Caseli, Maria das Graças V. Nunes and Mikel L. Forcada. 2008. Automatic Induction of Bilingual resources from aligned parallel corpora: Application to shallow-transfer machine translation. *Machine Translation*, 20:pp. 227-245.

Michael Denkowski and Alon Lavie. 2011. Meteor 1.3: *Automatic Metric for Reliable Optimization and Evaluation of Machine Translation Systems*. EMNLP 2011 Workshop on Statistical Machine Translation, Edinburgh, UK, pp. 85-91.

Ioannis Dologlou, Stella Markantonatou, George Tambouratzis, Olga Yannoutsou, Athanasia Fourla and Nikos Ioannou. 2003. *Using Monolingual Corpora for Statistical Machine Translation: The METIS System*. Proceedings of the EAMT- CLAW 2003 Workshop, Dublin, Ireland, pp. 61-68.

Richard O. Duda, Peter E. Hart and David G. Scott. 2001. *Pattern Classification (2nd edition)*. Wiley Interscience, New York, U.S.A.

David Gale and Lloyd S. Shapley. 1962. College Admissions and the Stability of Marriage. *American Mathematical Monthly*, 69:pp. 9-14.

John Hutchins. 2005. Example-Based Machine Translation: a Review and Commentary. *Machine Translation*, 19:pp. 197-211.

Alexandre Klementiev, Ann Irvine, Chris Callison-Burch and David Yarowsky. 2012. *Toward Statistical Machine Translation without Parallel Corpora*. Proceedings of EACL2012, Avignon, France, 23-25 April, pp. 130-140.

Philip Koehn. 2010. *Statistical Machine Translation*. Cambridge University Press, Cambridge.

John Lafferty, Andrew McCallum and Fernando Pereira. 2001. *Conditional Random Fields: Probabilistic Models for Segmenting and Labelling Sequence Data*. Proceedings of ICML 2011, Bellevue, Washington, USA, pp. 282-289.

Harry Mairson. 1992. The Stable Marriage Problem. *The Brandeis Review*, 12:1.

Stella Markantonatou, Sokratis Sofianopoulos, Olga Giannoutsou and Marina Vassiliou. 2009. Hybrid Machine Translation for Low- and Middle- Density Languages. *Language Engineering for Lesser-Studied Languages, S. Nirenburg (ed.)*, IOS Press, pp. 243-274.

NIST 2002. *Automatic Evaluation of Machine Translation Quality Using n-gram Co-occurrences Statistics*.

Kishore Papineni, Salim Roukos, Todd Ward, and Wei-Jing Zhu. 2002. *BLEU: A Method for Automatic Evaluation of Machine Translation*. Proceedings of the *40th ACL Meeting*, Philadelphia, USA, pp. 311-318.

Jan Pomikálek and Pavel Rychlý. 2008. *Detecting co-derivative documents in large text collections*. Proceedings of LREC2008, Marrakech, Morrocco, pp.1884-1887.

Prokopis Prokopidis, Byron Georgantopoulos and Harris Papageorgiou. 2011. *A suite of NLP tools for Greek*. Proceedings of the 10th ICGL Conference, Komotini, Greece, pp. 373-383.

Felipe Sanchez-Martinez and Mikel L. Forcada. 2009. Inferring Shallow-transfer Machine translation Rules from Small Parallel Corpora. *Journal of Artificial Intelligence Research,* 34:pp. 605-635.

Helmut Schmid. 1994. *Probabilistic Part-of-Speech Tagging Using Decision Trees*. Proceedings of International Conference on New Methods in Language Processing, Manchester, UK, pp. 44-49.

Temple F. Smith and Michael S. Waterman. 1981. Identification of Common Molecular Subsequences. *Journal of Molecular Biology*, 147:195-197.

Matthew Snover, Bonnie Dorr, Richard Schwartz, Linnea Micciulla and John Makhoul. 2006. *A Study of Translation Edit Rate with Targeted Human Annotation*. Proceedings of the 7th AMTA Conference, Cambridge, MA, USA, pp. 223-231.

Sokratis Sofianopoulos, Marina Vassiliou and George Tambouratzis. 2012. *Implementing a language-independent MT methodology*. Proceedings of the 1st Workshop on Multilingual Modeling (held within the ACL-2012 Conference), Jeju, Republic of Korea, pp.1-10.

Jinsong Su, Hua Wu, Haifeng Wang, Yidong Chen, Xiaodong Shi, Huailin Dong and Qun Liu. 2011. *Translation Model Adaptation for Statistical Machine Translation with Monolingual Topic Information*. Proceedings of the 50th ACL Meeting, Jeju, Republic of Korea, pp. 459–468.

George Tambouratzis, Fotini Simistira, Sokratis Sofianopoulos, Nikos Tsimboukakis and Marina Vassiliou. 2011. *A resource-light phrase scheme for language-portable MT*. Proceedings of the 15th EAMT Conference, Leuven, Belgium, pp. 185-192.

Author Index